BA

JAPANESE KANJI

VOLUME 1

HIGH-FREQUENCY KANJI AT YOUR COMMAND!

TIMOTHY G. STOUT & KAORI HAKONE
Illustrated by KINUKA UCHIDA

TUTTLE Publishing
Tokyo | Rutland, Vermont | Singapore

Published by Tuttle Publishing, an imprint of Periplus Editions (HK) Ltd.

www.tuttlepublishing.com

ISBN 978-4-8053-1048-9

Distributed by

North America, Latin America & Europe
Tuttle Publishing
364 Innovation Drive
North Clarendon, VT 05759-9436 U.S.A.
Tel: 1 (802) 773-8930; Fax: 1 (802) 773-6993
info@tuttlepublishing.com
www.tuttlepublishing.com

Japan
Tuttle Publishing
Yaekari Building, 3rd Floor
5-4-12 Osaki, Shinagawa-ku
Tokyo 141 0032
Tel: (81) 3 5437-0171; Fax: (81) 3 5437-0755
sales@tuttle.co.jp
www.tuttle.co.jp

Asia Pacific
Berkeley Books Pte. Ltd.
61 Tai Seng Avenue #02-12
Singapore 534167
Tel: (65) 6280-1330; Fax: (65) 6280-6290
inquiries@periplus.com.sg
www.periplus.com

First edition
14 13 12 11   5 4 3 2 1

Printed in Singapore

Contents

Introduction

Welcome to the study of Japanese kanji characters—a most challenging and rewarding part of the Japanese language. The aim of this book is to help you master the most important kanji for beginners. The kanji in this book are included on many important national and international exams—from the International Baccalaureate to the Advanced Placement Japanese Exam—and reflect a synthesis of all of the most commonly used college level beginning Japanese textbooks. Whether you are a college student, high school student, or simply interested in Japanese, this book can help you.

This book is designed for students who have completed a basic level of Japanese study, equivalent to one year of high school or one semester of college. Romaji is used, but you will get much more benefit from this book if you master hiragana and katakana, as well as beginning level vocabulary and grammar.

There are 1,945 common use kanji characters in Japanese, and 410 of them are often considered core for Japanese exams. Although large in number, these 410 kanji can be learned in a relatively short time with good instruction and consistent effort. Japanese elementary and secondary students spend many years learning the kanji characters by rote learning. This book, however, teaches them in a way that reduces study time and monotony.

This book uses both traditional as well as unique new methods to make the kanji characters easier to learn. The traditional methods include extensive writing practice, drills, and quizzes. The methods unique to this book include over one hundred reading passages and comprehension questions similar in format to those on many Japanese exams; numerous and engaging practice sections; and original mnemonics, illustrated by a Japanese artist, presented with each kanji.

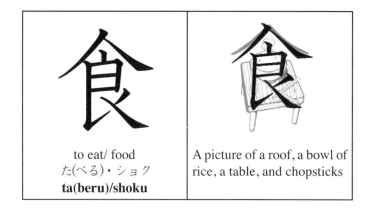

食 to eat/ food た(べる)・ショク **ta(beru)/shoku**	 A picture of a roof, a bowl of rice, a table, and chopsticks

Mnemonic illustrations associate the shape of the kanji characters with things already known to most learners, making the kanji easier to learn and remember. Using mnemonics is a proven, though often ignored, method of foreign language instruction. Some kanji characters are complex, so it makes sense to use mnemonics to ease the burden on memory, and improve the pace and quality of learning.

How to Use this Book

This book is organized into 22 lessons, each containing 5 to 15 kanji characters, beginning with the most basic and simple to write kanji, and reflecting the general progression of typical Japanese programs. There are abundant exercises in each lesson to help reinforce the newly learned kanji. Naturally, these exercises promote reading and writing proficiency, but some also provide speaking and listening practice as well (see the "Review Questions" at the end of each lesson). The key to mastering kanji is to learn to write them, study the most useful vocabulary, and practice them extensively in a variety of interesting and comprehensible contexts.

Write, Write, Write!

One of the best ways to learn kanji characters is simply to write them repeatedly. Nearly every page in this book provides extensive opportunities to write the kanji. There are simple drills and engaging exercises that promote kanji proficiency. Don't be tempted to skip over these valuable chances to improve your handwriting as well as to really learn and internalize the kanji.

Vocabulary Building

Since most kanji vocabulary are compound words (with two or more kanji characters), rather than learn them in isolation, it is best to learn kanji through actual vocabulary. This book presents between three and six useful words for each kanji character. Try to learn them all. Perhaps the most important thing you can do to improve your Japanese proficiency is to steadily increase your vocabulary.

Read, Read, Read!

This book teaches 205 kanji characters (plus 18 additional non-core kanji), and provides reading passages related to each one. The reading passages are level-appropriate for the ability and interests of high school students. Take the time to read these passages, and try to answer the comprehension questions that follow them. Learning to read, after all, is one of the main purposes for studying the kanji characters.

In the back of the book you will find answers to the reading comprehension questions. The table of contents also lists all of the kanji characters, grouped by common theme, for easy reference.

Two Ways to Pronounce Kanji Characters

Kanji characters often have multiple meanings and pronunciations, because the Japanese language has changed considerably in the past 1,500 years. Students often express anxiety over having to learn more than one meaning and pronunciation for kanji characters, but on the other hand, this also means there are one half or fewer kanji characters to learn than would otherwise be the case.

There are two basic ways that kanji characters can be read: the **on-yomi** or Chinese pronunciation, and the **kun-yomi** or Japanese pronunciation. Before the Japanese began to borrow Chinese characters, there was no written language of Japan. By the

6th century, Chinese characters were widely used in Japan. They became known as **kanji**, "**kan**" meaning the Han Dynasty, and "**ji**" meaning characters. The Japanese used kanji characters to represent Japanese words and ideas, but also adopted many Chinese words and their pronunciation (or their best approximation of them). Today, although the meanings of many kanji characters are mutually understood by Japanese and Chinese people, the pronunciations are somewhat different.

As you encounter each kanji notice the different meanings and pronunciations that it may have. For instance, in the example on page 4 the kanji 食 (food, eat) would include た(べる) and ショク. But rather than learning these pronunciations in isolation, they are presented in meaningful vocabulary items. Not all kanji have both Japanese and Chinese pronunciations, and sometimes they have additional special pronunciations. This is a challenging part of learning Japanese kanji, but if you try to learn the example vocabulary it will make this task less challenging.

This book teaches the most useful 3 to 6 vocabulary associated with each character, or about 1,000 vocabulary items in total. The words with the **kun-yomi** or Japanese pronunciation are introduced first in most cases. Students are often familiar with these words and only need to learn the kanji. The words with **on-yomi** or Chinese pronunciations tend to be more advanced, and they are presented second.

How to Write Kanji Characters

There are few better ways to learn kanji characters than by simply writing them by hand over and over. Using the correct type of line makes your characters look accurate and authentic. There are five basic types of lines: stops, abbreviated stops, sweeps, stop-sweeps, and checks.

1. **Stop:** This is a line that comes to a stop before the writing tool is removed from the page. Stops come in varying lengths and directions, and some even change direction midway.

one river seven mouth woman

2. **Abbreviated Stop:** This line is shorter than a regular stop, and sometimes looks like a dot.

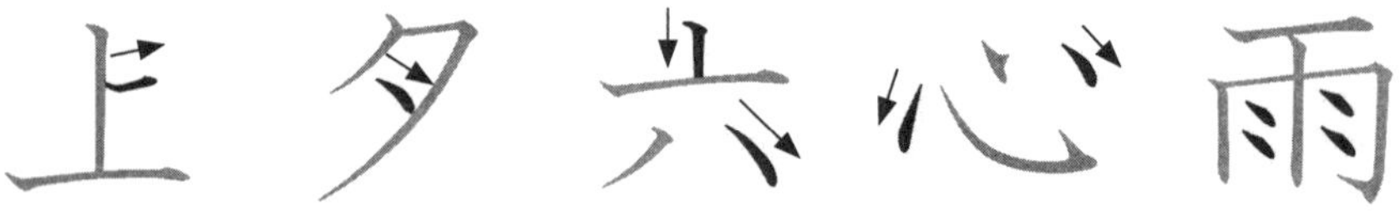

up early evening six heart rain

3. **Sweep:** This is a line that tapers off as the writing tool is gradually removed from the paper.

eight thousand white water western

4. **Stop sweep:** This line stops midway, changes direction, and then tapers off like a sweep. This leaves the end of the line a bit thicker than the rest of it.

person big against foot, leg near

5. **Check:** This line is made by removing the writing tool from the paper, as it changes direction, leaving a hook-shaped mark on the end of the line.

power nine older brother hand to lack

Kanji Stroke Order

Not only do students need to use the correct types of lines, they also need to write them in the correct order. Using correct stroke order makes your kanji look natural, particularly when writing them quickly. Experienced Japanese writers can tell when a kanji has been written out of order.

In this book the correct stroke order is provided with each new kanji character. Note these stroke order sections carefully. Like hiragana and katakana, kanji are usually written from left to right and from top to bottom. There are several general rules for writing kanji:

- Kanji are written from left to right. [川 is a useful example; see p. 40.]

- Kanji are written from top to bottom. [三, 言; see pp. 12 and 122.]

- When horizontal and vertical lines cross, the horizontal line goes first, and then the vertical line. [十, 未; see pp. 18 and 274.]

- When there is a left-middle-right arrangement and the middle is the longest, it is written first. [小, 水; see pp. 62 and 32.]

- When outside lines surround a character, the outside lines are written first. [月; see p. 30.]

- When the center of a kanji is surrounded by a box, the center is written before the bottom line. [日, 田, 国; see pp. 30, 38 and 218.]

- Lines that cover the outside, but not the top, are written last. [近; see p. 84.]

Some kanji do not follow these general rules, so pay careful attention to the stroke order sequence of each kanji as it is introduced. Using correct stroke order may seem awkward or unnatural at first, but it makes a big difference in the way the kanji look to Japanese people. With practice you will soon be producing natural looking kanji characters without having to think about stroke order at all.

The writing practice boxes in this book are on the small side, which can be helpful to some learners in keeping their strokes' lengths and relative positions more precise and consistent. But if you find that the larger writing spaces available in the lessons' Practice sections work better for you, remember that you should feel free to practice your writing on separate sheets of paper. It's impossible to practice your character writing *too* much!

Focus on Meaning

As you learn Japanese kanji characters you will be developing skills that are shared among over 1.5 billion people, including Japanese, Chinese, and others. One reason that alphabet-based writing systems have not replaced these characters is because of several advantages they have. One such advantage is a focus on meaning. In English, for example, readers can pronounce most words, but occasionally need to look up the meaning in a dictionary. In Japanese, on the other hand, readers occasionally come across characters they cannot pronounce, but they understand the meaning, so they do not need to stop reading to look it up.

The aim of this book is to help you master the most important kanji for beginners, particularly to be able to read more and more materials in Japanese. You will naturally be able to read more characters than you be able to write. As you focus on the meaning, you will be able to read and comprehend many sentences you may not be able to write, let alone read aloud. In each lesson you will encounter several reading passages that will help you practice this skill.

Do not worry if you cannot pronounce every character in the reading passages. Understanding the meaning of the characters is more important for reading. You will know this skill is developing, if you can answer the reading comprehension questions correctly.

Contents of the CD-ROM

The CD-ROM contains a program for reviewing the kanji characters introduced in this book. It has a vocabulary quiz section and a reading comprehension section. Using a multiple-choice format, you can get immediate, interactive feedback on how well you are progressing through each lesson.

In addition to the quiz program, the CD-ROM also contains a set of flash cards for all of the kanji characters and vocabulary introduced in this book, and a few extra vocabulary items as a bonus. The front displays the kanji and the useful vocabulary associated with it, and the back displays the corresponding hiragana, romaji, and English for each card.

The card files are provided in two different page setups, so that you may select your preferred way of printing them. One set is formatted to print double-sided if your printer allows that (i.e., the card "pages" are sequenced with each card-fronts page followed immediately by its corresponding card-backs page). The other format has all card-fronts in a group, and all card-backs in a separate group.

Card stock paper works best for printing out flash cards. Not only does it last longer, it also makes it impossible to accidentally see the answer through the paper. You may want to print out multiple sets of flash cards, one side only, for playing games like Memory. One advantage of having the flash cards on the CD-ROM is your ability to print as many copies as you wish.

Also, please note that Japanese has many homonyms. For instance, the word spelled in hiragana as にかい can mean 二回 (two times) and 二階 (second floor). This is one reason why kanji characters are important to the Japanese language. As you progress in your Japanese studies, you will encounter some words that share the same sound as words you have already learned, but have different meanings. This is the case with some of the words on the flash cards. Luckily there are kanji characters in most cases to help minimize this confusion!

For best results, try studying a few at a time, adding more cards as they become easy. Some students prefer to divide their cards into two piles as they study: the cards they already know and the cards they are still working on mastering. By focusing on the stack of flash cards you are still learning, you will use your study time more efficiently.

One Step at a Time

The Japanese have a saying, "A journey of a thousand miles begins with one step" 千里の道も一歩から "**senri no michi mo ippo kara**." This applies to learning kanji. You are taking the first steps toward mastering written Japanese. The list on the table of contents may seem vast at this point, but taking kanji one character at a time, one lesson at a time, you will make great progress. Most experienced students will tell you it is not easy, but worth it. When you look back, you will be impressed by all the ground you have covered. All the best to you in this journey!

1 一 One

Stroke order: 一

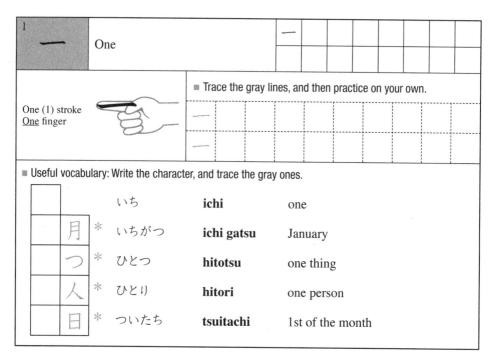

One (1) stroke
<u>One</u> finger

■ Trace the gray lines, and then practice on your own.

一

一

■ Useful vocabulary: Write the character, and trace the gray ones.

一		いち	**ichi**	one
一月	*	いちがつ	**ichi gatsu**	January
一つ	*	ひとつ	**hitotsu**	one thing
一人	*	ひとり	**hitori**	one person
一日	*	ついたち	**tsuitachi**	1st of the month

2 二 Two

Stroke order: 一 二

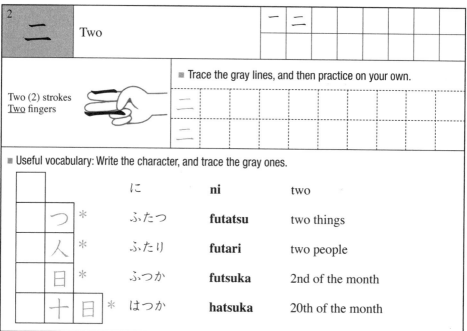

Two (2) strokes
<u>Two</u> fingers

■ Trace the gray lines, and then practice on your own.

二

二

■ Useful vocabulary: Write the character, and trace the gray ones.

二		に	**ni**	two
二つ	*	ふたつ	**futatsu**	two things
二人	*	ふたり	**futari**	two people
二日	*	ふつか	**futsuka**	2nd of the month
二十日	*	はつか	**hatsuka**	20th of the month

* An asterisk denotes vocabulary with kanji that have not yet been introduced.

Reading 1-A

よし子さんは、二月二十日から一週間(しゅうかん)、北海道(ほっかいどう)に行(い)きました。一日目はつかれて何(なに)もできませんでしたが、二日目からはスキーをしたり、温泉(おんせん)に入ったり、カラオケに行(い)ったりして、とても楽(たの)しかったです。来年(らいねん)の冬(ふゆ)は、スノーボードを習(なら)いたいです。

Yoshiko san wa, nigatsu hatsuka kara isshūkan, hokkaidō ni ikimashita. Ichinichime wa tsukarete nanimo dekimasendeshita ga, futsukame kara wa sukii o shitari, onsen ni haittari, karaoke ni ittari shite, totemo tanoshikatta desu. Rainen no fuyu wa, sunōbōdo o naraitai desu.

Questions 1-A

1. Yoshiko came home on (A. February 10, B. February 27, C. October 20, D. October 27).
2. Yoshiko could not do anything on the first day because (A. she was too excited, B. she had a cold, C. she was tired, D. it was very far).
3. Apart from skiing, how did Yoshiko enjoy her trip? (A. Bathing in a hot spring, B. Snowboarding, C. Riding a bullet train, D. Eating sushi).
4. Yoshiko is looking forward to (A. going skiing again, B. having a Japanese bath next winter, C. going to Hokkaido again, D. learning snowboarding next winter).

3 三 Three

Stroke order: 一 二 三

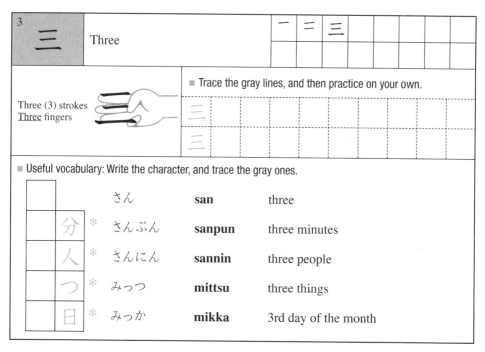

Three (3) strokes
Three fingers

■ Trace the gray lines, and then practice on your own.

三
三

■ Useful vocabulary: Write the character, and trace the gray ones.

三		さん	**san**	three
三分	*	さんぷん	**sanpun**	three minutes
三人	*	さんにん	**sannin**	three people
三つ	*	みっつ	**mittsu**	three things
三日	*	みっか	**mikka**	3rd day of the month

4 四 Four

Stroke order: 丨 冂 冂 四 四

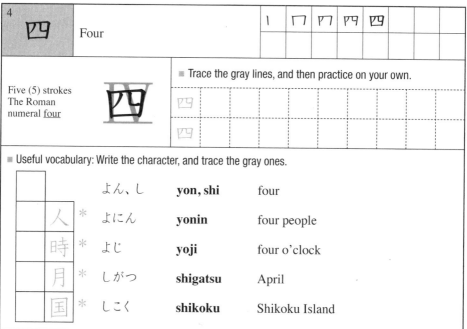

Five (5) strokes
The Roman
numeral four

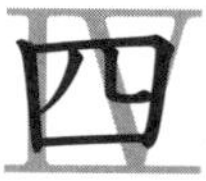

■ Trace the gray lines, and then practice on your own.

四
四

■ Useful vocabulary: Write the character, and trace the gray ones.

四		よん、し	**yon, shi**	four
四人	*	よにん	**yonin**	four people
四時	*	よじ	**yoji**	four o'clock
四月	*	しがつ	**shigatsu**	April
四国	*	しこく	**shikoku**	Shikoku Island

* An asterisk denotes vocabulary with kanji that have not yet been introduced.

Reading 1-B

ぼくはグレッグです。大阪にいる中学三年生の太郎くんに一月からメールを送っています。太郎くんに日本語と英語でメールを書くので、いい勉強になります。日本の中学校のことや太郎くんの趣味について話ができるので、とてもおもしろいです。太郎くんは、三月に中学を卒業して、四月から高校生になるそうです。

Boku wa Gureggu desu. Ōsaka ni iru chūgaku sannensei no Tarō kun ni ichigatsu kara mēru o okutte imasu. Tarō kun ni nihongo to eigo de mēru o kaku node, ii benkyō ni narimasu. Nihon no chūgakkō no koto ya Tarō kun no shumi ni tsuite hanashi ga dekiru node, totemo omoshiroi desu. Tarō kun wa, sangatsu ni chūgaku o sotsugyō shite, shigatsu kara kōkōsei ni naru sō desu.

Questions 1-B

1. What grade is Tarō in? (A. 3rd, B. 6th, C. 9th, D. 12th)
2. When did Greg begin writing his Japanese pen pal? (A. January, B. March, C. June, D. September)
3. What language did Greg use to write his pen pal? (A. Japanese, B. Japanese and English, C. mostly English, D. English)
4. When does the school year begin in Japan? (A. January, B. April, C. August, D. September)

5 五 Five

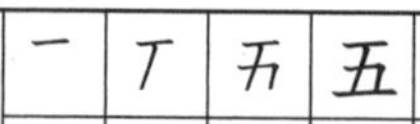

Four (4) strokes
To "go" down
five streets

■ Trace the gray lines, and then practice on your own.

五 五

■ Useful vocabulary: Write the character, and trace the gray ones.

五	ご	**go**	five
五月*	ごがつ	**gogatsu**	May
五番目*	ごばんめ	**gobanme**	5th
五日*	いつか	**itsuka**	5th day of the month
五つ	いつつ	**itsutsu**	five things

6 六 Six

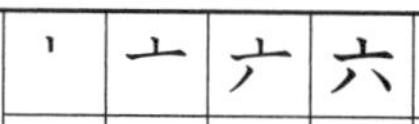

Four (4) strokes
Playing "roku"
and roll on your
six strings

■ Trace the gray lines, and then practice on your own.

六 六

■ Useful vocabulary: Write the character, and trace the gray ones.

六	ろく	**roku**	six
六月*	ろくがつ	**rokugatsu**	June
六番目*	ろくばんめ	**rokubanme**	6th
六つ	むっつ	**muttsu**	six things
六日*	むいか	**muika**	6th day of the month

* An asterisk denotes vocabulary with kanji that have not yet been introduced.

Reading 1-C

日本(にほん)では五月にゴールデンウイークがあります。学校(がっこう)もお父(とう)さんの仕事(しごと)も休(やす)みだったので、家族(かぞく)で山(やま)に行(い)ってピクニックをすることにしました。その朝(あさ)、私(わたし)も弟(おとうと)もワクワクして六時(じ)におきました。お母(かあ)さんは、おむすびを六つ作(つく)ってくれました。山(やま)の上(うえ)で食(た)べたおむすびは、おいしかったです。

Nihon dewa gogatsu ni gōrudenwiiku ga arimasu. Gakkō mo otōsan no shigoto mo yasumi datta node, kazoku de yama ni itte pikunikku o suru koto ni shimashita. Sono asa, watashi mo otōto mo wakuwaku shite rokuji ni okimashita. Okāsan wa, omusubi o muttsu tsukutte kuremashita. Yama no ue de tabeta omusubi wa, oishikatta desu.

Questions 1-C

1. What month is Golden Week in Japan? (A. March, B. May, C. July, D. September)
2. Where did the narrator's family go for Golden Week? (A. the mountains, B. the river, C. the beach, D. the countryside)
3. What time did the narrator wake up? (A. 4 o'clock, B. 5 o'clock, C. 6 o'clock, D. 7 o'clock)
4. How many rice balls did the narrator's mother make? (A. four, B. five, C. six, D. seven)

7 七 Seven

Stroke order: 一 七

Two (2) strokes
A peeled ba"nana"
looks like this.

■ Trace the gray lines, and then practice on your own.

七 七

■ Useful vocabulary: Write the character, and trace the gray ones.

□	なな、しち	**nana, shichi**	seven
□十 *	ななじゅう	**nanajū**	seven
□百円 *	ななひゃくえん	**nanahyaku en**	700 yen
□五三 *	しちごさん	**shichigosan**	7-5-3 Festival
□日 *	なのか	**nanoka**	7th day of the month
□つ	ななつ	**nanatsu**	seven things

8 八 Eight

Stroke order: ノ 八

Two (2) strokes
A person sneezing,
"hachi"(oo)!"

■ Trace the gray lines, and then practice on your own.

八 八

■ Useful vocabulary: Write the character, and trace the gray ones.

□	はち	**hachi**	eight
□日 *	ようか	**yōka**	8th day of the month
□分 *	はっぷん	**happun**	eight minutes
お□つ	おやつ	**oyatsu**	between meal snack
□百屋 *	やおや	**yaoya**	vegetable stand

* An asterisk denotes vocabulary with kanji that have not yet been introduced.

Reading 1-D

けい子さんは晩ご飯に、サラダを食べたいと思いました。だから、駅前の八百屋で、レタスときゅうりとにんじんを買いました。トマトも買うつもりでしたが、四つで七百円もしたので、買いませんでした。かわりに、八十円のセロリを買いました。

Keiko san wa bangohan ni, sarada o tabetai to omoimashita. Dakara, ekimae no yaoya de, retasu to kyūri to ninjin o kaimashita. Tomato mo kau tsumori deshita ga, yottsu de nana hyakuen mo shita node, kaimasen deshita. Kawari ni, hachijūen no serori o kaimashita.

Questions 1-D

1. Where did Keiko get the ingredients for dinner? (A. the grocery store, B. the farmers' market, C. the vegetable stand, D. her vegetable garden)
2. What did Keiko buy first? (A. tomatoes, lettuce, and cucumbers, B. lettuce, cucumbers, and carrots, C. cucumbers, carrots, and tomatoes, D. carrots, tomatoes, and lettuce)
3. How much did the tomatoes cost? (A. 400 yen for four, B. 400 yen for seven, C. 700 yen for four, D. 700 yen for seven)
4. How much did the celery cost? (A. 80 yen, B. 100 yen, C. 110 yen, D. 180 yen)

9

九

Nine

Stroke order: ノ 九

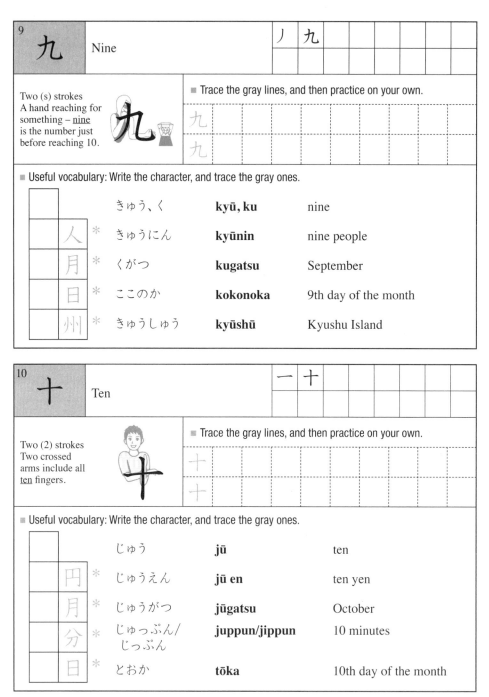

Two (s) strokes
A hand reaching for something – nine is the number just before reaching 10.

■ Trace the gray lines, and then practice on your own.

九
九

■ Useful vocabulary: Write the character, and trace the gray ones.

		きゅう、く	**kyū, ku**	nine
人	*	きゅうにん	**kyūnin**	nine people
月	*	くがつ	**kugatsu**	September
日	*	ここのか	**kokonoka**	9th day of the month
州	*	きゅうしゅう	**kyūshū**	Kyushu Island

10

十

Ten

Stroke order: 一 十

Two (2) strokes
Two crossed arms include all ten fingers.

■ Trace the gray lines, and then practice on your own.

十
十

■ Useful vocabulary: Write the character, and trace the gray ones.

		じゅう	**jū**	ten
円	*	じゅうえん	**jū en**	ten yen
月	*	じゅうがつ	**jūgatsu**	October
分	*	じゅっぷん/じっぷん	**juppun/jippun**	10 minutes
日	*	とおか	**tōka**	10th day of the month

* An asterisk denotes vocabulary with kanji that have not yet been introduced.

Reading 1-E

一男(かずお)くんは、夏休(なつやす)みにお母(かあ)さんと妹(いもうと)と九州へ行(い)きました。その時(とき)、初(はじ)めて新幹線(しんかんせん)に乗(の)りました。そして十日間(とおかかん)いとこの家(うち)に泊(と)まりました。いとこの家族(かぞく)はみんなで六人ですが、家はとても広(ひろ)いので、せまいと思(おも)いませんでした。

泊(と)まる (to stay at)

Kazuo kun wa, natsuyasumi ni okāsan to imōto to kyūshū e ikimashita. Sono toki, hajimete shinkansen ni norimashita. Soshite tōkakan itoko no uchi ni tomarimashita. Itoko no kazoku wa minna de rokunin desu ga, uchi wa totemo hiroi node, semai to omoimasen deshita.

Questions 1-E

1. When did Kazu visit his cousins? (A. during winter break, B. during spring break, C. during summer vacation, D. during fall holiday)
2. Who did Kazu travel with? (A. his father and little sister, B. his father and little brother, C. his mother and little sister, D. his mother and little brother)
3. How many people are in Kazu's cousin's family? (A. six, B. seven, C. eight, D. nine)
4. Where does Kazu most likely live? (A. Hokkaido, B. not in Hokkaido, C. Kyushu, D. not in Kyushu)

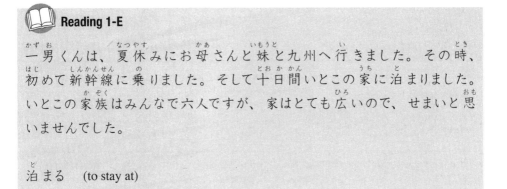

11 百 Hundred

Stroke order: 一 丆 丆 百 百 百

Six (6) strokes
Military captain of 100 wearing a kabuto (beetle) helmet.

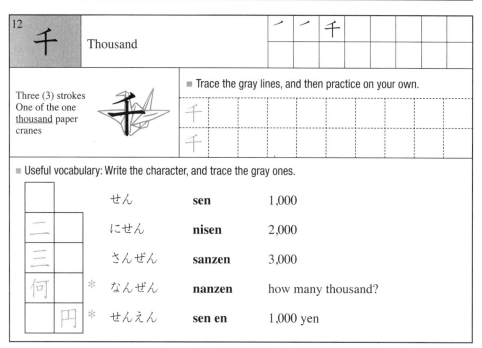

■ Trace the gray lines, and then practice on your own.

百
百

■ Useful vocabulary: Write the character, and trace the gray ones.

			ひゃく	**hyaku**	100
三			さんびゃく	**sanbyaku**	300
八			はっぴゃく	**happyaku**	800
	円	*	ひゃくえん	**hyaku en**	100 yen
	年	*	ひゃくねん	**hyakunen**	century, 100 years

12 千 Thousand

Stroke order: 丿 丿 千

Three (3) strokes
One of the one thousand paper cranes

■ Trace the gray lines, and then practice on your own.

千
千

■ Useful vocabulary: Write the character, and trace the gray ones.

			せん	**sen**	1,000
二			にせん	**nisen**	2,000
三			さんぜん	**sanzen**	3,000
何		*	なんぜん	**nanzen**	how many thousand?
	円	*	せんえん	**sen en**	1,000 yen

* An asterisk denotes vocabulary with kanji that have not yet been introduced.

Reading 1-F

私(わたし)は来週(らいしゅう)ドイツから来た友達(ともだち)と日光(にっこう)へ行(い)くことにしました。母(はは)はおこづかいを三千円(えん)くれるそうです。電車(でんしゃ)のきっぷは千六百三十円で、おべんとうは六百円です。のこりの七百円ぐらいで、家(か)族(ぞく)におみやげを買(か)うつもりです。

Watashi wa raishū doitsu kara kita tomodachi to nikkō e iku koto ni shimashita. Haha wa okozukai o sanzen en kureru sō desu. Densha no kippu wa sen roppyaku sanju en de, obentō wa roppyaku en desu. Nokori no nanahyakuen gurai de, kazoku ni omiyage o kau tsumori desu.

Questions 1-F

1. With whom is the writer going to Nikko? (A. a tour group, B. a friend, C. a parent, D. classmates)
2. How much is the train fare? (A. 1,360 yen, B. 1,630 yen, C. 3,130 yen, D. 3,630 yen)
3. How much will lunch cost? (A. 500 yen, B. 600 yen, C. 700 yen, D. 800 yen)
4. For whom will the writer buy souvenirs? (A. friends, B. classmates, C. teachers, D. family)

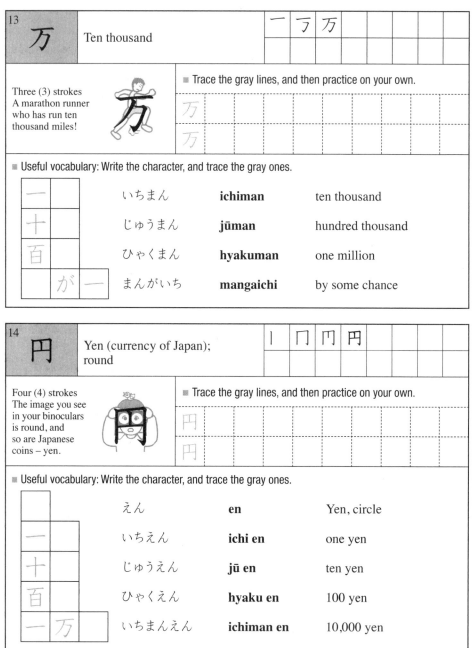

13 万 Ten thousand

Stroke order: 一 ㇆ 万

Three (3) strokes
A marathon runner who has run ten thousand miles!

■ Trace the gray lines, and then practice on your own.

万
万

■ Useful vocabulary: Write the character, and trace the gray ones.

一 □	いちまん	**ichiman**	ten thousand
十 □	じゅうまん	**jūman**	hundred thousand
百 □	ひゃくまん	**hyakuman**	one million
□ が 一	まんがいち	**mangaichi**	by some chance

14 円 Yen (currency of Japan); round

Stroke order: 丨 冂 冂 円

Four (4) strokes
The image you see in your binoculars is round, and so are Japanese coins – yen.

■ Trace the gray lines, and then practice on your own.

円
円

■ Useful vocabulary: Write the character, and trace the gray ones.

□	えん	**en**	Yen, circle
一 □	いちえん	**ichi en**	one yen
十 □	じゅうえん	**jū en**	ten yen
百 □	ひゃくえん	**hyaku en**	100 yen
一 万 □	いちまんえん	**ichiman en**	10,000 yen

Reading 1-G

日本では十六才でバイクの運転免許が取れます。たろうさんは十六才の誕生日に十三万円のバイクがほしいそうです。お父さんが半分の六万五千円、おじいさんとおばあさんが四万円を払ってくれるそうです。のこりの二万五千円はたろうさんが払うつもりです。

払う (to pay)

Nihon dewa jūrokusai de baiku no unten menkyo ga toremasu. Tarō san wa jūrokusai no tanjōbi ni jūsanman en no baiku ga hoshii sō desu. Otōsan ga hanbun no rokuman gosen en, ojiisan to obāsan ga yonmanen o haratte kureru sō desu. Nokori no niman gosen en wa Tarō san ga harau tsumori desu.

Questions 1-G

1. How old must one be to get a motorcycle license in Japan? (A. 16 years old, B. 17 years old, C. 18 years old, D. 20 years old)
2. How much does the motorcycle that Taro wants cost? (A. 90,000 yen, B. 110,000 yen, C. 130,000 yen, D. 150,000 yen)
3. How much will his father pay? (A. 55,000 yen, B. 60,000 yen, C. 65,000 yen, D. 70,000 yen)
4. How much does Taro need to pay? (A. 15,000 yen, B. 25,000 yen, C. 35,000 yen, D. 45,000 yen)

Lesson 1 Practice

A. Kanji Review

Write these kanji characters. You may refer to the mnemonic pictures for hints. (There is an answer key in the back of the book.)

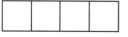

 one	 two	 three	 four	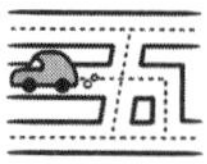 five	 six	 seven
1.	2.	3.	4.	5.	6.	7.
 eight	 nine	 ten	 hundred	 thousand	 ten thousand	 yen, circle
8.	9.	10.	11.	12.	13.	14.

B. Vocabulary Review

The following words and phrases use kanji related to numbers. Write the underlined words in kanji, and write the other parts in hiragana.

1. Vegetable stand (**ya o ya**)
2. best in the world (**se ka i ichi**)
3. One by one (**hito tsu hito tsu**)
4. Olympics (**go ri n**)
5. Triangle (**san ka ku**)
6. Square (**shi ka ku**)
7. Second (**da i ni**)
8. A turkey (**shichi me n chō**)

9. Always rebound from failure (**<u>nana</u> ko ro bi <u>ya</u> o ki**)

10. Red Cross (**se ki <u>jū</u> ji**)

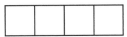

11. Bamboo flute (**sha ku <u>hachi</u>**)

12. 7-5-3 Festival (**<u>shichi</u> <u>go</u> <u>san</u>**)

13. 10 yen coin (**<u>jū</u> <u>en</u> dama**)

14. Firstly (**da i <u>ichi</u> ni**)

C. Ordering at a Japanese Restaurant

Numbers are written both in kanji and Arabic numerals in Japan. As a general rule kanji are used when writing vertically, and Arabic numerals when writing horizontally. Japanese restaurant menus are usually written vertically, as the one below.

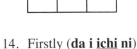

しょうゆラーメン	六百二十五円
みそラーメン	六百七十五円
やきそば	五百五十円
チャーハン	五百七十五円
かつどん	七百八十円
ぎゅうどん	八百三十円
カレーライス	六百円
しゃぶしゃぶ	千四百九十円

Refer to the menu above to tell the price of each of these items.

1. Yakisoba ___550 yen___
2. Shōyu-rāmen __________
3. Katsudon __________
4. Fried rice __________
5. Miso-rāmen __________
6. Japanese style hot pot __________
7. Beef bowl __________
8. Curry rice __________

9. What is the most expensive item on the menu? ______________________

10. If you had 1,000 yen for lunch, what would you order? ______________________

11. What is the change you'd receive? ______________________

D. Writing Japanese Addresses

When writing addresses, Arabic numerals are used for the seven-digit Japanese zip code (郵便番号), but kanji are typically used for other numbers. Complete the following addresses by writing the correct kanji, as indicated.

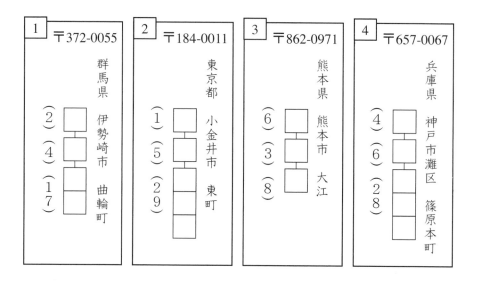

1	2	3	4
〒372-0055	〒184-0011	〒862-0971	〒657-0067
群馬県	東京都	熊本県	兵庫県
伊勢崎市	小金井市	熊本市	神戸市灘区
曲輪町	東町	大江	篠原本町
□ (2) – □ (4) – □□ (17)	□ (1) – □ (5) – □□□ (29)	□ (6) – □ (3) – □ (8)	□ (4) – □ (6) – □□□ (28)

E. Large Numbers in Japanese

Western numbers are based on three-digit units (i.e., thousand, million, billion, trillion), but Japan's and most Asian numbers are based on four-digit units (i.e., ten thousand = **man**, hundred million = **oku**, one trillion = **chō**). Although the last two units are not included in the list of core kanji they are included here briefly for illustration.

1 一 (**ichi**)	10 十 (**jū**)	100 百 (**hyaku**)	1,000 千 (**sen**)
10,000 万 (**man**)	100,000 十万 (**jū-man**)	1,000,000 百万 (**hyaku-man**)	10,000,000 千万 (**sen-man**)
100,000,000 億 (**oku**)	1,000,000,000 十億 (**jū-oku**)	10,000,000,000 百億 (**hyaku-oku**)	100,000,000,000 千億 (**sen-oku**)
1,000,000,000,000 兆 (**chō**)			

In English we do not commonly use numbers larger than the trillions, and this is also the case in Japanese.

If you give a large number to a Japanese person the first thing they usually do, is divide it into four-digit chunks. Take the following example.

301,139,947 (Population of the United States, July 2007)
3 | **01,13** | **9,947**
三億| 百十三万| 九千九百四十七 人 (にん = people)

Since the first number is in the ones' place of the third chunk, it represents the value of **oku**, here it is **san-oku**. Then, there is a zero in the thousands' place of the second chunk; zeros are ignored. Next, there is a one in the hundreds' place, a one in the tens' place, and a three in the ones' place. These represent the values of **hyaku jū san-man**. Finally, there is a nine in the thousands' place, a nine in the hundreds' place, a four in the tens' place and a seven in the ones' place. These are handled just as in Western numbers, namely **kyū-sen, kyū-hyaku yon-ju nana**.

Again, one trick is to parse numbers into four-digit chunks. Also, recall that the zeros in large western numbers are not written in kanji. Try these.

A. 73,500,000 ______________________________

B. 6,009,070 ______________________________

C. 80,021,100 ______________________________

Now, let's go in the other direction, from Japanese to Arabic numerals. This is a bit tricky, but one helpful method for doing this is to make a line for each place value. Look at this example.

一万二千三百八十八 (Mount Fuji's height in feet)

___ ___ , ___ ___ ___

The highest value is in the ten thousands' place, so the first line is drawn for the ten thousands' place, and a line is drawn for each of the smaller place values. Then, the actual values are written in the appropriate blanks. First, 1 is written in the ten thousands' place, 2 in the thousands' place, 3 in the hundreds' place, 8 in the tens' place, and 8 in the ones' place (12,388 ft.).

F. Time and Cost

The following table gives the time and cost of train travel from Tokyo Station to popular tourist destinations in Japan. Read the table and then write the times and costs in English below.

	Time	Cost
日光 Nikko	二じかん十二ふん Example: 2 hours 20 minutes	五千六百三十円 Example: 5,630 yen
鎌倉 Kamakura	五十五ふん	八百九十円
京都 Kyoto	二じかん二十一ぷん	一万三千七百二十円
横浜 Yokohama	二十四ぷん	四百五十円
奈良 Nara	三じかん三十四ぷん	一万四千八百三十円
広島 Hiroshima	三じかん二十五ふん	三万五千三百円
姫路 Himeji	三じかん八ぷん	一万九千十円

(Source: http://transit.goo.ne.jp/index.html Viewed August 2008)

G. Most Populous Cities in the World

Below are the 10 most populous cities in the world, listed out of order. Read the population figures, write them in Arabic numerals on the right, and then write the correct rankings on the left using kanji characters.

Note: 人 = people.

Ranking	City	Population (Kanji)	Population (Arabic numerals)
四	ブラジル、サンパウロ	千七百七十一万千人	17,711,000
	インド、カルカッタ	千二百九十万人	
	メキシコ、メキシコシティ	千八百十三万千人	
	日本(にほん)、東京(とうきょう)	二千八百二万五千人	
	アメリカ、ロサンゼルス	千三百十二万九千人	
	中国(ちゅうごく)、上海(しゃんはい)	千四百十七万三千人	
	アメリカ、ニューヨーク	千六百六十二万六千人	
	アルゼンチン、ブエノスアイレス	千二百四十三万千人	
	ナイジェリア、ラゴス	千三百四十八万八千人	
	インド、ムンバイ	千八百四万二千人	

(Source: http://www.worldatlas.com/citypops.htm Viewed August 2008)

15 日	Sun, day, Sunday	丨	冂	日	日				

Four (4) strokes
A sun with a
wide smile

■ Trace the gray lines, and then practice on your own.

日									
日									

■ Useful vocabulary: Write the character, and trace the gray ones.

□		ひ	**hi**	day
二□		ふつか	**futsuka**	2nd day of the month
□本	*	にほん	**nihon**	Japan
□曜□	*	にちようび	**nichiyōbi**	Sunday
休□	*	きゅうじつ	**kyūjitsu**	holiday, day off
今□	*	きょう	**kyō**	today

16 月	Moon, month, Monday	丿	冂	月	月				

Four (4) strokes
A crescent moon,
eyes closed
and smiling

■ Trace the gray lines, and then practice on your own.

月									
月									

■ Useful vocabulary: Write the character, and trace the gray ones.

□		つき	**tsuki**	moon
□曜日	*	げつようび	**getsuyōbi**	monday
今□	*	こんげつ	**kongetsu**	this month
一□		いちがつ	**ichigatsu**	January
何□	*	なんがつ	**nangatsu**	what month
一か□		いっかげつ	**ikkagetsu**	one month
生年□日	*	せいねんがっぴ	**seinengappi**	date of birth

* An asterisk denotes vocabulary with kanji that have not yet been introduced.

Reading 2-A

こうへいさんは、四か月間アメリカでホームステイをしました。そして今月二日に日本に帰ってきました。今日、はるなさんはこうへいさんを呼んでパーティーをします。こうへいさんはアメリカの写真を見せながら、アメリカのことを話してくれるそうです。

呼ぶ　よぶ (to invite, call out)

Kōhei san wa, yonkagetsukan amerika de hōmusutei o shimashita. Soshite kongetsu futsuka ni nihon ni kaette kimashita. Kyō, Haruna san wa Kōhei san o yonde pātii o shimasu. Kōhei san wa Amerika no shashin o misenagara, amerika no koto o hanashite kureru sō desu.

Questions 2-A

1. How long was Kōhei's homestay in America? (A. two months, B. four months, C. six months, D. eight months)
2. When did Kōhei return to Japan? (A. today, B. this week, C. on the 2nd, D. on the 4th)
3. When is Haruna having a party? (A. today, B. tomorrow, C. Sunday, D. Monday)
4. What will Kōhei bring to the party? (A. souvenirs, B. candy, C. food, D. photos)

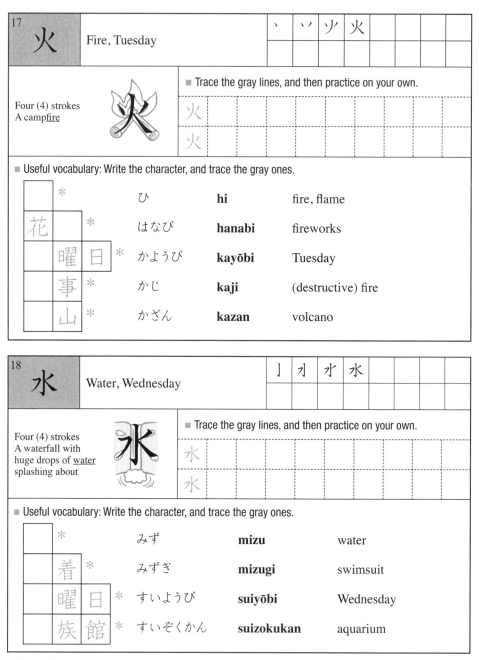

17 火 Fire, Tuesday

丶	丷	⺍	火

Four (4) strokes
A campfire

■ Trace the gray lines, and then practice on your own.

火
火

■ Useful vocabulary: Write the character, and trace the gray ones.

*	ひ	**hi**	fire, flame
花 *	はなび	**hanabi**	fireworks
曜日 *	かようび	**kayōbi**	Tuesday
事 *	かじ	**kaji**	(destructive) fire
山 *	かざん	**kazan**	volcano

18 水 Water, Wednesday

亅	刁	氺	水

Four (4) strokes
A waterfall with huge drops of water splashing about

■ Trace the gray lines, and then practice on your own.

水
水

■ Useful vocabulary: Write the character, and trace the gray ones.

*	みず	**mizu**	water
着 *	みずぎ	**mizugi**	swimsuit
曜日 *	すいようび	**suiyōbi**	Wednesday
族館 *	すいぞくかん	**suizokukan**	aquarium

* An asterisk denotes vocabulary with kanji that have not yet been introduced.

Reading 2-B

りさんとゆうかさんは先週(せんしゅう)の火曜(よう)日から今週(こんしゅう)の水曜日までハワイ旅行(りょこう)をしました。そこで火山や水族館(すいぞくかん)に行(い)ったり、ショッピングセンターで水着(みずぎ)を買(か)ったり、泳(およ)いだりしました。ひどい日焼(ひや)けもしましたが、楽(たの)しかったそうです。

日焼(ひや)け　ひやけ　(sunburn, suntan)

Risa san to Yūka san wa senshū no kayōbi kara konshū no suiyōbi made hawai ryokō o shimashita. Soko de kazan ya suizokukan ni ittari, shoppingusentā de mizugi o kattari, oyoidari shimashita. Hidoi hiyake mo shimashita ga, tanoshikatta sō desu.

Questions 2-B

1. Risa and Yūka went to Hawaii (A. from last Wednesday to this Tuesday, B. from last Wednesday to this Wednesday, C. from last Tuesday to this Tuesday, D. from last Tuesday to this Wednesday)
2. While in Hawaii they (A. saw a fire dancer and went to an aquarium, B. went to an aquarium and saw fireworks, C. saw fireworks and a volcano, D. saw a volcano and went to an aquarium).
3. Risa and Yūka bought their swimsuits (A. in Hawaii, B. in Japan, C. at the Duty-Free shop, D. through a mail order catalogue)
4. They had a fun trip, but (A. they got seasick, B. they lost a piece of luggage, C. they got sunburned, D. they got food poisoning)

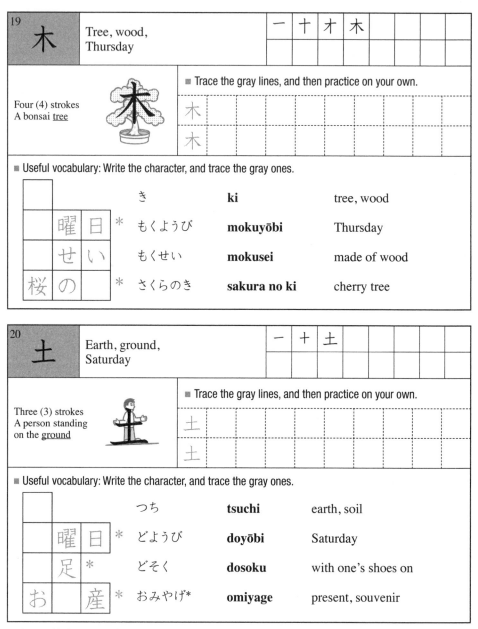

19 木	Tree, wood, Thursday	一	十	才	木

Four (4) strokes
A bonsai tree

■ Trace the gray lines, and then practice on your own.

木
木

■ Useful vocabulary: Write the character, and trace the gray ones.

[ ]		き	**ki**	tree, wood
[ ]曜日	*	もくようび	**mokuyōbi**	Thursday
[ ]せい		もくせい	**mokusei**	made of wood
桜の[ ]	*	さくらのき	**sakura no ki**	cherry tree

20 土	Earth, ground, Saturday	一	十	土

Three (3) strokes
A person standing on the ground

■ Trace the gray lines, and then practice on your own.

土
土

■ Useful vocabulary: Write the character, and trace the gray ones.

[ ]		つち	**tsuchi**	earth, soil
[ ]曜日	*	どようび	**doyōbi**	Saturday
[ ]足	*	どそく	**dosoku**	with one's shoes on
お[ ]産	*	おみやげ*	**omiyage**	present, souvenir

* An asterisk denotes vocabulary with kanji that have not yet been introduced.

Reading 2-C

春休(はるやす)みにゆうきさんはひめじ城(じょう)に行(い)きました。ひめじ城には、桜(さくら)の木がたくさんありました。ゆうきさんは桜の花(はな)がとてもきれいだと思(おも)いました。ひめじ城の中(なか)には土足(どそく)で入(はい)ってはいけませんだから。ゆうきさんは、スリッパをはかなければなりませんでした。お土産(みやげ)に、おせんべいを買(か)ってかえりました。

ひめじ城(じょう) (Himeji castle)

Haruyasumi ni Yūki san wa himeji jō ni ikimashita. Himeji jō niwa, sakura no ki ga takusan arimashita. Yūki san wa sakura no hana ga totemo kirei da to omoimashita. Himeji jō no naka niwa dosoku de haitte wa ikemasen dakara. Yūki san wa, surippa o hakanakereba narimasen deshita. Omiyage ni, osenbei o katte kaerimashita.

Questions 2-C

1. When did Yūki visit Himeji Castle? (A. spring break, B. summer vacation, C. fall holiday, D. winter vacation)
2. What did Yūki see at Himeji Castle? (A. tourists, B. school children, C. cherry blossoms, D. museums)
3. What is not allowed inside the castle? (A. taking pictures, B. eating food, C. purchasing souvenirs, D. wearing shoes)
4. What did Yūki buy for a souvenir? (A. candy, B. postcards, C. rice crackers, D. buckwheat noodles)

21 王	King	一	T	干	王				

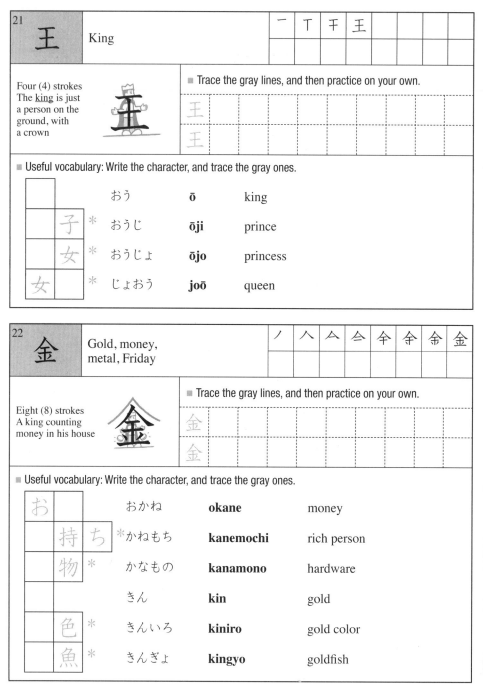

Four (4) strokes
The king is just a person on the ground, with a crown

■ Trace the gray lines, and then practice on your own.

王
王

■ Useful vocabulary: Write the character, and trace the gray ones.

			おう	**ō**	king
	子	*	おうじ	**ōji**	prince
	女	*	おうじょ	**ōjo**	princess
女		*	じょおう	**joō**	queen

22 金	Gold, money, metal, Friday	ノ	人	亼	今	全	弁	余	金

Eight (8) strokes
A king counting money in his house

■ Trace the gray lines, and then practice on your own.

金
金

■ Useful vocabulary: Write the character, and trace the gray ones.

お				おかね	**okane**	money
	持	ち	*	かねもち	**kanemochi**	rich person
	物		*	かなもの	**kanamono**	hardware
				きん	**kin**	gold
	色		*	きんいろ	**kiniro**	gold color
	魚		*	きんぎょ	**kingyo**	goldfish

* An asterisk denotes vocabulary with kanji that have not yet been introduced.

Reading 2-D

あやかさんはイギリスに旅行(りょこう)しました。バッキンガムきゅうでんではイギリス女王(じょおう)のはたが見(み)えました。それは、中(なか)に女王がいらっしゃるという意味(いみ)です。あやかさんは、バッキンガムきゅうでんはとても広(ひろ)いと思(おも)いました。だから女王はイギリスで最(もっと)も金持ちかもしれないと考(かんが)えました。

はた	(flag)	きゅうでん		(palace)
いらっしゃる	(is, exist – honorific)	考(かんが)える	かんがえる	(to think, consider)

Ayaka san wa igirisu ni ryokō shimashita. Bakkingamu kyūden dewa igirisu joō no hata ga miemashita. Sore wa, naka ni joō ga irassharu to iu imi desu. Ayaka san wa, Bakkingamu kyūden wa totemo hiroi to omoimashita. Dakara joō wa igirisu de mottomo kanemochi kamoshirenai to kangaemashita.

Questions 2-D

1. What palace did Ayaka visit in England? (A. Kensington Palace, B. Buckingham Palace, C. Hampton Court Palace, D. Kew Palace)
2. What did Ayaka see at the palace? (A. the Changing of the Guard, B. the Crown Prince, C. the Crown Jewels, D. the Queen's flag)
3. What did Ayaka think about the palace? (A. it is spacious, B. it is richly decorated, C. it is busy with visitors, D. it is filled with artwork)
4. What did Ayaka think about the Queen of England? (A. she is the richest person in England, B. she might be the richest person in England, C. she is the richest person in the world, D. she might be the richest queen in the world)

23 山	Mountain	丨	山	山				

Three (3) strokes
A three-peaked mountain

■ Trace the gray lines, and then practice on your own.

山									
山									

■ Useful vocabulary: Write the character, and trace the gray ones.

□	やま	**yama**	mountain
□ふじ□	ふじさん	**fujisan**	Mount Fuji
□々*	やまやま	**yamayama**	a lot, many mountains
□もり	やまもり	**yamamori**	a heap

24 田	Rice field	丨	冂	冊	用	田		

Five (5) strokes
A rice field

■ Trace the gray lines, and then practice on your own.

田									
田									

■ Useful vocabulary: Write the character, and trace the gray ones.

□んぼ	たんぼ	**tanbo**	rice field

* An asterisk denotes vocabulary with kanji that have not yet been introduced.

Reading 2-E

なつみさんはバードウォッチングが好(す)きです。先週(せんしゅう)なつみさんは学校(がっこう)のうらの田んぼに行(い)きました。でも、そこには鳥(とり)があまりいませんでした。だから、なつみさんは今週(こんしゅう)山に行きます。そこではたくさん鳥が見(み)えるでしょう。

バードウォッチング (bird watching)

Natsumi san wa bādowocchingu ga suki desu. Senshū Natsumi san wa gakkō no ura no tanbo ni ikimashita. Demo, soko niwa tori ga amari imasen deshita. Dakara, Natsumi san wa konshū yama ni ikimasu. Soko dewa takusan tori ga mieru deshō.

Questions 2-E

1. Where did Natsumi go bird watching last week? (A. in the mountains behind the school, B. in the rice fields behind the school, C. in the rice fields behind the mountains, D. in the mountains behind the rice fields)
2. How successful was bird watching last week? (A. there were many birds, B. there were some birds, C. there were not very many birds, D. there were no birds at all)
3. Where is Natsumi going bird watching this week? (A. in the rice fields behind the school, B. in the mountains, C. at the beach, D. along the river behind the school)
4. Why did Natsumi choose this week's location? (A. because the her classmates are going there, B. because there may be more birds there, C. because there are fewer people there, D. because her teacher suggested it)

25 川	River	ノ	川	川					

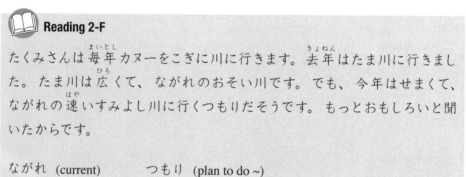

Three (3) strokes
A river

■ Trace the gray lines, and then practice on your own.

川								
川								

■ Useful vocabulary: Write the character, and trace the gray ones.

□	かわ	**kawa**	river
小□	おがわ	**ogawa**	brook, stream
～□	～かわ/がわ	**~kawa/ gawa**	suffix for rivers

Reading 2-F

たくみさんは毎年(まいとし)カヌーをこぎに川に行きます。去年(きょねん)はたま川に行きました。たま川は広(ひろ)くて、ながれのおそい川です。でも、今年はせまくて、ながれの速(はや)いすみよし川に行くつもりだそうです。もっとおもしろいと聞いたからです。

ながれ (current)　　つもり (plan to do ~)

Takumi san wa maitoshi kanū o kogi ni kawa ni ikimasu. Kyonen wa tamagawa ni ikimashita. Tamagawa wa hirokute, nagare no osoi kawa desu. Demo, kotoshi wa semakute, nagare no hayai sumiyoshikawa ni iku tsumori da sō desu. Motto omoshiroi to kiita kara desu.

Questions 2-F

1. How often does Takumi go on canoe trips? (A. monthly, B. every six months, C. annually, D. every few years)
2. How was the Tamagawa River? (A. wide and swift, B. wide and slow, C. narrow and swift, D. narrow and slow)
3. How is the Sumiyoshi River? (A. wide and swift, B. wide and slow, C. narrow and swift, D. narrow and slow)
4. The Sumiyoshi River is probably (A. more challenging than the Tama River, B. about the same as the Tama River, C. less challenging than the Tama River, D. cannot tell from the reading)

Lesson 2 Practice

A. Kanji Review

Write these kanji characters. The mnemonic pictures may offer some hints.

 sun	 moon mon	 fire	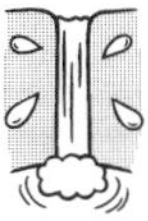 water	 tree	 earth
1.	2.	3.	4.	5.	6.
 king	 gold	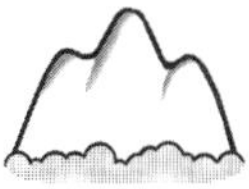 mountain	 rice field	 river	
7.	8.	9.	10.	11.	

B. Vocabulary Review

Try writing these words with the appropriate kanji.

1. ____ 曜(よう) ____ (Thursday)
2. ____ んぼ (rice paddy)
3. ____ 足(そく) (with one's shoes on)
4. ____ 着(ぎ) (swimsuit)
5. ____ ____ (volcano)
6. (お)____ (money)
7. ____ 女 (princess)
8. 小(お) ____ (brook, stream)
9. 積(つみ) ____ (building blocks)
10. 花(はな) ____ (fireworks)
11. ____ 魚(ぎょ) (goldfish)
12. 休(きゅう) ____ (holiday)
13. 桜(さくら)の ____ (cherry blossom tree)

C. Campout Story, Fill in the Blank

Read the following campout story, and fill in the blanks with these appropriate nature-related kanji characters: 日, 月, 火, 水, 木, 金, 土, 川, and 山. Use each kanji character only once. The glossary below may help with any unfamiliar vocabulary.

先週(せんしゅう)ビルさんの家族(かぞく)は三日間(かん)（1）________にキャンプに行(い)きました。（2）________がたくさんあって、とてもきれいな所(ところ)でした。一日目(め)に（3）________で魚釣(さかなつ)りをしたり、ハイキングをしたり、楽(たの)しい時間(じかん)をすごしました。夜(よる)になると（4）________がきれいに見(み)えたそうです。お父(とう)さんはビルさんに一人で焚(た)き火(び)を起(お)こさせました。そして寝(ね)る前(まえ)に（5）________で（6）________を消(け)しました。起きたら、ビルさんはさいふがないのに気づきました。お（7）________が入(はい)っていましたので、心配(しんぱい)して探(さが)しましたが、見つかりませんでした。さいごの（8）________に焚き火の近(ちか)くの（9）________土の上(うえ)にさいふをみつけました、うれしかったです。

Glossary

一日目 (first day)	魚釣(さかなつ)り (fishing)	焚(た)き火(び) (campfire)
起(お)こす (to start, build)	二日目 (second day)	さいふ (wallet)
気づく (to realize)	心配(しんぱい)する (to worry, be anxious)	
探(さが)す (to look for, search)		

D. Guess the Kanji

Which of the nature related kanji characters fit the following descriptions? Write the most appropriate kanji: 日月火水木金土川山田. Use each kanji character only once. The glossary below may help with any unfamiliar vocabulary.

1. 人(ひと)はこれを飲(の)みます。________
2. 高(たか)いところ。________

3. これをほしい人がたくさんいます。 ________

4. これで家(いえ)を建(た)てます。 ________

5. 夜(よる)の空(そら)にあります。 ________

6. ここから米(こめ)ができます。 ________

7. ここでカヌーをこぐことができます。 ________

8. 木をこれに埋(う)めます。 ________

9. 昼間(ひるま)の空(そら)にあります。 ________

10. バーベキューをする時に使います。 ________

空(そら) sky
お米(こめ) uncooked rice
埋(う)め to plant, bury

E. Months of the Year

As you may know, some nature related kanji are also used for time words, such as the days of the week and months of the year. Try writing the months in kanji below. This is done by adding the kanji for month 月 to the numbers of the months 1-12 in kanji, as in the example below. 月＝がつ

January 一月	February	March	April
May	June	July	August
September	October	November	December

F. Calendar with Kanji

Label the following calendar in kanji characters. Use the correct kanji for the days of the week, and use numbers for the dates. Label the month on the top of the calendar.

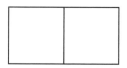

(Sunday)	(Monday)	(Tuesday)	(Wednesday)	(Thursday)	(Friday)	(Saturday)
1 一日	2 __日	3 __日	4 __日	5 __日	6 __日	7 __日
8 __日	9 __日	10 __日	11 __ __日	12 __ __日	13 __ __日	14 __ __日
15 __ __日	16 __ __日	17 __ __日	18 __ __日	19 __ __日	20 __ __日	21 ______日
22 ______日	23 ______日	24 ______日	25 ______日	26 ______日	27 ______日	28 ______日
29 ______日	30 ______日	31 ______日				

G. Japanese Last Names

These names can be written with the kanji characters you have learned so far. Try writing them.

1. かなやま (gold, mountain) ____ ____
2. やまだ (mountain, rice paddy) ____ ____
3. たがわ (rice paddy, river) ____ ____
4. きやま (tree, mountain) ____ ____

5. やまかわ (mountain, river) ____ ____

6. かねだ (gold, rice paddy) ____ ____

7. かわだ (river, rice paddy) ____ ____

8. つちだ (earth, rice paddy) ____ ____

9. みた (three, rice field) ____ ____

H. Annual Japanese Festivals and Holidays

Japanese people have many annual festivals and national holidays. On national holidays school and public offices are closed. Try to read the following calendar of annual events and write the dates in English below. Some annual events change from year to year (i.e., 2nd Monday of October). Also, note that ごろ means "around" or "about."

National Holiday	Date	Festival	Date
New Year's Day 一月一日		New Year 一月一日〜三日	
Coming of Age Day 一月のだい二月曜(よう)日		Bean Sowing Festival 二月三日	
Constitution Day 二月十一日		Girls' Day 三月三日	
Vernal Equinox 三月二十一日ごろ		Cherry Blossom Viewing 四月のはじめごろ	
Shōwa Day 四月二十九日		Golden Week 四月二十九日から一週間	
Constitution Day 五月三日		Boys' Day 五月五日	
Greenery Day 五月四日		Star Festival 七月七日	

Children's Day 五月五日		Bon Festival 八月十五日ごろ	
Marine Day 七月だい三月曜(よう)日		7-5-3 Festival 十一月十五日	
Respect for the Aged Day 九月のだい三月曜(よう)日		Ōmisoka 十二月三十一日	
Autumnal Equinox 九月二十三日ごろ			
Health and Sports Day 十月のだい二月曜(よう)日			
Culture Day 十一月三日			
Labor Thanksgiving Day 十一月二十三日			
Emperor's Birthday 十二月二十三日			

I. Review Questions

Try writing these sentences in Japanese using kanji whenever appropriate. Each sentence has at least one new kanji from this lesson. Then, compare your translations with the answer key at the end of the book.

1. What month is your birthday? ______________________________

2. When is the next holiday? ______________________________

3. What are you doing on Friday? ______________________________

4. Have you ever seen a volcano before? ______________________________

J. Interview Your Partner

Foreign language study is always enhanced when you study with others. Pick a partner who will help you try hard and do your best. Take turns asking the above questions with your partner. Try to answer as fully and appropriately as you can. For best results, you should elaborate on your answers whenever possible.

26 人 Person

Stroke order: ノ 人

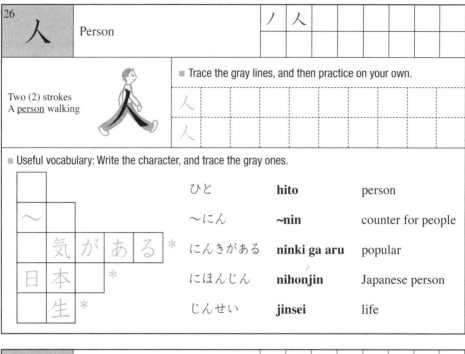

Two (2) strokes
A person walking

■ Trace the gray lines, and then practice on your own.

人
人

■ Useful vocabulary: Write the character, and trace the gray ones.

□	ひと	**hito**	person
～□	～にん	**~nin**	counter for people
□気がある *	にんきがある	**ninki ga aru**	popular
日本□ *	にほんじん	**nihonjin**	Japanese person
□生 *	じんせい	**jinsei**	life

27 力 Power

Stroke order: フ 力

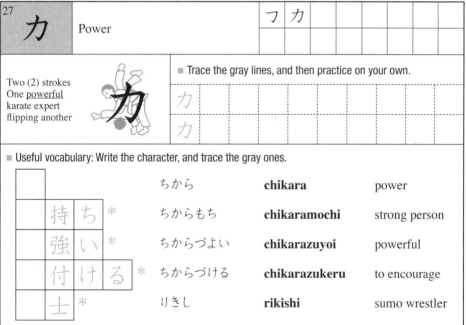

Two (2) strokes
One powerful karate expert flipping another

■ Trace the gray lines, and then practice on your own.

力
力

■ Useful vocabulary: Write the character, and trace the gray ones.

□	ちから	**chikara**	power
□持ち *	ちからもち	**chikaramochi**	strong person
□強い *	ちからづよい	**chikarazuyoi**	powerful
□付ける *	ちからづける	**chikarazukeru**	to encourage
□士 *	りきし	**rikishi**	sumo wrestler

* An asterisk denotes vocabulary with kanji that have not yet been introduced.

Reading 3-A

たけしくんのお母さんはアメリカ人で、お父さんは日本人です。たけしくんのお父さんは力持ちで、前はプロレスの選手でした。でもたけしくんは高校の野球部に入っています。とても上手で人気がある選手です。

Takeshi kun no okāsan wa amerikajin de, otōsan wa nihonjin desu. Takeshi kun no otōsan wa chikaramochi de, mae wa puroresu no senshu deshita. Demo Takeshi kun wa kōkō no yakyūbu ni haitteimasu. Totemo jōzu de ninki ga aru senshu desu.

Questions 3-A

1. What nationality/ies are Takashi's mother and father? (A. both Japanese, B. both American, C. American and Japanese, respectively, D. Japanese and American, respectively)
2. What was Takashi's father's former job? (A. professional wrestling, B. television personality, C. professional baseball, D. movie actor)
3. What sport does Takeshi play at school? (A. wrestling, B. baseball, C. jūdo, D. archery)
4. What is Takeshi's level of skill? (A. beginner, B. not bad, C. very good, D. professional)

28 男 Male

Stroke order: 丨 冂 冂 田 田 男 男

Seven (7) strokes
A powerful <u>man</u> working in the rice field

■ Trace the gray lines, and then practice on your own.

男
男

■ Useful vocabulary: Write the character, and trace the gray ones.

男	おとこ	**otoko**	male
男の人*	おとこのひと	**otokonohito**	man
男子*	だんし	**danshi**	boy, formal
男子校*	だんしこう	**danshikō**	boys' school
男性*	だんせい	**dansei**	man, male

29 父 Father

Stroke order: ノ ハ 父 父

Four (4) strokes
A <u>father</u> swinging an ax

■ Trace the gray lines, and then practice on your own.

父
父

■ Useful vocabulary: Write the character, and trace the gray ones.

お父さん	おとうさん	**otōsan**	father
父	ちち	**chichi**	my father
父の日	ちちのひ	**chichi no hi**	Father's Day
父母*	ふぼ	**fubo**	father and mother, parents

* An asterisk denotes vocabulary with kanji that have not yet been introduced.

Reading 3-B

りょうさんは、男子校に行っています。今年は六月十九日が父の日でした。父の日の前の金曜日にお父さんがりょうさんの学校に来ました。そしてりょうさんの授業を全部見て帰りました。お父さんはりょうさんにいい大学に入ってほしいと思っています。

Ryō san wa, danshikō ni itteimasu. Kotoshi wa rokugatsu jūkunichi ga chichi no hi deshita. Chichi no hi no mae no kinyōbi ni otōsan ga Ryō san no gakkō ni kimashita. Soshite Ryō san no jugyō o zenbu mite kaerimashita. Otōsan wa Ryō san ni ii daigaku ni haitte hoshii to omotteimasu.

Questions 3-B

1. When was Father's Day? (A. the 6th, B. the 9th, C. the 10th, D. the 19th)
2. When did Ryō's father visit his school? (A. Monday, B. Tuesday, C. Thursday, D. Friday)
3. How many classes did Ryō's father visit? (A. one of Ryō's classes, B. half of Ryō's classes, C. all of Ryō's classes, D. all but the last of Ryō's classes)
4. What is Ryō's father concerned about? (A. Ryō's busy schedule, B. Ryō's behavior at school, C. Ryō's grades, D. Ryō's future college)

30 女 Female

Stroke order: く 女 女

Three (3) strokes
A girl skipping

■ Trace the gray lines, and then practice on your own.

女

女

■ Useful vocabulary: Write the character, and trace the gray ones.

□	おんな	**onna**	female
□の人 *	おんなのひと	**onnanohito**	woman
□子校 *	じょしこう	**joshikō**	girls' school
男□	だんじょ	**danjo**	men and women
□性 *	じょせい	**josei**	woman, female

31 母 Mother

Stroke order: 𠃋 𠃊 母 母 母

Five (5) strokes
A mother holding her child
(Notice the kanji for female is part of the kanji for mother)

■ Trace the gray lines, and then practice on your own.

母

母

■ Useful vocabulary: Write the character, and trace the gray ones.

お□さん	おかあさん	**okāsan**	mother
□	はは	**haha**	my mother
□の日	はははのひ	**haha no hi**	Mother's Day
□国語 *	ぼこくご	**bokokugo**	one's mother tongue

* An asterisk denotes vocabulary with kanji that have not yet been introduced.

Reading 3-C

かなさんは山川高校に行っています。山川高校は昔女子校でした。今は男子もいますが、まだ少ないです。その学校でかなさんは空手部に入っています。あまり上手ではありませんが、お母さんはいつも大会におうえんに来てくれます。

Kana san wa yamakawa kōkō ni itteimasu. Yamakawa kōkō wa mukashi joshikō deshita. Ima wa danshi mo imasu ga, mada sukunai desu. Sono gakkō de Kana san wa karatebu ni haitteimasu. Amari jōzu dewa arimasen ga, okāsan wa itsumo taikai ni ōen ni kite kuremasu.

Questions 3-C

1. What is the name of the school that Kana attends? (A. Yamada High School, B. Yamakawa High School, C. Kawada High School, D. Kawayama High School)
2. Kana's high school used to be a (A. girls' school, B. private girls' school, C. coed school, D. private coed school)
3. Now Kana's school is attended by (A. many boys and girls, B. many boys but few girls, C. many girls but few boys, D. few boys and girls)
4. When Kana has karate tournaments, her mother (A. usually cannot attend, B. sometimes attends, C. usually attends, D. always attends)

32 子 Child

㇇	了	子					

Three (3) strokes
A child reaching out his arms

■ Trace the gray lines, and then practice on your own.

子									
子									

■ Useful vocabulary: Write the character, and trace the gray ones.

	ど	も			こども	**kodomo**	child
男	の				おとこのこ	**otokonoko**	boy
女	の				おんなのこ	**onnanoko**	girl
	犬	*			こいぬ	**koinu**	puppy
一	人	っ			ひとりっこ	**hitorikko**	only child
双		*			ふたご	**futago**	twins

33 好 Like

く	女	女	女ㇷ	好	好		

Six (6) strokes
Children like their mothers

■ Trace the gray lines, and then practice on your own.

好									
好									

■ Useful vocabulary: Write the character, and trace the gray ones.

	き	な				すきな	**suki na**	like, favorable (adj.)
お		み	焼	き	*	おこのみやき	**okonomiyaki**	savory hotcakes

* An asterisk denotes vocabulary with kanji that have not yet been introduced.

Reading 3-D

なおきさんは高校三年生です。なおきさんの家の近くにペットショップがあります。なおきさんは毎日ペットショップの前に立ち止まって子犬たちを見ます。子犬たちを見ていると、子どもの時にかっていた犬を思い出します。

立ち止まって (to stop walking)

Naoki san wa kōkō sannensei desu. Naoki san no ie no chikaku ni petto shoppu ga arimasu. Naoki san wa mainichi petto shoppu no mae ni tachidomatte koinu tachi o mimasu. Koinu tachi o miteiru to, kodomo no toki ni katteita inu o omoidashimasu.

Questions 3-D

1. What grade is Naoki in? (A. 3rd grade, B. 6th grade, C. 9th grade, D. 12th grade)
2. Where is the pet shop? (A. near Naoki's house, B. near Naoki's school, C. halfway between Naoki's house and school, D. near the train station)
3. What does Naoki do at the pet shop? (A. enters the pet shop, and looks around, B. talks to the pet shop owner about the puppies, C. talks with his friends about the puppies, D. looks at the puppies through the front window)
4. What do the puppies in the pet shop remind Naoki of? (A. when he owned a dog, B. that he always wanted a dog C. that he was afraid of dogs, D. that he did not like dogs)

34 方

Person (polite), this one, direction

Four (4) strokes
This is the distinguished person who ran ten thousand miles

■ Trace the gray lines, and then practice on your own.

■ Useful vocabulary: Write the character, and trace the gray ones.

この		このかた	**kono kata**	this person (polite)
し		しかた	**shikata**	how to do
夕	*	ゆうがた	**yūgata**	early evening
面	*	ほうめん	**hōmen**	direction
両	*	りょうほう	**ryōhō**	both

35 々

Noun pluralizer

Three (3) strokes
A person bent over in repetitious labor (Not technically a kanji, but used when writing kanji)

■ Trace the gray lines, and then practice on your own.

■ Useful vocabulary: Write the character, and trace the gray ones.

一	いちにち	**ichinichi**	one by one, separately
日	ひび	**hibi**	daily, day after day
月	つきづき	**tsukizuki**	every month
人	ひとびと	**hitobito**	people, each person
方	かたがた	**katagata**	people (honorific)

* An asterisk denotes vocabulary with kanji that have not yet been introduced.

Reading 3-E

ゆうとさんは中華料理(ちゅうかりょうり)と日本(にほん)料理が好きで、ぎょうざやチャーハン、やきそばなどを作(つく)るのがとくいです。毎日夕方(まいにちゆうがた)になると買(か)い物(もの)に行(い)って、晩(ばん)ご飯(はん)を作ります。将来(しょうらい)コックになりたいそうです。

中華料理(ちゅうかりょうり) (Chinese cooking)
作(つく)る (to make)

Yūto san wa chūkaryōri to nihonryōri ga suki de, gyōza ya chāhan, yakisoba nado o tsukuru no ga tokui desu. Mainichi yūgata ni naru to kaimono ni itte, bangohan o tsukurimasu. Shōrai kokku ni naritai sō desu.

Questions 3-E

1. What kind of cooking does Yūto like? (A. Chinese and Japanese cooking, B. Japanese and Thai cooking, C. Thai and Korean cooking, D. Korean and Chinese cooking)
2. How often does Yūto go grocery shopping? (A. every day, B. twice a week, C. every week, D. twice a month)
3. What dishes is Yūto good at making? (A. sweet and sour, gyōza, and fried rice, B. gyōza, fried rice, and stir-fry noodles, C. fried rice, stir-fry noodles, and sweet and sour, D. stir-fry noodles, sweet and sour, and gyōza)
4. What are Yūto's future plans? (A. to learn to cook fried rice, B. to learn to cook Chinese food, C. to manage a restaurant, D. to become a cook)

Lesson 3 Practice

A. Kanji Review

Write these words in kanji characters. The mnemonic pictures may offer some hints.

 person	 power	 male	 father	 female
1.	2.	3.	4.	5.
 mother	 child	 like	 Person, this one, direction	 Noun pluralizer
6.	7.	8.	9.	10.

B. Vocabulary Review

Try writing these words with the appropriate kanji.

1. ____ ども (child)
2. お ____ さん (mother)
3. ____ 本(ほん) ____ (Japanese person)
4. ____ きな (like)
5. ____ の ____ (boy)
6. ____ の ____ (man)
7. ____ の ____ (Father's Day)
8. ____ の ____ (woman)
9. 両(りょう) ____ (both)
10. ____ ____ 校 (boys' school)
11. ____ ____ (father and mother)
12. ____ の ____ (girl)
13. ____ ____ (men and women)
14. ____ 強(つよ)い (powerful)
15. ____ 犬 (puppy)
16. ____ 生 (life)

17. お ____ さん (father)

18. ____ の ____ (Mother's Day)

19. ____ 持(も)ち (powerful person)

20. ____ ____ (people, each person)

C. Common Japanese Last Names

Try writing these common Japanese last names with the appropriate kanji characters.

1. はった (eight, rice paddy) ____ ____
2. せんだ (thousand, rice paddy) ____ ____
3. かねこ (gold, child) ____ ____
4. みよし (three, like) ____ ____
5. やぎ (eight, tree) ____ ____
6. つちだ (earth, rice paddy) ____ ____
7. みき (three, tree) ____ ____

D. Nationalities

To express nationality in Japanese the kanji 人 (pronounced じん) is added as a suffix to the country name. For instance, an Australian is called オーストラリア人. Try writing these nationalities.

1. Australian (おーすとらりあじん)	オーストラリア人	2. Brazilian (ぶらじるじん)	
3. Canadian (かなだじん)		4. Chinese (ちゅうごくじん)	
5. Egyptian (えじぷとじん)		6. French (ふらんすじん)	
7. German (どいつじん)		8. Indian (いんどじん)	
9. Israeli (いすらえるじん)		10. Japanese (にほんじん)	

11. Korean (かんこくじん)		12. Mexican (めきしこじん)	
13. Saudi Arabian (さうじあらびあじん)		14. Spaniard (すぺいんじん)	
15. British (いぎりすじん)		16. American (あめりかじん)	

E. Review Questions

Try writing these sentences in Japanese using kanji whenever appropriate. Each sentence has at least one new kanji from this lesson. Then, compare your translations with the answer key at the end of the book.

1. How many people are in your family? ______________________________

____

2. How many boys are there? ______________________________

____

3. What is your father's name? ______________________________

____

4. Is your father strong? ______________________________

____

5. Who is more strict, your father or mother? ______________________________

____

6. What nationality are you? ______________________________

____

7. Are there Japanese people at your school? ______________________________

____

8. Who is popular at your school? ______________________________

____

9. What did you give to your mother on Mother's Day last year? ____________

____

10. Do you do homework every day? ____________________

____

11. Do you have a puppy? ____________________________

____

12. Which do you prefer, cats or dogs? __________________

____

13. Do you like classical music or rock? _________________

____

14. Do you prefer Japanese food or French food? ____________

____

15. Do you know how to cook Japanese food? ______________

____

F. Interview Your Partner

Take turns asking the above questions with your partner. Try to answer as fully and appropriately as you can. For best results, you should elaborate on your answers whenever possible.

36 小 Small

Stroke order: 亅 小 小

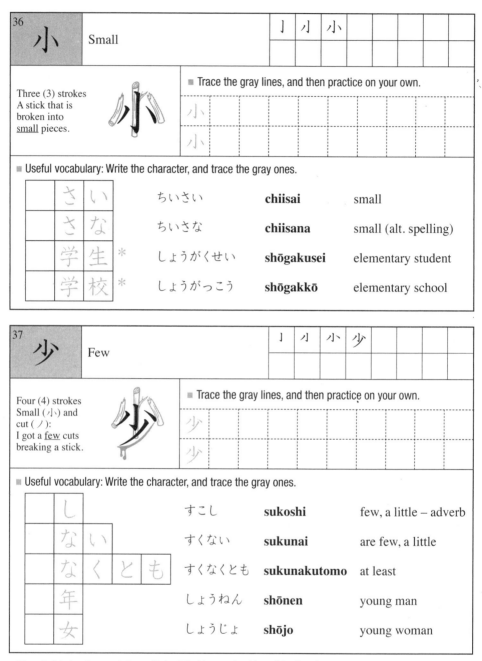

Three (3) strokes
A stick that is broken into small pieces.

■ Trace the gray lines, and then practice on your own.

小

小

■ Useful vocabulary: Write the character, and trace the gray ones.

さい	ちいさい	**chiisai**	small
さな	ちいさな	**chiisana**	small (alt. spelling)
学生 *	しょうがくせい	**shōgakusei**	elementary student
学校 *	しょうがっこう	**shōgakkō**	elementary school

37 少 Few

Stroke order: 亅 小 小 少

Four (4) strokes
Small (小) and cut (ノ):
I got a few cuts breaking a stick.

■ Trace the gray lines, and then practice on your own.

少

少

■ Useful vocabulary: Write the character, and trace the gray ones.

し	すこし	**sukoshi**	few, a little – adverb
ない	すくない	**sukunai**	are few, a little
なくとも	すくなくとも	**sukunakutomo**	at least
年	しょうねん	**shōnen**	young man
女	しょうじょ	**shōjo**	young woman

* An asterisk denotes vocabulary with kanji that have not yet been introduced.

Reading 4-A

れんさんは、子どものころ小さい町（まち）に住（す）んでいました。近（ちか）くの大きい町まで少なくとも一時間（じかん）かかりました。れんさんの小学校はとても小さくて生徒（せいと）はみんなで二十人くらいでした。生徒が少ないので年上（としうえ）のせいとも年下（としした）のせいとみんなれんさんの友だちでした。

年上（としうえ） older, senior　　年下（としした） younger, junior

Ren san wa, kodomo no koro chiisai machi ni sunde imashita. Chikaku no ōkii machi made sukunakutomo ichijikan kakarimashita. Ren san no shōgakkō wa totemo chiisakute seito wa minna de nijūnin kurai deshita. Seito ga sukunai node toshiue no seito mo toshishita no seito minna Ren san no tomodachi deshita.

Questions 4-A

1. Where did Ren live when he was a child? (A. a small home, B. a big home, C. a small town, D. a big city)
2. This passage is written about when Ren was attending (A. elementary school, B. middle school, C. high school, D. college)
3. How many students were in his school? (A. 20, B. 200, C. 800, D. 1200)
4. What kind of friends did Ren have? (A. mostly the same age, B. mostly the same age and younger, C. mostly the same age and older, D. friends of various ages)

38 中 Middle

Stroke order: 丨 冂 口 中

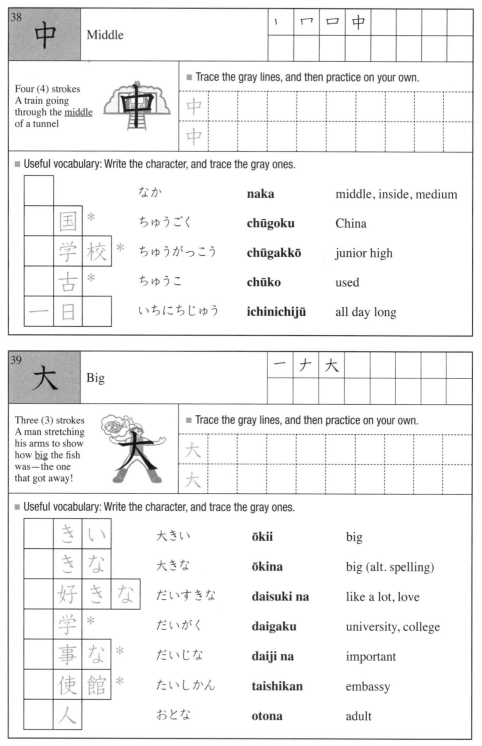

Four (4) strokes
A train going through the middle of a tunnel

■ Trace the gray lines, and then practice on your own.

中 中

■ Useful vocabulary: Write the character, and trace the gray ones.

				なか	**naka**	middle, inside, medium
	国	*		ちゅうごく	**chūgoku**	China
	学	校	*	ちゅうがっこう	**chūgakkō**	junior high
	古	*		ちゅうこ	**chūko**	used
一	日			いちにちじゅう	**ichinichijū**	all day long

39 大 Big

Stroke order: 一 ナ 大

Three (3) strokes
A man stretching his arms to show how big the fish was—the one that got away!

■ Trace the gray lines, and then practice on your own.

大 大

■ Useful vocabulary: Write the character, and trace the gray ones.

	き	い		大きい	**ōkii**	big
	き	な		大きな	**ōkina**	big (alt. spelling)
	好	き	な	だいすきな	**daisuki na**	like a lot, love
	学	*		だいがく	**daigaku**	university, college
	事	な	*	だいじな	**daiji na**	important
	使	館	*	たいしかん	**taishikan**	embassy
	人			おとな	**otona**	adult

* An asterisk denotes vocabulary with kanji that have not yet been introduced.

Reading 4-B

リンさんは中国人です。大学でべんきょうするために日本に来ました。中学校の時に日本にりゅうがくして、日本が大好きになりました。その時から大人になって、日本にもどって来ることはリンさんの大きなゆめでした。

Rin san wa chūgokujin desu. Daigaku de benkyō suru tame ni nihon ni kimashita. Chūgakkō no toki ni nihon ni ryūgaku shite, nihon ga daisuki ni narimashita. Sono toki kara otona ni natte, nihon ni modotte kuru koto wa Rin san no ōkina yume deshita.

Questions 4-B

1. Where did Rin study abroad during junior high school? (A. China, B. Japan, C. Australia, D. USA)
2. Where is Rin attending college? (A. China, B. Japan, C. Australia, D. USA)
3. When did Rin begin making college plans? (A. junior high, B. high school, C. after high school graduation, D. Rin is still undecided)
4. What does Rin think about Japan? (A. it is a good place to visit, but not to live, B. it is a good place to live, C. it is very expensive, D. it is very humid during the summer)

40 夕	Early evening	ノ	ク	夕

Three (3) strokes
A crescent moon in the early evening

■ Trace the gray lines, and then practice on your own.

夕
夕

■ Useful vocabulary: Write the character, and trace the gray ones.

べ	ゆうべ	**yūbe**	last evening
方	ゆうがた	**yūgata**	evening
食	ゆうしょく	**yūshoku**	dinner
七	たなばた	**tanabata**	The Star Festival

41 多	Many	ノ	ク	夕	夕	多	多

Six (6) strokes
At first, this character meant many moons, or a long time, but now it simply means many.

■ Trace the gray lines, and then practice on your own.

多
多

■ Useful vocabulary: Write the character, and trace the gray ones.

い	おおい	**ōi**	many
数	たすう	**tasū**	large number, multitude
分	たぶん	**tabun**	probably, maybe
少	たしょう	**tashō**	somewhat, more or less
目的	たもくてき	**tamokuteki**	multipurpose

Reading 4-C

七月七日は七夕(たなばた)です。今年(ことし)かずおさんは、弟(おとうと)のたくとくんをつれて、えんにちに行(い)きました。屋台(やたい)が多く出(で)ていました。たくとくんは金魚(きんぎょ)すくいをしてみました。一回目(かいめ)に、一ぴきすくいました。

えんにち (temple or shrine festival)
屋台(やたい) (booth)
金魚(きんぎょ)すくい (goldfish scooping game)

Shichigatsu nanoka wa tanabata desu. Kotoshi Kazuo san wa, otōto no Takuto kun o tsurete, ennichi ni ikimashita. Yatai ga ōku deteimashita. Takuto kun wa kingyo sukui o shitemimashita. Ikkaime ni, ippiki sukuimashita.

Questions 4-C

1. When is the Star Festival held? (A. spring, B. summer, C. autumn, D. winter)
2. Who did Kazuo take to the Star Festival? (A. his little sister, B. his little brother, C. his friend, D. his girlfriend)
3. How many festival booths were there? (A. one, B. a few, C. ten, D. many)
4. How did Takuto do on the goldfish game? (A. he did not scoop any, B. he scooped one with Kazuo's help, C. he scooped one on his first try, D. he scooped one on his second try)

42 内 Inside

Stroke order: 丨 冂 内 内

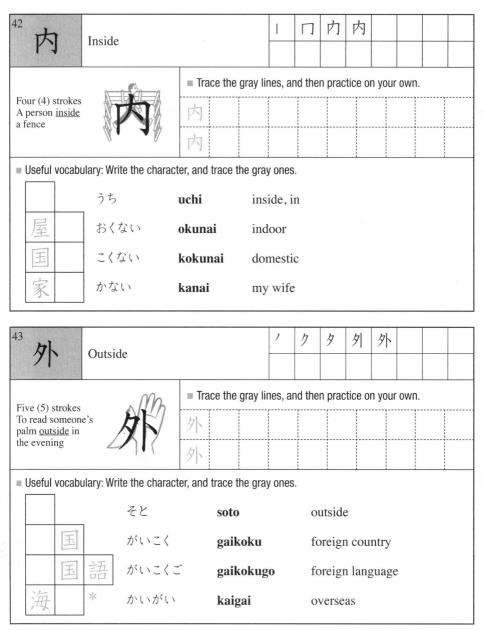

Four (4) strokes
A person inside
a fence

■ Trace the gray lines, and then practice on your own.

内
内

■ Useful vocabulary: Write the character, and trace the gray ones.

内	うち	**uchi**	inside, in
屋内	おくない	**okunai**	indoor
国内	こくない	**kokunai**	domestic
家内	かない	**kanai**	my wife

43 外 Outside

Stroke order: ノ ク タ 夘 外

Five (5) strokes
To read someone's
palm outside in
the evening

■ Trace the gray lines, and then practice on your own.

外
外

■ Useful vocabulary: Write the character, and trace the gray ones.

外	そと	**soto**	outside
外国	がいこく	**gaikoku**	foreign country
外国語	がいこくご	**gaikokugo**	foreign language
海外 *	かいがい	**kaigai**	overseas

* An asterisk denotes vocabulary with kanji that have not yet been introduced.

Reading 4-D

ともこさんは、郵便局(ゆうびんきょく)に年賀(ねんが)はがきを出(だ)しに行(い)きました。海外(かいがい)へ四まい、国内(こくない)へ四十まい送(おく)りました。おしょうがつの間(あいだ)、ともこさんのかぞくはあまり外へ出(で)かけません。ともこさんは家(うち)でゆっくりするのを楽(たの)しみにしています。

郵便局(ゆうびんきょく)	(post office)	年賀(ねんが)はがき	(New Year's cards)
楽(たの)しみにする	(to look forward to)		

Tomoko san wa, yūbinkyoku ni nengahagaki o dashi ni ikimashita. Kaigai e yonmai, kokunai e yonjū mai okurimashita. Oshōgatsu no aida, Tomoko san no kazoku wa amari soto e dekakemasen. Tomoko san wa uchi de yukkuri suru no o tanoshimi ni shiteimasu.

Questions 4-D

1. How many New Year's cards did Tomoko mail? (A. 4 domestic and 14 international, B. 4 international and 14 domestic, C. 4 international and 40 domestic, D. 4 domestic and 40 international)
2. What does Tomoko's family do during the New Year's holiday? (A. have a party with their neighbors, B. go out to eat, C. visit relatives, D. spend a lot time at home)
3. What is Tomoko looking forward to? (A. going out with friends, B. visiting with relatives, C. reading a good book, D. relaxing)
4. Would you suppose Tomoko has more foreign friends or more Japanese friends? (A. more foreign friends than Japanese friends, B. more Japanese friends than foreign friends, C. about the same number of foreign and Japanese friends, D. probably no foreign friends)

44 上

Up, above, on

Stroke order: 丨 ⺊ 上

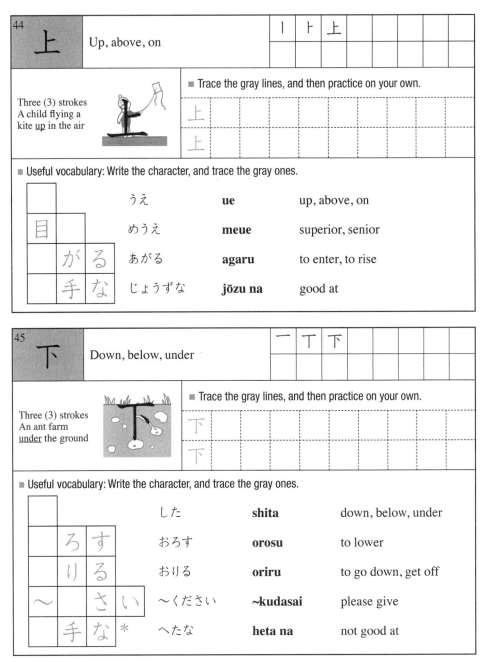

Three (3) strokes
A child flying a
kite up in the air

■ Trace the gray lines, and then practice on your own.

上									
上									

■ Useful vocabulary: Write the character, and trace the gray ones.

□	うえ	**ue**	up, above, on
目□	めうえ	**meue**	superior, senior
□がる	あがる	**agaru**	to enter, to rise
□手な	じょうずな	**jōzu na**	good at

45 下

Down, below, under

Stroke order: 一 丅 下

Three (3) strokes
An ant farm
under the ground

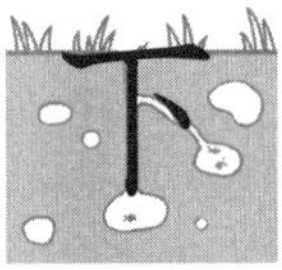

■ Trace the gray lines, and then practice on your own.

下									
下									

■ Useful vocabulary: Write the character, and trace the gray ones.

□	した	**shita**	down, below, under
□ろす	おろす	**orosu**	to lower
□りる	おりる	**oriru**	to go down, get off
～□さい	～ください	**~kudasai**	please give
□手な *	へたな	**heta na**	not good at

* An asterisk denotes vocabulary with kanji that have not yet been introduced.

Reading 4-E

はるきさんは英会話(えいかいわ)の学校(がっこう)に行(い)っています。ばしょは上田ビルの一かいです。はるきさんは英語(えいご)があまり上手ではありませんが、友達(ともだち)のゆうすけさんはとても上手です。英会話の学校のあとで、二人でよく七かいに行って、夕食(しょく)にラーメンを食(た)べます。

英会話(えいかいわ) (English conversation)

ばしょ (place)

Haruki san wa eikaiwa no gakkō ni itte imasu. Basho wa ueda biru no ikkai desu. Haruki san wa eigo ga amari jōzu dewa arimasen ga, tomodachi no Yūsuke san wa totemo jōzu desu. Eikaiwa no gakkō no atode, futari de yoku nanakai ni itte, yūshoku ni rāmen o tabemasu.

Questions 4-E

1. Where is the English conversation school located? (A. the Uchida building, B. the Ueda building, C. the Kawada building, D. the Shimoda building)
2. Who is taking an English conversation class? (A. Haruki, B. Haruki and his friend, C. Haruki's friend, D. the passage does not say)
3. What is Haruki's English skill level? (A. he is very good at English, and so is his friend, B. he is very good at English, but his friend is not, C. he is not very good at English, but his friend is, D. he is not very good at English, and neither is his friend)
4. What kind of food do Haruki and his friend like? (A. French food, B. Korean food, C. Italian food, D. Japanese food)

46 工 Craft

Stroke order: 一 T 工

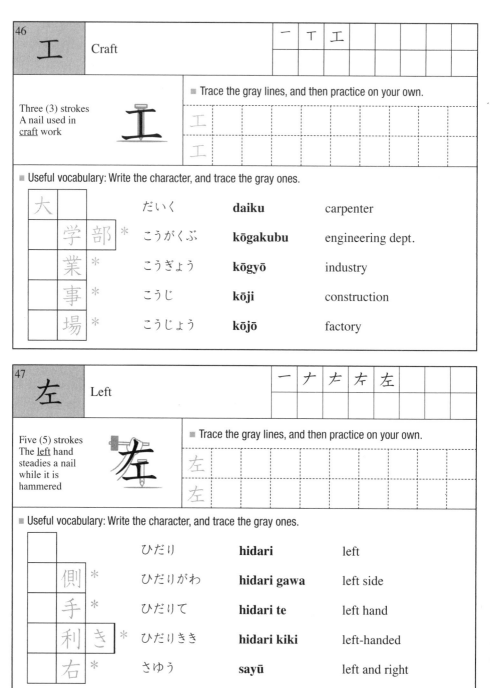

Three (3) strokes
A nail used in
craft work

■ Trace the gray lines, and then practice on your own.

工
工

■ Useful vocabulary: Write the character, and trace the gray ones.

大 □	だいく	**daiku**	carpenter
□ 学部 *	こうがくぶ	**kōgakubu**	engineering dept.
□ 業 *	こうぎょう	**kōgyō**	industry
□ 事 *	こうじ	**kōji**	construction
□ 場 *	こうじょう	**kōjō**	factory

47 左 Left

Stroke order: 一 ナ ￼ 左 左

Five (5) strokes
The left hand
steadies a nail
while it is
hammered

■ Trace the gray lines, and then practice on your own.

左
左

■ Useful vocabulary: Write the character, and trace the gray ones.

□	ひだり	**hidari**	left
□ 側 *	ひだりがわ	**hidari gawa**	left side
□ 手 *	ひだりて	**hidari te**	left hand
□ 利き *	ひだりきき	**hidari kiki**	left-handed
□ 右 *	さゆう	**sayū**	left and right

* An asterisk denotes vocabulary with kanji that have not yet been introduced.

Reading 4-F

ひろしさんは左利(き)で、とてもきようです。今(いま)、高校三年生(こうこうさんねんせい)で、ぎじゅつのクラスが大好きです。ひろしさんのクラスは学校(がっこう)のプールの左側(がわ)にものおきをつくっていて、たのしそうです。ひろしさんはそつぎょうした後(あと)、大工になるつもりです。

きよう (dexterous)　　ぎじゅつ (craft, technology, engineering)

Hiroshi san wa hidarikiki de, totemo kiyō desu. Ima, kōkō sannensei de, gijutsu no kurasu ga daisuki desu. Hiroshi san no kurasu wa gakkō no pūru no hidari gawa ni monooki o tsukutteite, tanoshisō desu. Hiroshi san wa sotsugyō shita ato, daiku ni naru tsumori desu.

Questions 4-F

1. Hiroshi is: (A. a high school senior, B. a college freshman, C. a college senior, D. a construction worker)
2. What is being constructed? (A. a shed to the right of the pool, B. a shed to the left of the pool, C. a pool to the right of the shed, D. a pool to the left of the shed)
3. What is Hiroshi planning to become? (A. a home designer, B. a construction company owner, C. a construction materials retailer, D. a carpenter)
4. What is Hiroshi good at? (A. studying, B. swimming, C. building, D. painting)

48 右	Right	ノ	ナ	才	右	右

Five (5) strokes
The right hand is used for hammering or picking up a stone

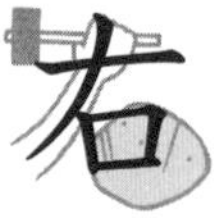

■ Trace the gray lines, and then practice on your own.

右

右

■ Useful vocabulary: Write the character, and trace the gray ones.

	みぎ	**migi**	right
側	みぎがわ	**migi gawa**	right side
手	みぎて	**migi te**	right hand
利き	みぎきき	**migi kiki**	right-handed
左	さゆう	**sayū**	left and right

Reading 4-G

ゆうたさんはハワイで車(くるま)の運転(うんてん)めんきょを取(と)りました。ハワイではどうろの右側(がわ)を運転しますが、日本では、どうろの左側を運転します。ゆうたさんは日本に帰(かえ)ってきた時(とき)にちゅういしなければなりませんでした。ある時ゆうたさんは、どうろの右側を運転してしまいました。あぶなかったけれど、じこにはあいませんでした。

運転(うんてん)	(to drive)	運転(うんてん)めんきょ	(driver's license)
ちゅういする	(be careful)	じこ	(traffic accident)

Yūta san wa hawai de kuruma no unten menkyo o torimashita. Hawai dewa dōro no migi gawa o unten shimasu ga, nihon dewa, dōro no hidari gawa o unten shimasu. Yūta san wa nihon ni kaette kita toki ni chūi shinakereba narimasen deshita. Aru toki Yūta san wa, dōro no migi gawa o unten shite shimaimashita. Abunakatta keredo, jiko niwa aimasen deshita.

Questions 4-G

1. Where did Yūta learn to drive? (A. Korea, B. Singapore, C. Hawaii, D. Guam)
2. What is one difference between driving there and Japan? (A. there are many bicycles on the streets there, B. people drive on the right side of the road there, C. people tend to drive fast there, D. traffic is very heavy there)
3. What did Yūta have to be careful about? (A. not speeding, B. not stopping abruptly, C. not suddenly turning, D. not driving on the wrong side of the road)
4. What happened when Yūta broke a traffic law? (A. it was dangerous, but he did not have an accident, B. he had a small accident, C. he wrecked his car, D. he was severely injured)

Lesson 4 Practice

A. Kanji Review

Write these words in kanji, referring to the mnemonic pictures if necessary.

 small	 few	 medium	 big	 early evening	 many	 inside
1.	2.	3.	4.	5.	6.	7.
 outside	 up, on	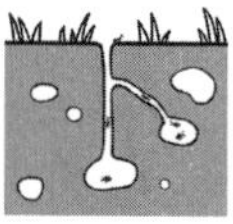 down, under	 craft	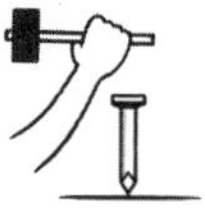 left	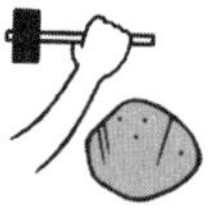 right	
8.	9.	10.	11.	12.	13.	

B. Opposites

Using kanji that you have learned so far write a kanji that means the opposite of the one below.

1. 下	2. 男	3. 少	4. 父
5. 大	6. 外	7. 小人	8. 右

C. Vocabulary Review

Try writing these words with the appropriate kanji characters.

1. ____ ____ ____ (いちにちじゅう all day long)
2. ____学生 (しょうがくせい elementary student)
3. ____ ____ (たなばた Tanabata festival)
4. ____事な (だいじな important)

5. ____ ____ (としうえ superior, senior)
6. ____ 数 (たすう majority, large number)
7. ____ 事 (こうじ construction)
8. ____ りる (おりる to go down, get off)
9. ____ 利き (みぎきき right-handed)
10. ____ 利き (ひだりきき left-handed)
11. ____ ろす (おろす to lower)
12. ____ さい (ください please give)
13. ____ きい (おおきい big)
14. ____ ____ (しょうじょ young lady)
15. ____ 業 (こうぎょう industry)
16. ____ 学校 (ちゅうがっこう junior high)
17. ____ 数 (しょうすう minority, small number)
18. ____ 食 (ゆうしょく dinner)
19. ____ がる (あがる to rise, enter)
20. ____ なくとも (すくなくとも at least)
21. ____ 分 (たぶん probably, maybe)
22. 海 ____ (かいがい overseas)
23. ____ 古 (ちゅうこ used)
24. ____ 側 (みぎがわ right side)
25. 屋 ____ (おくない indoors)
26. ____ ____ 的 (たもくてき multipurpose)
27. ____ 国語 (がいこくご foreign language)
28. ____ 場 (こうじょう factory)
29. ____ 側 (ひだりがわ left side)
30. ____ げる (あげる to raise)
31. ____ ____ (ゆうべ evening, last night)
32. ____ 食 (がいしょく eating out)

D. Japanese Last Names

Write these common Japanese last names in kanji.

1. うちやま (inside, mountain) ____ ____
2. おがわ (small, river) ____ ____
3. たなか (rice field, middle) ____ ____
4. かわかみ (river, up) ____ ____
5. やました (mountain, down) ____ ____
6. おおかわ (big, river) ____ ____
7. しもだ (down, rice field) ____ ____
8. なかやま (middle, mountain) ____ ____
9. おおやま (big, mountain) ____ ____
10. うちだ (inside, rice field) ____ ____
11. みかみ (three, up) ____ ____
12. ただ (many, rice field) ____ ____
13. おだ (small, rice field) ____ ____
14. おおうち (big, inside) ____ ____
15. きうち (tree, inside) ____ ____
16. なかた (middle, rice field) ____ ____
17. やまなか (mountain, middle) ____ ____
18. おぐち／こぐち (small, mouth) ____ ____
19. きのした (tree, down) ____ ____

E. How Many?

Read these descriptions and answer the questions using either 多い or 少ない.

1. はるとさんは小さいころお父さんに何(なん)でもかってもらったので、おもちゃが（ 多い ）です。
2. 田中さんのりんごの木は小さいです。だからりんごは（　　　　　）ですね。

3. 昨日(きのう)だいどころにはドーナッツがたくさんありました。でも、夕べ おにいさんの友(とも)だちがあそびにきて、ほとんど (most) たべてしました。だから（　　　　　）です。

4. 月曜(よう)日に八百屋(やおや)にバナナがたくさんありました。でも、火曜日にセールがあったので、今(いま)バナナが（　　　　　）です。

5. ゆうとさんはテレビゲームが大好きです。いつもあたらしいのを買(か)います。だから（　　　　　）ですよ。

F. Which One?

Read these hints and guess which number is being described. Write your answer in kanji.

1. 上から二番(ばん)目で、左から二番(ばん)目です。 ___七___ です。
2. 一番(ばん)上で、右から　二番(ばん)目です。 ________ です。
3. 下から二番(ばん)目で、一番(ばん)左です。 ________ です。
4. 上から二番(ばん)目で、右から二番(ばん)目です。 ________ です。
5. 上から三番(ばん)目で、右から三番(ばん)目です。 ________ です。
6. 一番(ばん)上で、一番(ばん)左です。 ________ です。
7. 下から二番(ばん)目で、右から三番(ばん)目です。 ________ です。
8. 一番(ばん)下で、一番(ばん)右です。 ________ です。
9. 上から三番(ばん)目で、一番(ばん)右です。 ________ です。
10. 一番(ばん)下で、左から二番(ばん)目です。 ________ です。

1	2	3	4	5
6	7	8	9	10
11	12	13	14	15
16	17	18	19	20
21	22	23	24	25

G. Review Questions

Try writing these sentences in Japanese using kanji whenever appropriate. Each sentence has at least one new kanji from this lesson. Then, compare your translations with the answer key at the end of the book.

1. Do you prefer big cars or small cars? ________

2. Can you write hiragana with your left hand? ________

3. Are you right handed or left handed? ________

4. What is inside your backpack? ________

5. Do you have a lot of homework tonight? ________

6. What did you do last night? ________

7. Have you ever waited outside a movie theater for an hour? ________

8. Is your house big or small? ________

9. Are you good at sports? ________

10. Where do you prefer to exercise, inside or outside? ________

11. Sometimes do you watch TV all day long on weekends? ________

12. Will you play video games when you are an adult? ______________________

____

13. Do you love *anime*? ____

____

14. Do you know what *Tanabata* is? ______________________________________

____

15. Are you somewhat tired? ____

____

16. What are you not good at? ____

____

17. Are there many students taking Japanese at this school? ________________

____

18. Do you have any older siblings? ______________________________________

____

19. Do you know any carpenters? ____

____

H. Interview Your Partner

Take turns asking the above questions with your partner. Try to answer as fully and appropriately as you can. For best results, you should elaborate on your answers whenever possible.

49 家

House, home

Stroke order: 家 (10 strokes)

Ten (10) strokes
Thatched roof (宀)
and pig (豕):
In old Japan, pigs
were often allowed
in the house.

■ Trace the gray lines, and then practice on your own.

家
家

■ Useful vocabulary: Write the character, and trace the gray ones.

[ ]	いえ, うち	**ie, uchi**	house, home
[ ]族 *	かぞく	**kazoku**	family
[ ]庭 *	かてい	**katei**	household
[ ]計 *	かけい	**kakei**	family finances
作[ ] *	さっか	**sakka**	writer, author
専門[ ] *	せんもんか	**senmonka**	specialist, expert

50 入

Enter

Stroke order: ノ 入

Two (2) strokes
Opening *noren*
curtains

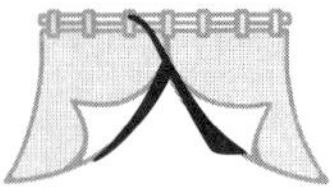

■ Trace the gray lines, and then practice on your own.

入
入

■ Useful vocabulary: Write the character, and trace the gray ones.

[ ]れる	いれる	**ireru**	to put in, insert
[ ]る	はいる	**hairu**	enter
[ ]学する *	にゅうがくする	**nyūgaku suru**	enroll at school
記[ ]する *	きにゅうする	**kinyū suru**	to write on a form

* An asterisk denotes vocabulary with kanji that have not yet been introduced.

Reading 5-A

ひなさんはしょうらい作家（さっか）になりたいそうです。大学（だいがく）の入学がんしょにもそう記入（きにゅう）しました。ひなさんの家族（かぞく）はおうえんしてくれています。家計（かけい）を上手（じょうず）にやりくりして、大学のじゅぎょうりょうをはらってくれるそうです。ひなさんはいい作家になれるようにがんばると言（い）っています。

入学（にゅうがく）がんしょ (school entrance application)
やりくりする (to manage)

Hina san wa shōrai sakka ni naritai sō desu. Daigaku no nyūgakugansho nimo sō kinyū shimashita. Hina san no kazoku wa ōen shite kureteimasu. Kakei o jōzu ni yarikuri shite, daigaku no jugyōryō o haratte kureru sō desu. Hina san wa ii sakka ni naru yō ni ganbaru to itte imasu.

Questions 5-A

1. What did Hina write on her college application? (A. she wants to become an author, B. she wants to become a business leader, C. she wants to become a teacher, D. she wants to become a carpenter)
2. Who is supportive of Hina's goals? (A. her best friend, B. her family, C. her teacher, D. her older sister)
3. How will Hina pay for college? (A. student loans, B. a scholarship, C. a part-time job, D. family assistance)
4. Which of the following is Hina's likely hobby? (A. reading, B. building, C. traveling, D. shopping)

51 出 Exit

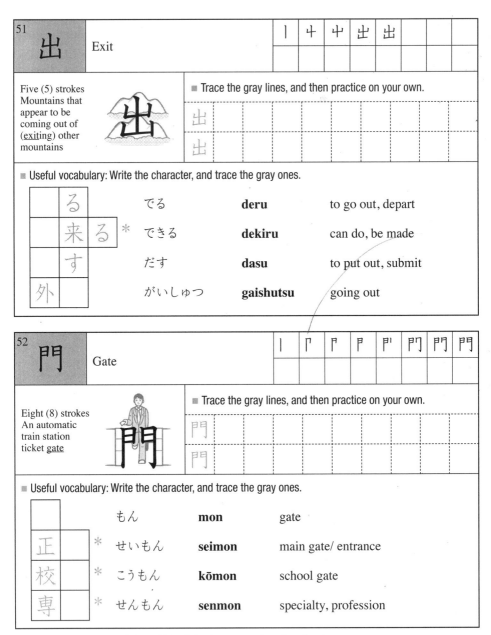

Five (5) strokes
Mountains that appear to be coming out of (exiting) other mountains

■ Trace the gray lines, and then practice on your own.

出
出

■ Useful vocabulary: Write the character, and trace the gray ones.

出る		でる	**deru**	to go out, depart
出来る	*	できる	**dekiru**	can do, be made
出す		だす	**dasu**	to put out, submit
外出		がいしゅつ	**gaishutsu**	going out

52 門 Gate

Eight (8) strokes
An automatic train station ticket gate

■ Trace the gray lines, and then practice on your own.

門
門

■ Useful vocabulary: Write the character, and trace the gray ones.

門		もん	**mon**	gate
正門	*	せいもん	**seimon**	main gate/ entrance
校門	*	こうもん	**kōmon**	school gate
専門	*	せんもん	**senmon**	specialty, profession

* An asterisk denotes vocabulary with kanji that have not yet been introduced.

Reading 5-B

はるきさんは山田専門学校に行っています。山田専門学校は、はるきさんの家から三十分くらいです。毎日九時に家を出て、ちかくのバスていでバスにのります。山田えきでおりて、えきまえの大きいみちをあるきます。二つ目のしんごうで右へまがると、がっこうの正門は左がわにあります。

せんもんがっこう
専門学校 (polytechnic college)

Haruki san wa yamada senmon gakkō ni itte imasu. Yamada senmon gakkō wa Haruki san no ie kara sanjuppun kurai desu. Mainichi kuji ni ie o dete, chikaku no basutei de basu ni norimasu. Yamada eki de orite, eki mae no ōkii michi o arukimasu. Futatsume no shingō de migi e magaru to, gakkō no seimon wa hidari gawa ni arimasu.

Questions 5-B

1. How far is it from Haruki's house to the college? (A. 30 minutes, B. 40 minutes, C. 50 minutes, D. one hour)
2. What time does Haruki leave in the morning? (A. 7:30, B. 8:00, C. 8:30, D. 9:00)
3. How does Haruki commute to college? (A. bus and walking, B. walking and train, C. train and taxi, D. taxi and bus)
4. The college entrance is (A. at the end of the street, B. on the right side of the street, C. on the left side of the street, D. across from the park)

53 開	Open	丨	𠃍	...	門	門	門	開	開

Twelve (12) strokes
A gate (門) and *torii* gate (开): A gate that is open as wide as a torii gate

開

■ Trace the gray lines, and then practice on your own.

開

開

■ Useful vocabulary: Write the character, and trace the gray ones.

□ける	あける	**akeru**	to open something
□く	あく	**aku**	something opens
□く	ひらく	**hiraku**	to open, hold (meeting)
□店*	かいてん	**kaiten**	store opening
□始*	かいし	**kaishi**	start, beginning
□会式*	かいかいしき	**kaikaishiki**	opening ceremony

54 閉	Close	丨	𠃍	...	門	閉	閉

Eleven (11) strokes
A gate (門) and age (才): A gate that is closed to anyone not old enough to enter

閉

■ Trace the gray lines, and then practice on your own.

閉

閉

■ Useful vocabulary: Write the character, and trace the gray ones.

□める	しめる	**shimeru**	to close something
□まる	しまる	**shimaru**	something closes
□じる	とじる	**tojiru**	to shut
□会式*	へいかいしき	**heikaishiki**	closing ceremony
□店*	へいてん	**heiten**	closing shop

* An asterisk denotes vocabulary with kanji that have not yet been introduced.

Reading 5-C

さきさんはリサイクルショップでアルバイトしています。毎(まい)あさ十時(じ)にみせを開(あ)けなければなりません。閉店時間(へいてんじかん)はよる八時(じ)ですが、さきさんはみせが閉まるまえにかえります。そしていつももう一人のてんいんがみせを閉めます。

てんいん (store clerk)

Saki san wa risaikuru shoppu de arubaito shite imasu. Maiasa jūji ni mise o akenakereba narimasen. Heiten jikan wa yoru hachiji desu ga, Saki san wa mise ga shimaru mae ni kaerimasu. Soshite itsumo mō hitori no tenin ga mise o shimemasu.

Questions 5-C

1. Where does Saki work? (A. a bicycle shop, B. an auto repair shop, C. a recycle shop, D. rental shop)
2. What time does Saki open the store? (A. 9:00, B. 9:30, C. 10:00, D. 10:30)
3. What time does the store close? (A. 6:00, B. 7:00, C. 8:00, D. 9:00)
4. When does Saki go home? (A. after the closing, B. after all the other store clerks, C. before the store closes, D. after lunchtime)

55 所 Place

一	ヿ	ヨ	戸	戸	所	所	所

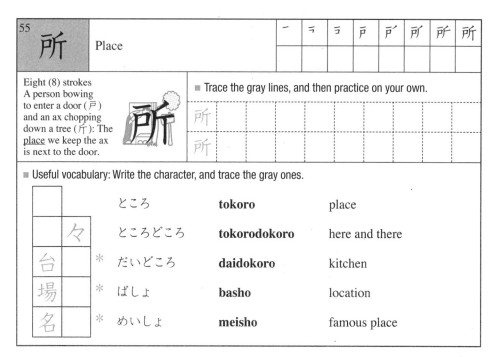

Eight (8) strokes
A person bowing to enter a door (戸) and an ax chopping down a tree (斤): The place we keep the ax is next to the door.

■ Trace the gray lines, and then practice on your own.

所
所

■ Useful vocabulary: Write the character, and trace the gray ones.

〔 〕	ところ	**tokoro**	place
〔 〕々	ところどころ	**tokorodokoro**	here and there
台〔 〕*	だいどころ	**daidokoro**	kitchen
場〔 〕*	ばしょ	**basho**	location
名〔 〕*	めいしょ	**meisho**	famous place

56 近 Near

ノ	厂	斤	斤	斤	近	近	

Seven (7) strokes
A path (⻌) and an ax chopping down a tree (斤): Cutting wood near the path

■ Trace the gray lines, and then practice on your own.

近
近

■ Useful vocabulary: Write the character, and trace the gray ones.

〔 〕い	ちかい	**chikai**	near, soon
〔 〕道*	ちかみち	**chikamichi**	shortcut
〔 〕所	きんじょ	**kinjo**	neighborhood
〔 〕代*	きんだい	**kindai**	modern times
〔 〕代的な*	きんだいてき	**kindaiteki**	modern
最〔 〕*	さいきん	**saikin**	recent

* An asterisk denotes vocabulary with kanji that have not yet been introduced.

Reading 5-D

だいすけさんは中国へ旅行して、名所をたくさん見ました。二〇〇八年の北京オリンピックの開会式の場所に近いホテルに泊まりました。北京には、むかしのたてものもありますが、近代的なたてものも多いです。

泊まる (to stay, lodge)

Daisuke san wa chūgoku e ryokō shite, meisho o takusan mimashita. Nisen hachi nen no pekin orinpikku no kaikaishiki no basho ni chikai hoteru ni tomarimashita. Pekin niwa, mukashi no tatemono mo arimasu ga, kindaiteki na tatemono mo ōi desu.

Questions 5-D

1. Where did Daisuke travel to recently? (A. Korea, B. Italy, C. China, D. England)
2. What did he do during his travels? (A. shopping, B. swimming, C. business, D. sightseeing)
3. What landmark was near his hotel? (A. Big Ben, B. an Olympics venue, C. the 38th parallel, D. Tower of Pisa)
4. What kind of buildings did Daisuke see? (A. mostly old buildings, B. old and new buildings, C. many new buildings, D. the passage does not provide this detail)

Lesson 5 Practice

A. Kanji Review

Write these words in kanji, referring to the mnemonic pictures if necessary.

 house	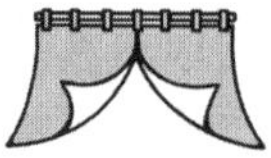 to enter	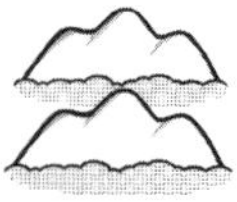 to exit	 gate
1.	2.	3.	4.
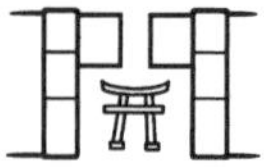 to open	 to close	 place	 near
5.	6.	7.	8.

B. Vocabulary Review

Try writing these words with the appropriate kanji.

1. ____ける (あける to open something)
2. ____ (ところ place)
3. ____口 (でぐち exit)
4. ____ (いえ、うち house, home)
5. ____れる (いれる to put in, insert)
6. 正 ____ (せいもん main gate)
7. ____める (しめる to close something)
8. ____ 代 (きんだい modern times)
9. 作 ____ (さっか writer, author)

10. ____ ____ (がいしゅつ going out)

11. ____ 会式 (かいかいしき opening ceremony)

12. 名 ____ (めいしょ famous place)

13. 校 ____ (こうもん school gate)

14. ____ 会式 (へいかいしき closing ceremony)

15. 最____ (さいきん recent)

16. 記 ____ する (きにゅうする to write on a form)

17. ____す (だす to put out, submit)

18. ____ 始 (かいし start, beginning)

19. 専 ____ (せんもん specialty, profession)

20. 台 ____ (だいどころ kitchen)

21. ____まる (しまる something closes)

22. ____ 庭 (かてい household)

23. 場____ (ばしょ location)

24. ____る (でる to go out, depart)

25. ____ 代的な (きんだいてき modern)

26. ____ 店 (へいてん closing shop)

27. ____ 来る (できる can do, be made)

28. ____学する (にゅうがくする to enroll in a school)

29. ____ ____ (きんじょ neighborhood)

30. ____ 計 (かけい family finances)

31. ____く (あく something opens)

32. ____ 族 (かぞく family)

33. ____口 (いりぐち entrance)

34. ____い (ちかい near, soon)

C. Opposites

Write a kanji that has the opposite meaning of the ones below.

1. 出 ____ 2. 上 ____ 3. 開 ____ 4. 左 ____

5. 男 ____ 6. 母 ____ 7. 小 ____ 8. 内 ____

D. Review Questions

Try writing these sentences in Japanese using kanji whenever appropriate. Each sentence has at least one new kanji from this lesson. Then, compare your translations with the answer key at the end of the book.

1. When did you enroll at this school? ____________________

____

2. What time do you leave the house in the morning? ____________________

____

3. Do you put your lunch in your backpack? ____________________

____

4. What time does the school open? ____________________

____

5. From which door (entrance) do you usually enter the school? ____________________

____

6. Did you already turn in today's homework? ____________________

____

7. Is your school a modern building? ____________________

____

8. Last summer did you visit any famous places? ____________________

____

9. Are the houses in your neighborhood big? ______________________

____

10. Is there a gate in front of your house? ______________________

____

11. Who usually takes out the trash at your home? ______________________

____

12. Do you prefer restaurant cooking or home cooking? ______________________

____

13. Until what time are you allowed to stay out? ______________________

____

14. Are there some good bird watching locations near here? ______________________

____

15. Can you do karate? ______________________

____

16. Did you watch the Olympics opening ceremonies (しき) on TV? ______________________

____

E. Interview Your Partner

Take turns asking the above questions with your partner. Try to answer as fully and appropriately as you can. For best results, you should elaborate on your answers whenever possible.

57 口 Mouth

Stroke order: 丨 ㄇ 口

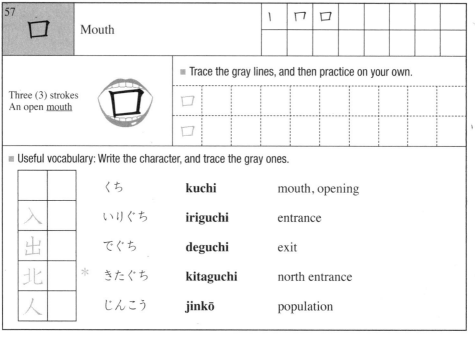

Three (3) strokes
An open mouth

■ Trace the gray lines, and then practice on your own.

口
口

■ Useful vocabulary: Write the character, and trace the gray ones.

		くち	**kuchi**	mouth, opening
入		いりぐち	**iriguchi**	entrance
出		でぐち	**deguchi**	exit
北	*	きたぐち	**kitaguchi**	north entrance
人		じんこう	**jinkō**	population

58 目 Eye(s)

Stroke order: 丨 冂 月 月 目

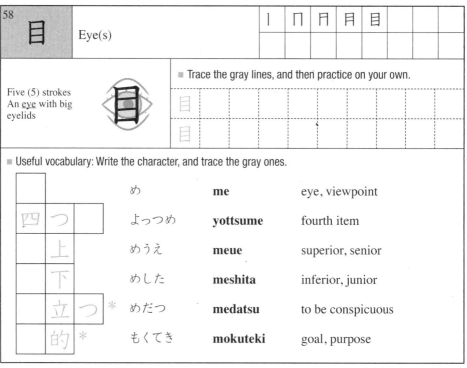

Five (5) strokes
An eye with big eyelids

■ Trace the gray lines, and then practice on your own.

目
目

■ Useful vocabulary: Write the character, and trace the gray ones.

		め	**me**	eye, viewpoint
四つ		よっつめ	**yottsume**	fourth item
上		めうえ	**meue**	superior, senior
下		めした	**meshita**	inferior, junior
立つ	*	めだつ	**medatsu**	to be conspicuous
的	*	もくてき	**mokuteki**	goal, purpose

* An asterisk denotes vocabulary with kanji that have not yet been introduced.

Reading 6-A

みきさんは、毎日友だちのゆみさんと電車で学校へ行きます。ある日、みきさんは、おそくおきたので、一人で学校に行きました。電車のドアが開いてすぐに、みきさんはえきの出口の方に走って行きました。すると、きゅうにだれかがみきさんの名前をよびました。みきさんは、こわかったけれど、後ろを見ました。それはゆみさんでした。みきさんとゆみさんは、いそいであるいたので、学校に間に合いました。

Miki san wa, mainichi tomodachi no Yumi san to densha de gakkō e ikimasu. Aru hi, miki san wa, osoku okita node, hitori de gakkō ni ikimashita. Densha no doa ga aite suguni, miki san wa eki no deguchi no hō ni hashitte ikimashita. Suru to, kyū ni dareka ga Miki san no namae o yobimashita. Miki san wa, kowakatta keredo, ushiro o mimashita. Sore wa Yumi san deshita. Miki san to Yumi san wa, isoide aruita node, gakkō ni maniaimashita.

Questions 6-A

1. When did this story take place? (A. on Sunday, B. last week, C. on a certain day, D. today)
2. Since Miki woke up late, what did she do? (A. she was late for school, B. she got a ride to school in her mother's car, C. she went to school alone, D. she skipped school)
3. Why did Miki run at the train station? (A. she saw her friend, B. she saw her teacher, C. she was late for school, D. she heard an alarm)
4. Why was Miki relieved? (A. because the alarm turned off, B. because she saw her teacher, C. because the train doors opened, D. because she saw her friend)

59 耳 Ear(s)

Stroke order: 一 丅 F F 圧 耳

Six (6) strokes
An ear with a big earlobe

■ Trace the gray lines, and then practice on your own.

耳
耳

■ Useful vocabulary: Write the character, and trace the gray ones.

□	みみ	**mimi**	ear
右□	みぎみみ	**migi mimi**	right ear
左□	ひだりみみ	**hidari mimi**	left ear
□が痛い *	みみがいたい	**mimi ga itai**	earache

60 手 Hand

Stroke order: ノ 二 三 手

Four (4) strokes
Five fingers on a hand (count the lines stemming from the vertical line)

■ Trace the gray lines, and then practice on your own.

手
手

■ Useful vocabulary: Write the character, and trace the gray ones.

□	て	**te**	hand
□品 *	てじな	**tejina**	magic trick
相□ *	あいて	**aite**	partner, opponent
選□ *	せんしゅ	**senshu**	athlete, player
上□な	じょうずな	**jōzu na**	good at
下□な	へたな	**heta na**	not good at, clumsy
苦□な *	にがてな	**nigate na**	not good at, dislike

* An asterisk denotes vocabulary with kanji that have not yet been introduced.

Reading 6-B

ゆいさんの学校(がっこう)にはピアスをしてはいけないというきそくがあります。目上の人に失礼(しつれい)だからだそうです。ゆいさんは先生(せんせい)たちを尊敬(そんけい)していますが、時々(ときどき)左耳にピアスをします。ピアスをすると目立ちますが、山田先生は気(き)付(づ)いていないようです。

失礼(しつれい) (impolite, rude)　　尊敬(そんけい) (respect)

Yui san no gakkō niwa piasu o shite wa ikenai to iu kisoku ga arimasu. Meue no hito ni shitsurei da kara da sō desu. Yui san wa sensei tachi o sonkei shiteimasu ga, tokidoki hidari mimi ni piasu o shimasu. Piasu o suru to medachimasu ga, Yamada sensei wa kizuiteinai yō desu.

Questions 6-B

1. How does Yui feel regarding her teachers? (A. she disrespects her teachers, B. she disrespects some of her teachers, C. she respects most of her teachers, D. she respects her teachers)
2. What is Yui's response to the school dress code? (A. she sometimes breaks the dress code, B. she never breaks the dress code, C. she likes the dress code, D. she never complains about the dress code)
3. What does Mr. Yamada do when students break the dress code? (A. he does not notice, B. he always catches them, C. he catches them, and gets angry, D. he catches them and sends them to the principal's office)
4. Yui is probably a: (A. teacher, B. college student, C. high school student, D. home school student)

61 心	Heart	Stroke order: 心 (4 strokes shown)

Four (4) strokes
The four chambers of a human heart

■ Trace the gray lines, and then practice on your own.

心									
心									

■ Useful vocabulary: Write the character, and trace the gray ones.

					こころ	**kokoro**	heart
	地	よ	い	*	ここちよい	**kokochiyoi**	comfortable
安		す	る	*	あんしんする	**anshin suru**	be relieved
	配	す	る	*	しんぱいする	**shinpai suru**	to worry
中					ちゅうしん	**chūshin**	center, middle

* An asterisk denotes vocabulary with kanji that have not yet been introduced.

Reading 6-C

桜(さくら)さんはチェスクラブに入(はい)っています。今日(きょう)ははじめての大会(たいかい)だったので少(すこ)しドキドキしていました。試合(しあい)の相手(あいて)はチェスがとても上手で桜さんは負(ま)けてしまいました。桜さんはつぎの大会ではがんばってかちたいと思(おも)っています。でも、はじめての大会がおわったので、今日は安心(あんしん)してねむれます。

ねむれる　(to be able to sleep)

Sakura san wa chesu kurabu ni haitteimasu. Kyō wa hajimete no taikai datta node sukoshi dokidoki shite imashita. Shiai no aite wa chesu ga totemo jōzu de Sakura san wa makete shimaimashita. Sakura san wa tsugi no taikai dewa ganbatte kachitai to omotte imasu. Demo, hajimete no taikai ga owatta node, kyō wa anshin shite nemuremasu.

Questions 6-C

1. When was Sakura's first chess tournament? (A. today, B. yesterday, C. last week, D. last year)
2. How nervous was Sakura about her first tournament? (A. she was not nervous at all, B. she was not very nervous, C. she was a little nervous, D. she was nervous)
3. What was the outcome of Sakura's chess match? (A. she won, even though her opponent was very good, B. she won because her opponent was not very good, C. she lost because her opponent was very good, D. she lost, even though her opponent was not very good)
4. Why was Sakura relieved after the tournament? (A. she did very well, B. it was over, C. her friend won, D. her team won)

Lesson 6 Practice

A. Kanji Review

Write these words in kanji, referring to the mnemonic pictures if necessary.

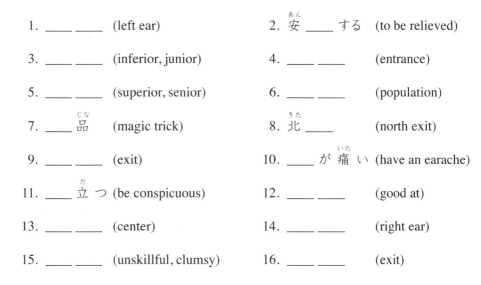

 mouth	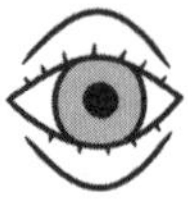 eyes	 ears	 hand	 heart
1.	2.	3.	4.	5.

B. Vocabulary Review

Try writing these words with the appropriate kanji.

1. ____ ____ (left ear)
2. 安(あん) ____ する (to be relieved)
3. ____ ____ (inferior, junior)
4. ____ ____ (entrance)
5. ____ ____ (superior, senior)
6. ____ ____ (population)
7. ____ 品(じな) (magic trick)
8. 北(きた) ____ (north exit)
9. ____ ____ (exit)
10. ____ が 痛(いた) い (have an earache)
11. ____ 立(だ) つ (be conspicuous)
12. ____ ____ (good at)
13. ____ ____ (center)
14. ____ ____ (right ear)
15. ____ ____ (unskillful, clumsy)
16. ____ ____ (exit)

C. More Japanese Vocabulary Related to the Body

The following words and phrases use kanji related to the body. Write the underlined words in kanji you have learned, and write the others in hiragana.

1. Bad eyesight (**<u>me</u>** ga war u i)

2. To be hard of hearing, deaf (**<u>mimi</u>** ga to o i)

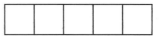

3. To be dizzy (**me** ga mawa ru)

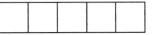

4. Tongue twister (ha ya **kuchi** ko to ba)

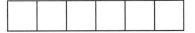

5. Driver (u n te n **shu**)

6. Player, athlete (se n **shu**)

7. Singer (ka **shu**)

8. Spicy hot (ka ra **kuchi**)

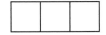

D. Guess the Kanji

Read the following hints and guess the correct kanji related to the body. Write it carefully in the space provided.

1. これで　ラジオを　ききます。 _______
2. これで　えんぴつを　もちます。 _______
3. これで たべものを　たべます。 _______
4. これで　テレビを　みます。 _______
5. これで　うれしい　きもちを　かんじます。 _______

E. Japanese Last Names

Here are some more names that include some of the kanji characters we have learned so far. Read the pronunciation, and try to write them in kanji.

1. やまぐち (mountain, mouth)	2. かわぐち (river, mouth)
3. たぐち (rice field, mouth)	4. みずぐち (water, mouth)

F. Review Questions

Try writing these sentences in Japanese using kanji whenever appropriate. Each sentence has at least one new kanji from this lesson. Then, compare your translations with the answer key at the end of the book.

1. Who is your favorite singer? ______

2. Do you have a favorite athlete? Who? ______

3. What are you good at? ______

4. What are you bad at? ______

5. In our Japanese class, who has bad eyesight? ______

6. Do you know any Japanese tongue twisters? ______

7. Do you have to raise your hand in Japanese class? ______

8. Can you do a magic trick? ______

9. Do you prefer spicy hot cooking or mild cooking? ______

10. Do you like the crust of bread (パンのみみ)? ______

11. What is the population of our city? ______________________________

____

G. Interview Your Partner

Take turns asking the above questions with your partner. Try to answer as fully and appropriately as you can. For best results, you should elaborate on your answers whenever possible.

62 寺	Temple	一	十	土	圭	寺	寺		

Six (6) strokes
A Buddhist priest ringing a temple bell

■ Trace the gray lines, and then practice on your own.

寺								
寺								

■ Useful vocabulary: Write the character, and trace the gray ones.

(お)	(お)てら	**(o)tera**	Buddhist temple
〜	〜でら、〜じ	**~dera, ~ji**	suffix for temples
清水 *	きよみずでら	**kiyomizu-dera**	Kiyomizu Temple
金閣 *	きんかくじ	**kinkaku-ji**	Kinkaku Temple

63 時	Time	丨	冂	日	日	日一	日十	日土	日圭
		時	時						

Ten (10) strokes
The sun tells when it is time to ring the temple bell

■ Trace the gray lines, and then practice on your own.

時								
時								

■ Useful vocabulary: Write the character, and trace the gray ones.

(時)	とき	**toki**	time, occasion, when~
(時)間 *	じかん	**jikan**	time, hour, leisure
一(時)	いちじ	**ichiji**	one o'clock, temporarily
八(時)	はちじ	**hachiji**	eight o'clock
何(時)ですか *	なんじですか	**nanji desu ka**	What time is it?

* An asterisk denotes vocabulary with kanji that have not yet been introduced.

Reading 7-A

めいさんはオーストラリアの友達(ともだち)がきた時にいっしょに京都(きょうと)のゆうめいなお寺を見(み)に行(い)きました。あさ八時にしんかんせんにのって、十時二十分(ぶん)に京都につきました。清水寺(きよみずでら)や金閣寺(きんかくじ)を見たあとで、夕方の六時にしんかんせんにのって八時二十分に東京(とうきょう)にかえってきました。

Mei san wa ōsutoraria no tomodachi ga kita toki ni isshoni kyōto no yūmei na otera o mi ni ikimashita. Asa hachiji ni shinkansen ni notte, jūji nijuppun ni kyōto ni tsukimashita. Kiyomizudera ya kinkakuji o mita atode, yūgata no rokuji ni shinkansen ni notte hachiji nijuppun ni tōkyō ni kaette kimashita.

Questions 7-A

1. Where did Mei take her Australian friend? (A. to Tokyo, B. to Kofu, C. to Fukuoka, D. to Kyoto)
2. What time did they board the bullet train? (A. 6 a.m., B. 8 a.m., C. 8:30 a.m., D. 10:20 a.m.)
3. What did they see while in Kyoto? (A. two shrines, B. two temples, C. one shrine and one temple, D. two shrines and two temples)
4. What time did they board the bullet train for home? (A. 6 p.m., B. 6:20 p.m., C. 8 p.m., D. 8:20 p.m.)

64 **半** Half

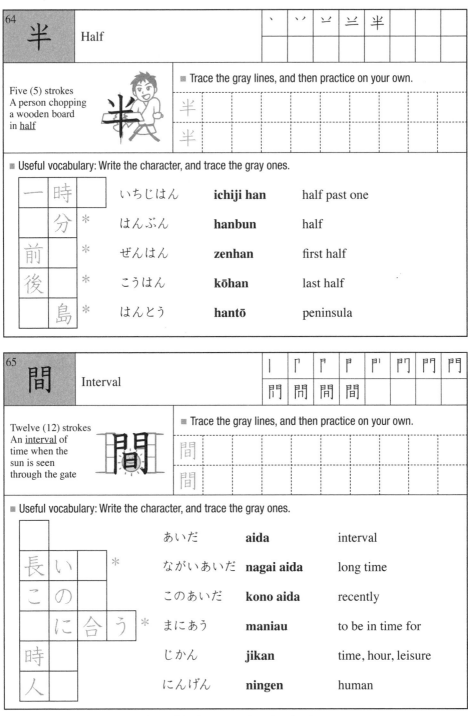

Five (5) strokes
A person chopping a wooden board in half

■ Trace the gray lines, and then practice on your own.

半
半

■ Useful vocabulary: Write the character, and trace the gray ones.

一時□		いちじはん	**ichiji han**	half past one
□分	*	はんぶん	**hanbun**	half
前□	*	ぜんはん	**zenhan**	first half
後□	*	こうはん	**kōhan**	last half
□島	*	はんとう	**hantō**	peninsula

65 **間** Interval

Twelve (12) strokes
An interval of time when the sun is seen through the gate

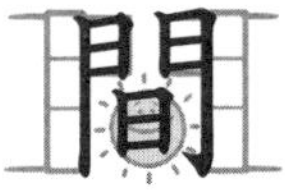

■ Trace the gray lines, and then practice on your own.

間
間

■ Useful vocabulary: Write the character, and trace the gray ones.

□		あいだ	**aida**	interval
長い□	*	ながいあいだ	**nagai aida**	long time
この□		このあいだ	**kono aida**	recently
□に合う	*	まにあう	**maniau**	to be in time for
時□		じかん	**jikan**	time, hour, leisure
人□		にんげん	**ningen**	human

* An asterisk denotes vocabulary with kanji that have not yet been introduced.

Reading 7-B

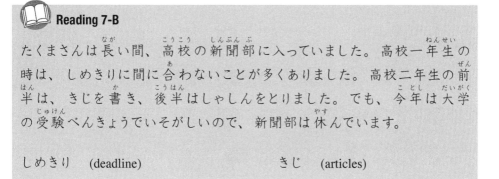

たくまさんは長(なが)い間、高校(こうこう)の新聞部(しんぶんぶ)に入っていました。高校一年生(ねんせい)の時は、しめきりに間に合(あ)わないことが多くありました。高校二年生の前(ぜん)半(はん)は、きじを書(か)き、後半(こうはん)はしゃしんをとりました。でも、今年(ことし)は大学(だいがく)の受験(じゅけん)べんきょうでいそがしいので、新聞部は休(やす)んでいます。

しめきり (deadline)　　きじ (articles)

Takuma san wa nagai aida, kōkō no shinbunbu ni haitte imashita. Kōkō ichinensei no toki wa, shimekiri ni maniawanai koto ga ōku arimashita. Kōkō ninensei no zenhan wa, kiji o kaki, kōhan wa shashin o torimashita. Demo, Kotoshi wa daigaku no juken benkyō de isogashii node, shinbunbu wa yasundeimasu.

Questions 7-B

1. How long was Takuma a member of the school newspaper club? (A. one year, B. two years, C. three years, D. Takuma did not join the newspaper club)
2. What year did Takuma sometimes have trouble meeting the deadlines? (A. freshman, B. sophomore, C. junior, D. senior)
3. What did Takuma do when he was a junior? (A. sold advertisements and delivered newspapers, B. delivered newspapers and wrote articles, C. wrote articles and took pictures, D. took pictures and sold advertisements)
4. What did Takuma do this year? (A. he does not participate in the newspaper club, B. he still participates in the newspaper club occasionally, C. he participated in the newspaper club for the first half of the year, D. he still participates fully in the newspaper club)

66 分	Minute, part, understand	ノ	八	分	分

Four (4) strokes
Separate (八) and blade (刀): To cut in parts. Scientists divide subjects into easy to understand parts.

■ Trace the gray lines, and then practice on your own.

分									
分									

■ Useful vocabulary: Write the character, and trace the gray ones.

□かる	わかる	**wakaru**	to understand
□ける	わける	**wakeru**	to divide
三□の一	さんぶんのいち	**sanbun no ichi**	one third
五□	ごふん	**gofun**	5 minutes
十□	じっぷん/じゅっぷん	**jippun/juppun**	10 minutes
十□な	じゅうぶんな	**jūbun na**	full, enough
自□ *	じぶん	**jibun**	oneself

67 今	Now	ノ	入	亼	今

Four (4) strokes
Noren curtains (𠆢) and katakana character *ra* (ラ): The ramen shop is open now!

■ Trace the gray lines, and then practice on your own.

今									
今									

■ Useful vocabulary: Write the character, and trace the gray ones.

□	いま	**ima**	now, soon
□月	こんげつ	**kongetsu**	this month
□年	ことし	**kotoshi**	this year
□日	きょう	**kyō**	today
□朝 *	けさ	**kesa**	this morning

* An asterisk denotes vocabulary with kanji that have not yet been introduced.

Reading 7-C

今年りささんがべんきょうしている数学(すうがく)のじゅぎょうはむずかしいです。まえは数学のしゅくだいを十分でできましたが、今は毎(まい)あさはやくおきてしゅくだいをしなければなりません。でも今朝(けさ)ねぼうしてしまって、しゅくだいをする時間が十分(じゅうぶん)ありませんでした。だから今はじゅぎょうに行きたくありません。

ねぼう (to sleep in)

Kotoshi Risa san ga benkyō shiteiru sūgaku no jugyō wa muzukashii desu. Mae was sūgaku no shukudai o juppun de dekimashita ga, ima wa maiasa hayaku okite shukudai o shinakereba narimasen. Demo kesa nebō shite shimatte, shukudai o suru jikan ga jūbun arimasen deshita. Dakara ima wa jugyō ni ikitaku arimasen.

Questions 7-C

1. How long did Risa's math homework used to take? (A. less than 10 minutes, B. 10 minutes, C. 30 minutes, D. about an hour)
2. How does Risa do her math homework? (A. right after school, B. late at night, C. early in the morning, D. early in the evening)
3. What happened this morning? (A. she was late for school, B. she did not finish her homework, C. she went to school early to get help on her homework, D. she called her friend to ask for help on her homework)
4. How did Risa feel about going to math class? (A. she wanted to go, B. she wanted to go, but she was late, C. did not want to go because her friend was late, D. she did not want to go because she did not finish her homework)

68 何 What

Stroke order: ノ 亻 亻 亻 亻 亻 何

Seven (7) strokes
A person (亻) and potential (可): <u>What</u> is that person lifting?

■ Trace the gray lines, and then practice on your own.

何
何

■ Useful vocabulary: Write the character, and trace the gray ones.

□	なに、なん	**nani, nan**	what, which
□～	なに、なん～	**nani, nan ~**	what, how many
□時ですか	なんじですか	**nanji desu ka**	what time is it?
□か	なにか	**nanika**	something, some, any
□度 *	なんど	**nando**	how many degrees, how many times
□人	なんにん	**nannin**	how many people

69 年 Year

Stroke order: ノ 𠂉 𠂉 𠂉 𠂉 年

Six (6) strokes
Pointing finger (𠂉) harvesting grain (㐄): The time appointed each <u>year</u> to harvest

■ Trace the gray lines, and then practice on your own.

年
年

■ Useful vocabulary: Write the character, and trace the gray ones.

□	とし	**toshi**	year
今□	ことし	**kotoshi**	this year
□上	としうえ	**toshiue**	older
来□ *	らいねん	**rainen**	next year
去□ *	きょねん	**kyonen**	last year

* An asterisk denotes vocabulary with kanji that have not yet been introduced.

Reading 7-D

今年せいやさんは、けんこうのために何かしようと思って、ウエイトリフティングをすることにしました。さいしょに三十キロのウエイトをあげてみました。でも、何度(なんど)やってみてもあげることができませんでした。それでせいやさんはもう少しかるいウエイトではじめることにしました。

けんこう (health) あげる (to lift)

Kotoshi Seiya san wa, kenkō no tame ni nanika shiyō to omotte, weitorifutingu o suru koto ni shimashita. Saisho ni sanjū kiro no weito o agete mimashita. Demo, nando yatte mitemo ageru koto ga dekimasen deshita. Sore de Seiya san wa mō sukoshi karui weito de hajimeru koto ni shimashita.

Questions 7-D

1. When did Seiya decide to improve his health? (A. last year, B. this year, C. last month, D. last week)
2. What is Seiya interested in? (A. losing weight, B. weightlifting, C. martial arts training, D. gymnastics)
3. What did Seiya begin with? (A. dieting, B. the parallel bars, C. heavy weights, D. karate)
4. What did Seiya do when he was not successful at first? (A. give up, B. try something less challenging, C. ask for help, D. keep trying until he succeeded)

70 回	Turn around, times (counter)	丨	冂	冂	冋	回	回		

Six (6) strokes
Two mouths (口):
How many times
have I told you…?

■ Trace the gray lines, and then practice on your own.

回									
回									

■ Useful vocabulary: Write the character, and trace the gray ones.

	る		まわる	**mawaru**	turn around, go around
	答	*	かいとう	**kaitō**	reply, answer
二		*	にかい	**nikai**	two times (counter)
二		目	にかいめ	**nikaime**	second time

71 毎	Every	ノ	⺊	乍	气	毎	毎		

Six (6) strokes
Pointing finger (⺈)
and mother (母):
Mother scolds me
every time I do
something wrong.

■ Trace the gray lines, and then practice on your own.

毎									
毎									

■ Useful vocabulary: Write the character, and trace the gray ones.

	日		まいにち	**mainichi**	every day
	週	*	まいしゅう	**maishū**	every week
	月		まいつき	**maitsuki**	every month
	年		まいねん/まいとし	**mainen/ maitoshi**	every year

* An asterisk denotes vocabulary with kanji that have not yet been introduced.

Reading 7-E

はるきさんは八代(やつしろ)という人口の少ないまちのしゅっしんです。でも、大きいまちが好きだそうです。今年の夏(なつ)はるきさんはニューヨークに行(い)きました。ニューヨークにいくのは二回目でした。はるきさんは、ゆうめいなびじゅつかんをぜんぶ回りました。そしてレストランでおいしいスパゲッティをたべました。

Haruki san wa yatsushiro toiu jinkō no sukunai machi no shusshin desu. Demo, ōkii machi ga suki da sō desu. Kotoshi no natsu Haruki san wa nyūyōku ni ikimashita. Nyūyōku ni iku nowa nikaime deshita. Haruki san wa, yūmei na bijutsukan o zenbu mawari mashita. Soshite resutoran de oishii supagetti o tabemashita.

Questions 7-E

1. Where does Haruki come from? (A. a large city called Yatsushiro, B. a small town called Yatsushiro, C. Tokyo, D. the passage does not say where Haruki is from)
2. What kind of places does he like? (A. big cities, B. foreign cities, C. small towns, D. port towns)
3. How many times has Haruki been to New York? (A. he has never been to New York before, B. he has been to New York once before, C. he has been to New York twice before, D. he has been to New York many times)
4. Where did Haruki go in New York? (A. he went to all the famous museums and ate at a restaurant, B. he ate at a restaurant and went to a Broadway play, C. he went to a Broadway play and visited the Statue of Liberty, D. he visited the Statue of Liberty and went to all the famous museums)

Lesson 7 Practice

A. Kanji Review

Write these words in kanji, referring to the mnemonic pictures if necessary.

 temple	 time	 half	 interval	 minute
1.	2.	3.	4.	5.
 now	 what	 year	 times	 every
6.	7.	8.	9.	10.

B. Vocabulary Review

Try writing these words with appropriate kanji and okurigana.

1. ____ ____ (one o'clock)
2. ____ ____ 合 ____ (to catch, in time)
3. ____ ____ ____ (to understand)
4. ____ ____ ____ ____ ____ (What time is it?)
5. ____ ____ (today)
6. 後(こう) ____ (last half)
7. 清(きよ) ____ ____ (Kiyomizu Temple)
8. ____ ____ (time)
9. 自(じ) ____ (self)
10. ____ 朝(さ) (this morning)

11. ____ 島(とう) (peninsula)

12. ____ 閣(かく) ____ (Kinkaku Temple)

13. ____ 度(ど) (how many degrees/times)

14. ____ ____ (half)

15. ____ ____ (enough)

16. ____ ____ (something)

C. Common Japanese Last Names

Try writing these common Japanese last names with the appropriate kanji characters.

1. はんだ (half, rice paddy) ____ ____
2. こいで (small, go out) ____ ____
3. てらうち (temple, inside) ____ ____
4. てらだ (temple, rice paddy) ____ ____
5. かどた (gate, rice paddy) ____ ____
6. いまがわ (now, river) ____ ____
7. たどころ (rice paddy, place) ____ ____
8. いまだ (now, rice paddy) ____ ____

D. Telling Time

Read these times, and write them in English.

1. 三時二十分 ____3:20____
2. 六時五十五分 ______:______
3. 十一時四十分 ______:______
4. 八時十分 ______:______
5. 一時五分 ______:______
6. 七時三十五分 ______:______
7. 四時半 ______:______
8. 十時二十五分 ______:______
9. 十二時五十分 ______:______
10. 九時四十五分 ______:______

E. Questions Words with 何 (なに, What?)

There are many question words with the kanji 何 in them. Try to match the following examples with their English meanings on the right. Write the appropriate question word in the blank on the left.

1. ________	How old?	何人
2. ________	What year?	何分
3. ________	What time?	何時
4. ________	What month?	何か月
5. ________	How many people? / What nationality?	何日
6. ________	How many times?	何時間
7. ________	How many minutes?	何さい
8. ________	What day?	何日間
9. ________	How many months?	何回
10. ________	How many hours?	何年
11. ________	How many days?	何月
12. ________	What day of the week?	何よう日

F. Ayaka's High School Class Schedule

Ayaka is a student at 寺田(Terada) High School. Below is her class schedule. Read over it and then answer the following questions.

1. What days does Ayaka have Art? ________
2. How many days per week does Ayaka attend school? ________
3. What time does she have Math on Mondays? ________
4. How many days per week does she have Music? ________
5. On what day does Ayaka have Physical Education after lunch? ________
6. What class does Ayaka take at 8:40 on Saturday? ________

7. What time does she have Social Studies on Thursday and Friday? ________

8. What class does Ayaka have on Friday at 1:20? ________________

9. How long is Ayaka's History class? ________________________

10. Which class does she have only once each week? ________________

	月	火	水	木	金	土
八時四十分～九時半	こくご	えいご	えいご	かがく	すうがく	たいいく
九時四十分～十時半	すうがく	こくご	おんがく	えいご	かがく	かがく
十時四十分～十一時半	おんがく	すうがく	すうがく	しゃかい	しゃかい	びじゅつ
十一時四十分～十二時半	たいいく	たいいく	しゃかい	こくご	こくご	ホームルーム
十二時三十分～一時二十分	ひるやすみ					
一時二十分～二時十分	かがく	れきし	びじゅつ	たいいく	えいご	
二時二十分～三時十分	しゃかい	れきし	こくご	おんがく	おんがく	

G. How Many Times?

How many times have you done the following things? Interview a partner and take turns asking and answering the following questions. Write your answers in kanji ("one time" is 一回). If you cannot recall exactly, make a realistic guess. If you have never done it, say 「(Action) たform+ことが　ありません」. If you have done it more times than you can count you may say 「なん回もしたことが　あります。」

	わたし	パートナー
1. なん回　ひこうきに　のったことが　ありますか。		

	わたし	パートナー
2. なん回　がいこく(foreign country)へ　いったことが　ありますか。		
3. なん回　日本(ほん)の　レストランで　たべたことが　ありますか。		
4. なん回　じてんしゃの　じこ(accident)に　あったことが　ありますか。		
5. なん回　キャンプへ　いったことが　ありますか。		
6. なん回　さいふ(wallet)を　なくした (to lose) ことが　ありますか。		
7. なん回　ゆうえんち(theme park)へ　いったことが　ありますか。		
8. なん回　山に　のぼった ことが　ありますか。		

H. Review Questions

Try writing these sentences in Japanese using kanji whenever appropriate. Each sentence has at least one new kanji from this lesson. Then, compare your translations with the answer key at the end of the book.

1. What time do you usually wake up? ______________________________

____

2. Are you always on time for your first period class? ______________________________

____

3. What classes do you have today? ______________________________

____

4. What days do you have Japanese class? ______________________________

____

5. What time do you have Japanese class? ______________________________

____

6. How many people are in your Japanese class? ______________________

____

7. What nationality is your Japanese teacher? ______________________

____

8. Do you understand Spanish? ______________________

____

9. Is the math homework hard this year? ______________________

____

10. What are you doing at 3:30 today? ______________________

____

11. Do you have enough money for a trip to Japan? ______________________

____

12. Do you listen to music for a long time every day? ______________________

____

13. Do you have a TV in your bedroom? ______________________

____

14. Did you walk to school by yourself when you were in elementary school?

____

15. Have you ever been to a Buddhist temple? ______________________

____

I. Interview Your Partner

Take turns asking the above questions with your partner. Try to answer as fully and appropriately as you can. For best results, you should elaborate on your answers whenever possible.

72 聞	Hear

Fourteen (14) strokes
Gate (門) and ear (耳): The ear is a gate that lets us hear sounds

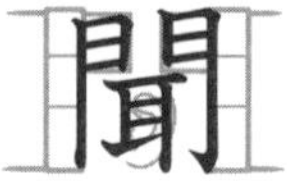

■ Trace the gray lines, and then practice on your own.

聞
聞

■ Useful vocabulary: Write the character, and trace the gray ones.

☐く		きく	**kiku**	to hear, listen, ask
☐き手		ききて	**kikite**	listener, audience
☐こえる		きこえる	**kikoeru**	can hear
新☐	*	しんぶん	**shinbun**	newspaper

73 見	See

Seven (7) strokes
Eye (目) and legs (ル): Figuratively, in order to see something, your eyes run over to it.

■ Trace the gray lines, and then practice on your own.

見
見

■ Useful vocabulary: Write the character, and trace the gray ones.

☐る		みる	**miru**	to see, look, watch
☐える		みえる	**mieru**	can see
☐方		みかた	**mikata**	point of view
花☐	*	はなみ	**hanami**	cherry blossom viewing
☐物	*	けんぶつ	**kenbutsu**	sightseeing, visit

* An asterisk denotes vocabulary with kanji that have not yet been introduced.

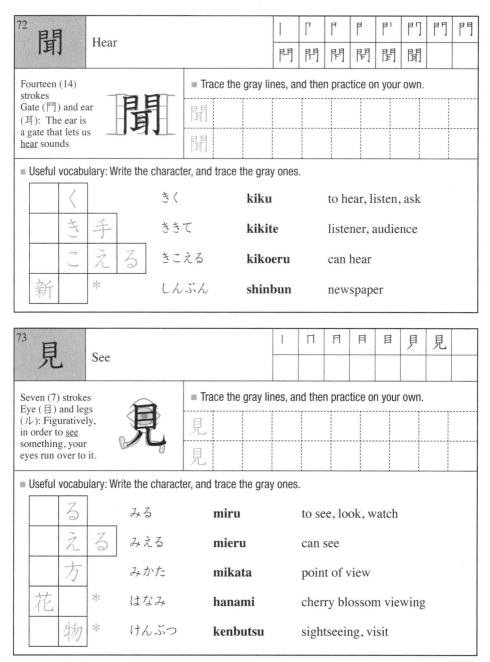

Reading 8-A

あつこさんは花見が大好きです。せんしゅうの土曜(よう)日に親友(しんゆう)のまみさんと、ともだちのまさしさんと代々木(よよぎ)こうえんにいって花見をしました。新聞によるとその日は代々木こうえんに花見にきた人が三千人もいたそうです。まさしさんは、こうえんからでんわでピザのはいたつをおねがいしました。はいたつの人は、あつこさんたちがどこにいるか分からなかったようです。まっていてもピザがこないので、まさしさんがもう一回でんわをしたら、すぐにきてくれました。

親友(しんゆう) best friend

Atsuko san wa hanami ga daisuki desu. Senshū no doyōbi ni shinyū no Mami san to, tomodachi no Masashi san to yoyogi kōen ni itte hanami o shimashita. Shinbun niyoru to sono hi wa yoyogi kōen ni hanami ni kita hito ga sanzennin mo ita sō desu. Masashi san wa, kōen kara denwa de piza no haitatsu o onegai shimashita. Haitatsu no hito wa, Atsuko san tachi ga doko ni iru ka wakaranakatta yō desu. Matteitemo piza ga konai node, Masashi san ga mō ikkai denwa o shitara, sugu ni kite kuremashita.

Questions 8-A

1. When did Atsuko go to the park? (A. Monday, B. Friday, C. Saturday, D. Sunday)
2. How many people were at the park according to the newspaper? (A. over 3,000 people that day, B. over 30,000 people that day, C. over 3,000 people that week, D. over 30,000 people that week)
3. What did Masashi order? (A. delivery Chinese food at home, B. delivery Chinese food at the park, C. delivery pizza at home, D. delivery pizza at the park)
4. How many times did Masashi have to call the delivery person? (A. once, B. twice, C. three times, D. many times)

74 思 Think

丨	冂	冂	田	田	田	思	思
思							

Nine (9) strokes
A picture of a brain (田) and heart (心): To think with your brain and heart

■ Trace the gray lines, and then practice on your own.

思								
思								

■ Useful vocabulary: Write the character, and trace the gray ones.

	う			おもう	**omou**	to think
	い	出		おもいで	**omoide**	memory
	い	出	す	おもいだす	**omoidasu**	to remember
意		*		いし	**ishi**	intention

75 言 Say

丶	亠	亠	言	言	言	言	

Seven (7) strokes
Someone saying something

■ Trace the gray lines, and then practice on your own.

言								
言								

■ Useful vocabulary: Write the character, and trace the gray ones.

	う	いう	**iu**	say, speak
方		ほうげん	**hōgen**	dialect

* An asterisk denotes vocabulary with kanji that have not yet been introduced.

Reading 8-B

ひできさんは、小さいころから、みんなと少しちがいました。いつも思っていることをはっきり言うからです。家（いえ）でも学校（がっこう）でもそうです。よく、クラスのみんなが聞きたくても聞けないことを聞いてしまいます。だから、クラスのみんなは、ひできさんがあたまがいいと思っています。

はっきり　clearly

Hideki san wa, chiisai koro kara, minna to sukoshi chigaimashita. Itsumo omotteiru koto o hakkiri iu kara desu. Ie demo gakkō demo sō desu. Yoku, kurasu no minna ga kikitakutemo kikenai koto o kiite shimaimasu. Dakara, kurasu no minna wa, Hideki san ga atama ga ii to omotte imasu.

Questions 8-B

1. What is Hideki's behavior like at school? (A. speaks his mind, except in school, B. speaks his mind, even in school, C. is a bit shy at school, D. is a bit shy, especially in school)
2. When does he ask questions? (A. he asks, even if they might be bad questions, B. he asks, unless they might be bad questions, C. he asks about things that no one else cares about, D. he asks too many questions)
3. What kinds of questions does Hideki ask? (A. he asks questions that no one is thinking about, B. he asks questions that other students have already asked, C. he asks questions without thinking, D. he asks questions that the others want to ask, but can not ask)
4. What does the class think about Hideki? (A. they think he is smart, B. they think he is not smart, C. they think he needs to say what he thinks more often, D. they think he needs to think about what he says more often)

76 語 Language

Fourteen (14) strokes
To say (言), intersection (五), and mouth (口): Language is when people exchange words.

■ Trace the gray lines, and then practice on your own.

語
語

■ Useful vocabulary: Write the character, and trace the gray ones.

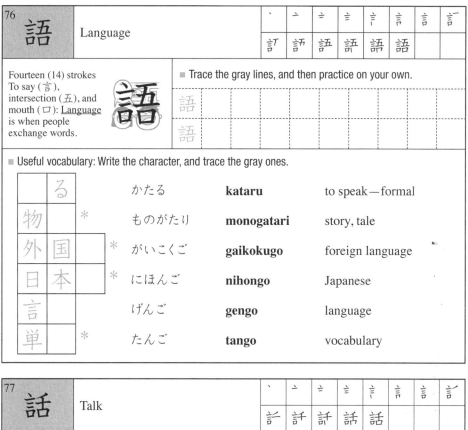

□る	かたる	**kataru**	to speak—formal
物□ *	ものがたり	**monogatari**	story, tale
外国□ *	がいこくご	**gaikokugo**	foreign language
日本□ *	にほんご	**nihongo**	Japanese
言□	げんご	**gengo**	language
単□ *	たんご	**tango**	vocabulary

77 話 Talk

Thirteen (13) strokes
To say (言), thousand (千), and mouth (口): A story that has been told (talk) a thousand times

■ Trace the gray lines, and then practice on your own.

話
話

■ Useful vocabulary: Write the character, and trace the gray ones.

□す	はなす	**hanasu**	to talk
□	はなし	**hanashi**	story, speech
笑い□ *	わらいばなし	**waraibanashi**	funny story
昔□ *	むかしばなし	**mukashibanashi**	folk tale
世□ *	せわ	**sewa**	care, help
神□ *	しんわ	**shinwa**	myth

* An asterisk denotes vocabulary with kanji that have not yet been introduced.

Reading 8-C

ちえこさんはアメリカでうまれて、アメリカにすんでいます。アメリカにいるちえこさんのかぞくに会うために、おばあさんが時どき、日本からあそびに来てくれます。ちえこさんは日本語があまり上手ではありませんが、今年学校(がっこう)で日本語を勉強(べんきょう)しています。だから、おばあさんはとてもうれしいそうです。日本語は少しむずかしいですが、おばあさんと日本語で話したいので、ちえこさんはがんばっています。

Chieko san wa amerika de umarete, amerika ni sunde imasu. Amerika ni iru Chieko san no kazoku ni au tame ni, obāsan ga tokidoki, nihon kara asobini kite kuremasu. Chieko san wa nihongo ga amari jōzu dewa arimasen ga, kotoshi gakkō de nihongo o benkyō shite imasu. Dakara, obāsan wa totemo ureshii sō desu. Nihongo wa sukoshi muzukashii desu ga, obāsan to nihongo de hanashitai node, Chieko san wa ganbatte imasu.

Questions 8-C

1. Where does Chieko live? (A. America, B. Japan, C. Australia, D. China)
2. How often does Chieko's grandmother come to visit? (A. sometimes, B. every year, C. every few years, D. never)
3. How is Chieko studying Japanese? (A. with her grandmother, B. school, C. weekends, D. she is not studying Japanese)
4. What does Chieko think about Japanese class? (A. it is difficult, but she will do her best, B. it is too easy, so she will change to another class, C. it is difficult, so she will change to another class, D. it is easy, but she will not change to another class)

78 会	Meet	ノ	入	亼	亽	会	会		

Six (6) strokes
Noren curtains (入) and simple form of say (言): When people gather to have their say, it is called a meeting.

■ Trace the gray lines, and then practice on your own.

会								
会								

■ Useful vocabulary: Write the character, and trace the gray ones.

	う		あう	**au**	to meet
	話		かいわ	**kaiwa**	conversation
	館	*	かいかん	**kaikan**	meeting hall
集		*	しゅうかい	**shūkai**	meeting
大			たいかい	**taikai**	conference, tournament
機		*	きかい	**kikai**	opportunity, occasion

* An asterisk denotes vocabulary with kanji that have not yet been introduced.

Reading 8-D

今日はまことさんのたっきゅう大会です。この大会でゆうしょうすれば、全(ぜん)日本(にほん)大会にいくことができます。だから、まことさんの友達(ともだち)はみんなで大会におうえんにいきました。まことさんのたっきゅうのあい手もつよかったから、しあいはながくて、みんなドキドキしました。でもまことさんはかちました。まことさんも友達もとてもうれしそうでした。

たっきゅう	table tennis	全日本(ぜんにほん)	all Japan
ゆうしょう	win a championship		

Kyō wa makoto san no takkyū taikai desu. Kono taikai de yūshō sureba, zennihon taikai ni iku koto ga dekimasu. Dakara, Makoto san no tomodachi wa minna de, taikai ni ōen ni kimashita. Makoto san no takkyū no aite mo tsuyokatta kara, shiai wa nagakute, minna dokidoki shimashita. Demo Makoto san wa kachimashita. Makoko san mo tomodachi mo totemo ureshisō desu.

Questions 8-D

1. When did Makoto compete in a table tennis tournament (A. yesterday, B. today, C. Friday, D. Sunday)
2. What would happen if Makoto were to win at the tournament? (A. he would win the All Japan Table Tennis Tournament, B. he would advance to the All Japan Table Tennis Tournament, C. he would win the All Asia Table Tennis Tournament, D. he would advance to the All Asia Table Tennis Tournament)
3. What kind of table tennis player was Makoto's opponent? (A. he was not good, B. he was good, C. he not good, but he won, D. he was good, but he made many mistakes)
4. Based on the passage what can you guess about Makoto? (A. he spends all of his time playing table tennis, B. he travels a lot playing in tournaments, C. he has good friends, D. he does not have friends)

Let's Review:

Write the English meaning of these words.

1. 見えます ____________________
2. 思い出す ____________________
3. 昔話 ____________________
4. 言語 ____________________
5. 会話 ____________________
6. 方言 ____________________
7. 聞こえる ____________________
8. 大会 ____________________
9. 話す ____________________
10. 物語 ____________________
11. 意思 ____________________
12. 日本語 ____________________
13. 花見 ____________________
14. 新聞 ____________________

Lesson 8 Practice

A. Kanji Review

Try writing these words with the appropriate kanji and okurigana characters.

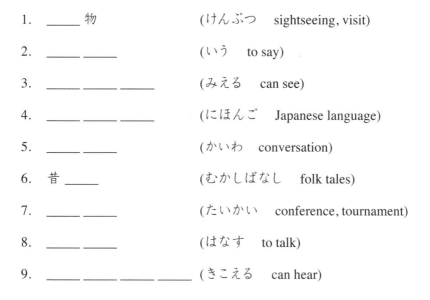

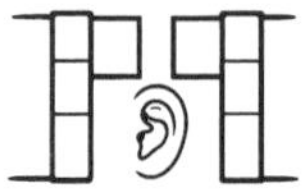 to hear	 to see	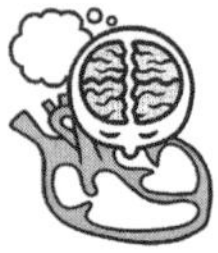 to think	 to say
1.	2.	3.	4.
 language	 to speak	 to meet	
5.	6.	7.	

B. Vocabulary Review

Try writing these words with the appropriate kanji and okurigana characters.

1. _____ 物 (けんぶつ sightseeing, visit)
2. _____ _____ (いう to say)
3. _____ _____ _____ (みえる can see)
4. _____ _____ _____ (にほんご Japanese language)
5. _____ _____ (かいわ conversation)
6. 昔 _____ (むかしばなし folk tales)
7. _____ _____ (たいかい conference, tournament)
8. _____ _____ (はなす to talk)
9. _____ _____ _____ _____ (きこえる can hear)

10. 花 _____ (はなみ cherry blossom viewing)

11. _____ _____ _____ _____ (おもいだす to remember)

12. _____ (はなし story, speech)

13. _____ _____ (ほうげん dialect)

14. 世 _____ (せわ care, help)

15. 機 _____ (きかい opportunity)

16. _____ _____ (かたる to speak – formal)

17. _____ _____ (おもう to think)

18. _____ _____ (きく to hear, listen, ask*)

19. 意 _____ (いし intention)

20. 物 _____ (ものがたり story, tale)

21. _____ 館 (かいかん meeting hall)

22. 笑 _____ _____ (わらいばなし funny story)

23. _____ _____ _____ (ききて listener, audience)

24. _____ _____ _____ (おもいで memory)

25. 集_____ (しゅうかい meeting)

26. _____ _____ (げんご language)

27. _____ _____ (みる to see)

28. 神 _____ (しんわ myth)

29. 単 _____ (たんご vocabulary)

30. 新 _____ (しんぶん newspaper)

31. _____ _____ (あう to meet)

32. _____ _____ _____ (がいこくご foreign language)

C. Odd One Out

Cross out the word that does not belong with the action word.

1. (えいが、山、テレビ、ラジオ) を見る。
2. (さよなら、やきとり、ありがとう、こんにちは、すみません) と言う。
3. (ともだち、せんせい、あたま、おかあさん) に会う。
4. (ラジオ、うた、はなし、木) を聞く。
5. (でんわ、日本語、イヤホン、ケータイでんわ) で話す

D. Languages of the World

The kanji for language is 語 (pronounced ご). It is generally added to the country name to write the language of that country. For instance, the Japanese language is called 日本語(にほんご). Below is listed the 10 most commonly spoken languages of the world, based on population (Wikipedia.com viewed October 2008). Write the names of the languages in English. Then, decide the correct ranking and write it in kanji.

Rank	Language	Language Name in Japanese	Number of Native-Speakers
五	Arabic	アラビア語	206,000,000
		ベンガル語	171,000,000
		中国語	873,000,000
		英(えい)語	309,350,000
		ドイツ語	95,400,000
		ヒンディー語	366,000,000
		日本語	122,400,000
		ポルトガル語	177,500,000
		ロシア語	145,000,000
		スペイン語	322,300,000

E. Which Part of the Body

Which part of the body do you use to do the following actions? Circle the most appropriate word.

1. (目、回、口、耳、あたま、あし) で話す
2. (あたま、耳、目、口、あし、手) で思う
3. (はな、口、耳、目、あし、ひざ) で見る
4. (あたま、あし、目、耳、はな、口) でたべる
5. (門、耳、目、手、はな、あし、回) で聞く
6. (心、目、耳、あたま、手、あし) でかく

F. Commonly Mistaken Kanji

Which kanji correctly expresses the meaning of the English word? Circle the most appropriate kanji character.

1. four	目	回	円	内	四	田
2. person	入	大	人	八	火	小
3. to open	閉	聞	門	開	間	耳
4. now	分	今	会	金	八	入
5. middle	中	口	十	木	千	田
6. thousand	少	十	千	下	上	半
7. eye	耳	内	四	目	回	口
8. big	木	大	小	父	八	入
9. listen, hear	門	開	間	耳	閉	聞
10. gold	会	今	金	分	八	人
11. small	少	木	八	入	小	人
12. to think	男	見	田	思	力	毎
13. ten thousand	方	力	分	万	九	タ

14. up, above	千	手	上	十	工	小
15. times (counter)	田	回	ロ	円	肉	内
16. gate	聞	回	間	開	閉	門
17. few	小	多	下	木	少	入
18. fire	水	火	人	入	半	小
19. water	水	半	木	火	小	少
20. inside	肉	回	ロ	目	内	田

G. Verbs, Matching

Match the English phrase on the right with the Japanese phrases on the left. Write the correct number on the line, and then fill in the blank with the appropriate verb using kanji and okurigana (the hiragana following the kanji). Also note, that although there is a specific kanji character 訊 used to express "to ask" most Japanese tend to use the familiar kanji character 聞 to express "hear," "listen," and "ask."

__1__ 母に (話す)	1. to talk to mother
_____ 友達（ともだち）に (　　　　)	2. to meet a person
_____ 日本語を (　　　　)	3. to see the mountains
_____ 金曜（よう）日だと (　　　　)	4. to think it is Friday
_____ 話を (　　　　)	5. to speak Japanese
_____ 中国（ごく）語を (　　　　)	6. to listen to music
_____ おんがくを (　　　　)	7. to think it is 1,000 yen
_____ 三時だと (　　　　)	8. to meet friend(s)
_____ 山を (　　　　)	9. to ask father
_____ 千円だと (　　　　)	10. to see a temple
_____ 上野 (の) えきで (　　　　)	11. to listen to a story

_____ 先生に (　　　　　)

_____ 人に (　　　　　)

_____ 大きいと (　　　　　)

_____ 父に (　　　　　)

_____ 寺を (　　　　　)

12. to speak Chinese

13. to think it is 3 o'clock

14. to meet at Ueno Station

15. to ask the teacher

16. to think (it) is big

H. Say, Think, and Ask

Match the following English phrases on the left with the Japanese phrases on the right. Write the correct number on the line, and then fill in the blank with the appropriate verb in kanji and okurigana (the hiragana that follows the kanji). Use correct the grammar.

1. (I) think we don't have any homework.
2. (He) says it is no good.
3. (I) will ask if the test is on Friday.
4. (I) think my science grade is good.
5. (I) think the game is on Saturday
6. (He) said that was too bad.
7. (She) asked why (I) was sad.
8. (She) said the party is tomorrow.
9. (He) asked who won the lacrosse game.
10. (I) think there is a lot of homework.

__1__ しゅくだいがないと (思う)

_____ パーティーはあしただと (　　　)

_____ なぜかなしいか (　　　　)

_____ しゅくだいが多いと(　　　)

_____ だれがラクロスのしあいにかったか (　　　　)

_____ 家は近いと (　　　　)

_____ だめだと (　　　　)

_____ かがくのせいせきはいいと (　　　)

_____ 「おげんきですか」と (　　　)

_____ それはざんねんだと(　　　)

11. (I) think the house is nearby. _____ 小テストは月曜(よう)日かどうか (　　　)

12. (He) said the concert is Thursday. _____ そのバンドが好きだと (　　　)

13. (She) said (she) likes that band. _____ しけんは金曜(よう)日かどうか (　　　)

14. (She) asked "How are you?" _____ コンサートは木曜(よう)日だと (　　　)

15. (He) asked if the quiz is on Monday. _____ しあいは土曜(よう)日だと (　　　)

I. Review Questions

Try writing these sentences in Japanese using kanji whenever appropriate. Each sentence has at least one new kanji from this lesson. Then, compare your translations with the answer key at the end of the book.

1. Do you like scary stories? ______________________________

____

2. How many times per month do you watch movies? ______________________________

____

3. How many hours per day do you talk on the telephone? ______________________________

____

4. What is your very first memory? ______________________________

____

5. Can you remember when you were 1 year old? ______________________________

____

6. How many years have you studied Japanese? ______________________

____

7. What languages can you speak? ______________________

____

8. Is your mother easy to talk with? ______________________

____

9. Does your father read the newspaper every day? ______________________

____

10. What can you see from your bedroom window? ______________________

____

11. What can you see from your Japanese classroom? ______________________

____

12. Have you ever played in a sports tournament? ______________________

____

13. Where did you meet your best friend (しんゆう)? ______________________

____

14. Do you always say directly （はっきり） what you think? ______________________

____

J. Interview Your Partner

Take turns asking the above questions with your partner. Try to answer as fully and appropriately as you can. For best results, you should elaborate on your answers whenever possible.

79 生	Life, birth	ノ	𠂉	牛	牛	生

Five (5) strokes
A plant growing (life) out of the ground

■ Trace the gray lines, and then practice on your own.

生

生

■ Useful vocabulary: Write the character, and trace the gray ones.

きる	いきる	**ikiru**	to live, exist
まれる	うまれる	**umareru**	to be born
～	なま～	**nama~**	raw~
人 *	じんせい	**jinsei**	life
年月日	せいねんがっぴ	**seinengappi**	date of birth
け花 *	いけばな	**ikebana**	flower arranging

80 先	Ahead	ノ	𠂉	屮	生	牛	先

Six (6) strokes
Simplified plant (⺧) and human feet (儿): The planting time comes ahead of harvesting time

■ Trace the gray lines, and then practice on your own.

先

先

■ Useful vocabulary: Write the character, and trace the gray ones.

に	さきに	**sakini**	ahead of, prior to
行き *	いきさき	**ikisaki**	destination
生	せんせい	**sensei**	teacher, doctor, etc.
月	せんげつ	**sengetsu**	last month

* An asterisk denotes vocabulary with kanji that have not yet been introduced.

Reading 9-A

ベスさんは２０００年１月１２日に生まれました。ニュージーランド人ですが、お父さんが東京(とうきょう)のインターナショナルスクールで働(はたら)いていたので、日本で生まれました。お父さんの学校(がっこう)の先生たちはみんなよろこんで、ベスさんとお母さんのおみまいに、びょういんにきてくれたそうです。ベスさんのお父さんもおにいさん三人も、女の子が生まれてよかったと思ったそうです。でも、ベスさんのお母さんが一番、むすめができてうれしかったようです。

おみまい　(to visit an ill person)

Besu san wa nisennen ichigatsu jūninichi ni umaremashita. Nyūjiirandojin desu ga, otōsan ga tōkyō no intānashonaru sukūru de hataraite ita node, nihon de umaremashita. Otōsan no gakkō no sensei tachi wa minna yorokonde, besu san to okāsan no mimai ni, byōin ni kite kureta sō desu. Besu san no otōsan mo oniisan sannin mo, onnanoko ga umarete yokatta to omotta sō desu. Demo, besu san no okāsan ga ichiban, musume ga dekite ureshikatta yō desu.

Questions 9-A

1. Where was Beth born? (A. New Zealand, B. Japan, C. America, D. Korea)
2. What is her birthday? (A. December 1, 2000, B. December 12, 2000, C. January 1, 2000, D. January 12, 2000)
3. How many siblings does Beth have? (A. one younger sister, B. one younger brother, C. three older sisters, D. three older brothers)
4. What was Beth's mother most thrilled about? (A. Beth was born in the year 2000, B. Beth was a girl, C. many people came to visit her in the hospital, D. Beth was born the same month as her mother)

81 私	I, myself

Stroke order: ノ ニ 千 禾 禾 私 私

Seven (7) strokes
Grain (禾) and to gather (厶):
To gather grain for <u>myself</u>

■ Trace the gray lines, and then practice on your own.

私
私

■ Useful vocabulary: Write the character, and trace the gray ones.

□	わたし	**watashi**	I, myself
□たち	わたしたち	**watashitachi**	we, us
□立 *	しりつ	**shiritsu**	private
□立学校 *	しりつがっこう	**shiritsu gakkō**	private school
□立大学 *	しりつだいがく	**shiritsu daigaku**	private college

82 友	Friend

Stroke order: 一 ナ 方 友

Four (4) strokes
A hand holding tool (ナ) and hand holding sticks (又):
The idea is simplified to just mean holding hands: <u>friends</u>

■ Trace the gray lines, and then practice on your own.

友
友

■ Useful vocabulary: Write the character, and trace the gray ones.

□だち	ともだち	**tomodachi**	friend, companion
□人	ゆうじん	**yūjin**	friend
親□ *	しんゆう	**shinyū**	best friend
□情 *	ゆうじょう	**yūjō**	friendship, fellowship

* An asterisk denotes vocabulary with kanji that have not yet been introduced.

Reading 9-B

トッドさんはアメリカ人で、ニールさんはカナダ人ですが、二人ともお父さんの仕事のために、日本にすむことになりました。二人が中学二年生の時に、東京にある私立校で同じクラスになり、友だちになりました。去年、トッドさんは、家族とアメリカに帰りました。でも、今年のなつやすみに二しゅう間、ニールさんに会いに東京に行きました。トッドさんとニールさんは、今はちがう国にいますが、今でもよくイーメールをしています。来年、ニールさんは、トッドさんに会いにアメリカにいくつもりです。

Toddo san wa amerikajin de, Niiru san wa kanadajin desu ga, futari tomo otōsan no shigoto no tame ni, nihon ni sumu koto ni narimashita. Futari ga chūgaku ninensei no toki ni, tōkyō ni aru shiritsukō de onaji kurasu ni nari, tomodachi ni narimashita. Kyonen, Toddo san wa, kazoku to amerika ni kaerimashita. Demo, kotoshi no natsuyasumi ni nishūkan, Niiru san ni ai ni tōkyō ni ikimashita. Toddo san to Niiru san wa, ima wa chigau kuni ni imasu ga, ima demo yoku iimēru o shite imasu. Rainen, Niiru san wa, Toddo san ni ai ni amerika ni iku tsumori desu.

Questions 9-B

1. When did Todd and Neale meet? (A. 6th grade, B. 7th grade, C. 8th grade, D. 9th grade)
2. To where did Todd's family move? (A. Canada, B. New Zealand, C. America, D. Australia)
3. When did Todd visit Neale? (A. winter vacation, B. spring break, C. summer vacation, D. fall holiday)
4. When will Neale visit Todd? (A. next month, B. next year, C. in two months, D. in two years)

83 学 Learn

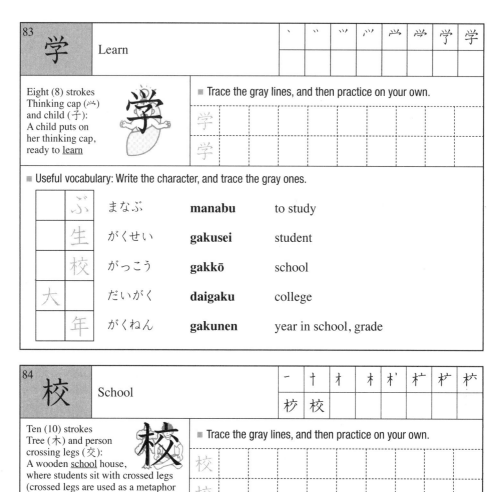

Eight (8) strokes
Thinking cap (⺍) and child (子):
A child puts on her thinking cap, ready to learn

■ Trace the gray lines, and then practice on your own.

学
学

■ Useful vocabulary: Write the character, and trace the gray ones.

ぶ	まなぶ	**manabu**	to study
生	がくせい	**gakusei**	student
校	がっこう	**gakkō**	school
大	だいがく	**daigaku**	college
年	がくねん	**gakunen**	year in school, grade

84 校 School

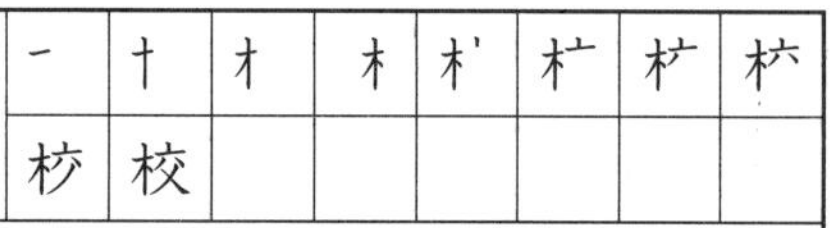

Ten (10) strokes
Tree (木) and person crossing legs (交):
A wooden school house, where students sit with crossed legs (crossed legs are used as a metaphor for the exchange of information)

■ Trace the gray lines, and then practice on your own.

校
校

■ Useful vocabulary: Write the character, and trace the gray ones.

学	がっこう	**gakkō**	school
小学	しょうがっこう	**shōgakkō**	elementary school
中学	ちゅうがっこう	**chūgakkō**	middle school
高	こうこう	**kōkō**	high school

* An asterisk denotes vocabulary with kanji that have not yet been introduced.

Reading 9-C

ちえさんは大学で英(えい)文学をべんきょうしながら、時々大学の文学ざっしにきじを書(か)いていました。大学をそつぎょうして、何年かはたらいた後(あと)で、三十さいでけっこんして、三人の子どもをうみました。子どもが英語を話せるようになってほしいと思っていたので、子どもを英会話きょうしつにつれて行(い)っています。ちえさんは、まだアメリカに行ったことがないけれど、いつか家族(かぞく)をつれて行きたいと思っています。

きじ　article　　　　そつぎょう　graduation

Chie san wa daigaku de eibungaku o benkyō shinagara, tokidoki daigaku no bungaku zasshi ni kiji o kaiteimashita. Daigaku o sotsugyō shite, nannen ka hataraita ato de, sanjussai de kekkon shite, san nin no kodomo o umimashita. Kodomo ga eigo o hanaseru yōni natte hoshii to omotte ita node, kodomo o eikaiwa kyōshitsu ni tsurete itte imasu. Chie san wa, mada amerika ni itta koto ga nai keredo, itsuka kazoku o tsurete ikitai to omotteimasu.

Questions 9-C

1. What did Chie study in college? (A. Japanese literature, B. English literature, C. education, D. international business)
2. When did Chie get married? (A. at age 23, B. at age 28, C. at age 30, D. at age 38)
3. What did Chie do so her children would learn English? (A. she hired a private tutor, B. she enrolled her children in an English class, C. she taught them English at home, D. she let them watch English language TV programs)
4. What are Chie's plans regarding travel to the United States? (A. she wants to travel there alone, B. she wants travel there with friends, C. she wants to travel there with her husband, D. she wants to travel there with her family).

85 本

Book, main, counter for long objects

Stroke order: 一 十 才 木 本

Five (5) strokes
Tree (木) and one (一): A <u>book</u> is written on paper, which is one part of a tree

■ Trace the gray lines, and then practice on your own.

本
本

■ Useful vocabulary: Write the character, and trace the gray ones.

	ほん	**hon**	book
一 のえんぴつ	いっぽんのえんぴつ	**ippon no enpitsu**	one pencil
日	にほん	**nihon**	Japan
日	ほんじつ	**honjitsu**	today
州 *	ほんしゅう	**honshū**	Honshū
当 *	ほんとう	**hontō**	truth, reality

86 字

Character, letter

Stroke order: 丶 丷 宀 宀 字 字

Six (6) strokes
Thatched roof (宀) and child (子): A child learns her first <u>letters</u> at home

■ Trace the gray lines, and then practice on your own.

字
字

■ Useful vocabulary: Write the character, and trace the gray ones.

	じ	**ji**	character
文	もじ	**moji**	character, letter
大文	おおもじ	**ōmoji**	capital letter
ローマ	ローマじ	**rōmaji**	Roman letters
数 *	すうじ	**sūji**	numbers
習 *	しゅうじ	**shūji**	calligraphy

* An asterisk denotes vocabulary with kanji that have not yet been introduced.

Reading 9-D

山本先生は、高校の数学(すう)の先生です。山本先生のわるいところは、先生がホワイトボードに書(か)く字が少しよみにくいことです。でも、先生はおもしろいし、じゅぎょうでたいせつなことを二、三回くりかえして教(おし)えてくれますから、じゅぎょうがよく分かります。教え方が上手だから、山本先生はとても人気(にんき)があります。

Yamamoto sensei wa, kōkō no sūgaku no sensei desu. Yamamoto sensei no warui tokoro wa, sensei ga howaitobōdo ni kaku ji ga sukoshi yominikui koto desu. Demo, sensei wa omoshiroi shi, jugyō de taisetsu na koto o ni, san kai kurikaeshite oshiete kuremasu kara, jugyō ga yoku wakarimasu. Oshie kata ga jōzu da kara, Yamamoto sensei wa totemo ninki ga arimasu.

Questions 9-D

1. According to the passage, what is Mr. Yamamoto's weakness? (A. his students have difficulty reading his writing, B. he has difficulty reading his students' writing, C. he allows too many questions during class, D. he does not allow enough questions during class)
2. Which of the following is true of Mr. Yamamoto's teaching style? (A. he often repeats himself, B. he provides lecture notes, C. he writes carefully on the whiteboard, D. he listens to numerous student comments)
3. What is Mr. Yamamoto particularly good at? (A. writing, B. explaining, C. listening, D. reading)
4. Which of the following is true of Mr. Yamamoto? (A. he is not well liked by his students, but he has good handwriting, B. he is not well liked by his students, and he has bad handwriting, C. he is well liked by his students, and he has good handwriting, D. he is well liked by his students, but he has bad handwriting)

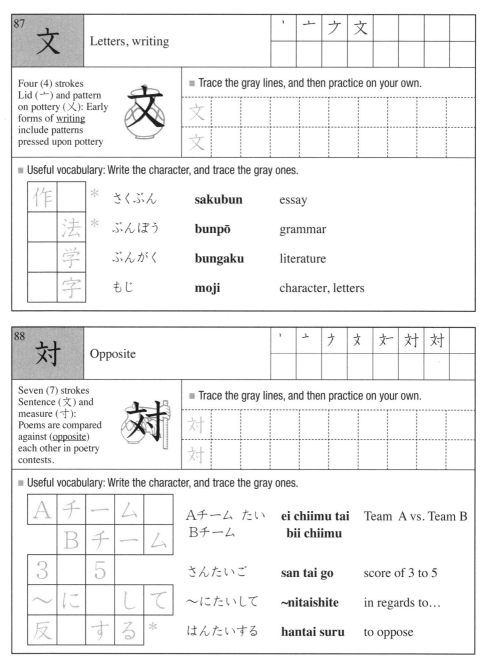

87 文 Letters, writing

丶	亠	ナ	文				

Four (4) strokes
Lid (亠) and pattern on pottery (乂): Early forms of writing include patterns pressed upon pottery

■ Trace the gray lines, and then practice on your own.

文								
文								

■ Useful vocabulary: Write the character, and trace the gray ones.

作		*	さくぶん	**sakubun**	essay
	法	*	ぶんぽう	**bunpō**	grammar
	学		ぶんがく	**bungaku**	literature
	字		もじ	**moji**	character, letters

88 対 Opposite

丶	亠	ナ	文	文	対	対	

Seven (7) strokes
Sentence (文) and measure (寸):
Poems are compared against (opposite) each other in poetry contests.

■ Trace the gray lines, and then practice on your own.

対								
対								

■ Useful vocabulary: Write the character, and trace the gray ones.

A	チ	ー	ム			Aチーム たい Bチーム	**ei chiimu tai bii chiimu**	Team A vs. Team B
	B	チ	ー	ム				
3		5				さんたいご	**san tai go**	score of 3 to 5
〜	に		し	て		〜にたいして	**~nitaishite**	in regards to…
反		す	る		*	はんたいする	**hantai suru**	to oppose

* An asterisk denotes vocabulary with kanji that have not yet been introduced.

Reading 9-E

まさしさんのりょうしんは日系一世(にっけいいっせい)で、まさしさんはハワイでそだちました。今、大学三年生で、ハワイの大学でべんきょうしています。日本語の文法(ぶんぽう)は少しむずかしいと思いますが、日本語が好きです。とくに日本の文化(ぶんか)に対して、きょうみを持っています。今年、まさしさんは、日本語スピーチコンテストに出て、しょうをもらいました。まさしさんも家族(かぞく)もとてもうれしそうでした。

日系一世(にっけいいっせい)　(first generation Japanese immigrant)

Masashi san no ryōshin wa nikkei issei de, Masashi san wa hawai de sodachimashita. Ima, daigaku sannensei de, hawai no daigaku de benkyō shite imasu. Nihongo no bunpō wa muzukashii to omoimasu ga, nihongo ga suki desu. Tokuni nihon no bunka ni taishite, kyōmi o motte imasu. Kotoshi, Masashi san wa, nihongo supiichi kontesuto ni dete, shō o moraimashita. Masashi san mo kazoku mo totemo ureshisō deshita.

Questions 9-E

1. Where are Masashi's parents from? (A. Hawaii, B. Japan, C. Singapore, D. Malaysia)
2. What does Masashi think about Japanese grammar? (A. it is very difficult, B. it is a bit difficult, C. it is not very difficult, D. it is not difficult at all)
3. What does Masashi seem to have an interest in? (A. Japanese culture, B. working in Japan, C. moving to Japan, D. Japanese business)
4. When did Masashi enter the speech contest? (A. in high school, B. last year, C. this year, D. he did not enter a speech contest)

89 書

Books, writing

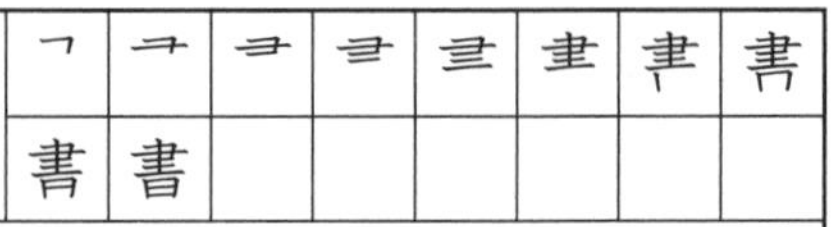

Ten (10) strokes
Hand holding a brush (⺻), sheets of paper (二), and an inkwell (日): A hand holding a brush, and writing with ink on paper

■ Trace the gray lines, and then practice on your own.

書
書

■ Useful vocabulary: Write the character, and trace the gray ones.

	く		かく	**kaku**	to write
手		き	てがき	**tegaki**	handwriting
図		館	* としょかん	**toshokan**	library
読		*	どくしょ	**dokusho**	reading
教	科		* きょうかしょ	**kyōkasho**	textbook

90 化

To change into

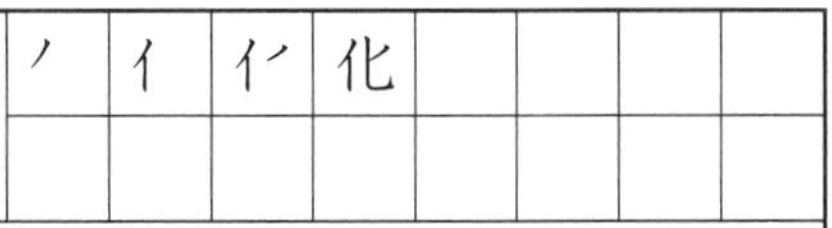

Four (4) strokes
A person standing (亻) and person sitting (匕): A person changing from a standing position to a sitting position

■ Trace the gray lines, and then practice on your own.

化
化

■ Useful vocabulary: Write the character, and trace the gray ones.

	け	る	ばける	**bakeru**	to change into something
	け	物	* ばけもの	**bakemono**	monster, ghost
文			ぶんか	**bunka**	culture
	石	*	かせき	**kaseki**	fossil
変		*	へんか	**henka**	change, transformation
	学		かがく	**kagaku**	chemistry

* An asterisk denotes vocabulary with kanji that have not yet been introduced.

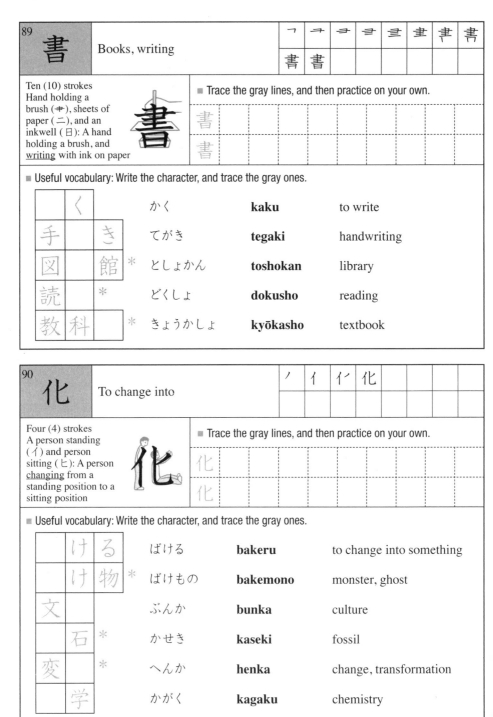

Reading 9-F

はなさんは、高校（こうこう）三年生で、文学にも化学にもきょうみがあります。よく図書館（としょかん）へいって、文学の本をよみますが、文学のレポートを書くのはあまり好きではありません。はなさんは、文学より、化学の方がもっと好きです。化学クラブに入っていて、去年（きょねん）、東京（とうきょう）大学の化学のコンテストにさんかしました。楽しかったし、とても勉強（べんきょう）になったので、大学で化学を勉強したいと思うようになりました。

さんか　to participate

Hana san wa, kōkō sannensei de, bungaku nimo kagaku nimo kyōmi ga arimasu. Yoku toshokan e itte, bungaku no hon o yomimasu ga, bungaku no repōto o kaku nowa amari suki dewa arimasen. Hana san wa, bungaku yori, kagaku no hō ga motto suki desu. Kagaku kurabu ni haitte ite, kyonen, tōkyō daigaku no kagaku no kontesuto ni sanka shimashita. Tanoshikatta shi, totemo benkyō ni natta node, daigaku de gakagu o benkyō shitai to omou yōni narimashita.

Questions 9-F

1. Where does Hana often spend her free time? (A. the Senior Lounge, B. the library, C. the high school athletic field, D. the science lab)
2. What is Hana's preference between chemistry and literature? (A. she does not like literature class or chemistry class, B. she likes literature class better than chemistry class, C. she likes chemistry class better than literature class, D. she likes both literature class and chemistry class about the same)
3. Which does Hana like more, reading or writing? (A. she likes reading books and writing essays for literature class, B. she likes reading books, but does not like writing essays for literature class, C. she does not like reading books, but likes writing essays for literature class, D. she does not like reading books or writing reports for literature class)
4. What club did she join? (A. the chemistry club, B. the literature club, C. the drama club, D. the book club)

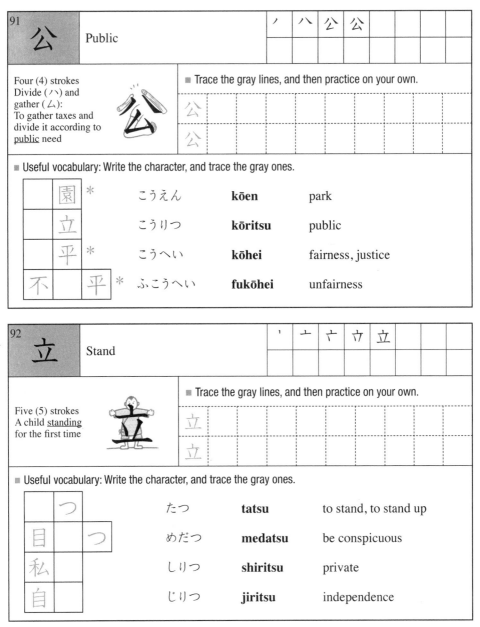

91 公	Public	ノ	八	公	公

Four (4) strokes
Divide (ハ) and gather (厶):
To gather taxes and divide it according to public need

■ Trace the gray lines, and then practice on your own.

公
公

■ Useful vocabulary: Write the character, and trace the gray ones.

園 *	こうえん	**kōen**	park
立	こうりつ	**kōritsu**	public
平 *	こうへい	**kōhei**	fairness, justice
不 平 *	ふこうへい	**fukōhei**	unfairness

92 立	Stand	丶	亠	亡	立	立

Five (5) strokes
A child standing for the first time

■ Trace the gray lines, and then practice on your own.

立
立

■ Useful vocabulary: Write the character, and trace the gray ones.

つ	たつ	**tatsu**	to stand, to stand up
目 つ	めだつ	**medatsu**	be conspicuous
私	しりつ	**shiritsu**	private
自	じりつ	**jiritsu**	independence

* An asterisk denotes vocabulary with kanji that have not yet been introduced.

Reading 9-G

はるさんは、十五さいです。最近(さいきん)、早く大人になりたいと思っています。そこで、かみのけをみどりにそめてみました。先週(せんしゅう)友達(だち)と公園(こうえん)へいったら、かみのけがとても目立ったようです。公園にいる人にじろじろ見られたり、子ども達(たち)に話しかけられたりしました。でも、はるさんは、気にしませんでした。

最近(さいきん) recently　　　そめる to dye

Haru san wa, jūgosai desu. Saikin, hayaku otona ni naritai to omotte imasu. Soko de, kaminoke o midori ni sometemimashita. Senshū tomodachi to kōen e ittara, kaminoke ga totemo medatta yō desu. Kōen ni iru hito ni jirojiro miraretari, kodomotachi ni hanashi kakeraretari shimashita. Demo, Haru san wa, ki ni shimasen deshita.

Questions 9-G

1. How old is Haru? (A. 15 years old, B. 16 years old, C. 17 years old, D. 18 years old)
2. Who did Haru go to the park with? (A. her family, B. her sister, C. her friends, D. her brother)
3. What was the response of the people at the park who saw her dyed hair? (A. they looked at her strangely, B. they mostly ignored her, C. the children mostly ignored her, D. no one else was at the park)
4. What does Haru think about others' opinions? (A. she worries too much about what others think, B. she tries to please her family too much, C. she does not mind what others think about her, D. she tries to please everyone)

Lesson 9 Practice

A. Kanji Review

Write the appropriate kanji character in each box below. Use the mnemonic pictures for hints if necessary.

 life, birth	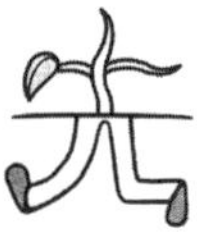 previous	 I, myself	 friend	 study	 school	 book
1.	2.	3.	4.	5.	6.	7.
 character	 letters	 against	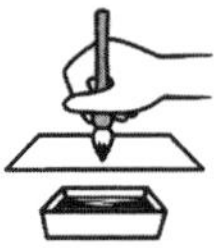 to write	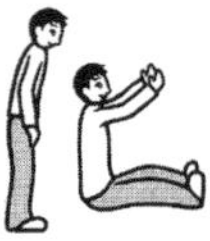 to change into	 public	 to stand
8.	9.	10.	11.	12.	13.	14.

B. Vocabulary Review

Try writing these vocabulary words with the appropriate kanji and okurigana characters.

1. ____ ____ 花 (いけばな flower arranging)
2. ____ ____ (だいがく college)
3. ____ ____ ____ (おおもじ capital letter)
4. ____ ____ (ぶんがく literature)
5. ____ ____ ____ (てんもんがく astronomy)
6. ____ ____ ____ (めだつ to stand out, be conspicuous)
7. 行 ____ ____ (いきさき destination)

8. ____ ____ ____ (しりつこう private school)

9. ____ ____ (まなぶ to learn)

10. ____ 正 (こうせい proofreading)

11. ____ 州 (ほんしゅう Honshū; main island)

12. ____ ____ (ぶんか culture)

13. ____ ____ ____ (おばけ monster, ghost)

14. 自 ____ (じりつ independence)

15. ____ ____ ____ (いきる to live, exist)

16. ____ ____ ____ (わたしたち we, us)

17. ____ ____ (がくせい college student)

18. ____ ____ ____ ____ (ローマじ Roman letter)

19. ____ ____ ____ ____ (にたいして towards)

20. ____ ____ (かく to write)

21. ____ ____ ____ (こうりつの public)

22. ____ ____ (じんせい life)

23. ____ ____ (にほん Japan)

24. ____ ____ ____ (しょうがっこう elementary school)

25. ____ ____ ____ ____ (しりつだいがく private university)

26. ____ ____ (せんげつ last month)

27. ____ ____ (ゆうじん friend – formal style)

28. ____ ____ (さきに ahead of, prior to)

29. ____ ____ ____ (ともだち friend – plain style)

30. ____ ____ (がっこう school)

31. ____ ____ (せんせい teacher, doctor)

C. Japanese Last Names

Try reading these Japanese last names. Match them by writing the correct number on each line.

1. 二見さん　_____ Tomoda san
2. 友田さん　_____ Hitomi san
3. 公文さん　_____ Futami san
4. 人見さん　_____ Tsuchimoto san
5. 土本さん　_____ Kumon san

D. Subjects of Study ～学(がく)

Match the names of the English and Japanese subjects of study. Write the appropriate name of the Japanese subject of study on the line, using kanji when possible.

1. ______________________ science　化学
2. ______________________ literature　すう学
3. ______________________ math　言語学
4. ______________________ astronomy　ぶつり学
5. ______________________ linguistics　文学
6. ______________________ electrical engineering　科(か)学
7. ______________________ chemistry　土木工学
8. ______________________ zoology　しゃ会学
9. ______________________ civil engineering　どうぶつ学
10. ______________________ physics　天(てん)文学
11. ______________________ civics　でんき工学

E. Types of Literature

Match the Japanese and English names of the following types of literature. Write the Japanese name of the type of literature on the appropriate line. A common word for ancient is 古(こ).

1.	______________________	German literature	中国文学
2.	______________________	French literature	国文学
3.	______________________	Chinese literature	ドイツ文学
4.	______________________	English literature	イギリス文学
5.	______________________	Japanese literature	仏(ふつ)文
6.	______________________	Ancient literature	古文

F. Japanese School System

The Japanese school system names each level of school a bit differently than some of the Western systems do. The activity below compares the Japanese and US. In Japan the numbering of each grade starts over in each school division (i.e., 7th grade is 中学一年, and 10th grade is 高校一年). Match the Japanese grade levels below with the appropriate Western school grade. Write the name of the Japanese grade level on the line.

1.	______________________	1st grade	小学三年
2.	______________________	2nd grade	高三年
3.	______________________	3rd grade	大学三年
4.	______________________	4th grade	小学一年
5.	______________________	5th grade	中学三年
6.	______________________	6th grade	大学四年
7.	______________________	7th grade	高一年
8.	______________________	8th grade	小学二年
9.	______________________	9th grade	中学二年
10.	______________________	10th grade	小学六年

11. ______________________ 11th grade 大学一年

12. ______________________ 12th grade 大学二年

13. ______________________ college freshman 小学四年

14. ______________________ college sophomore 中学一年

15. ______________________ college junior 高二年

16. ______________________ college senior 小学五年

G. Commonly Mistaken Kanji

Which kanji correctly expresses the meaning of the English word? Circle the most appropriate kanji character.

1. School	木	父	校	六	交	林
2. Friend	ナ	友	名	右	左	工
3. To write	事	早	東	雪	書	帰
4. To study	子	字	家	学	蛍	虫
5. Previous	先	生	見	兄	午	牛
6. Against	村	寸	文	射	守	対
7. Book	木	休	本	体	大	小
8. Public	分	公	ム	今	刀	力
9. Character	虫	学	宇	家	字	子
10. Life	生	王	先	土	玉	午
11. To stand	豆	六	口	国	文	立
12. Letters	交	立	文	父	校	木
13. To change into	花	北	比	化	カ	似
14. I, myself	科	私	ム	禾	料	数

H. Review Questions

Try writing these sentences in Japanese using kanji whenever appropriate. Each sentence has at least one new kanji from this lesson. Then, compare your translations with the answer key at the end of the book.

1. What kind of books do you like? ______
2. Do you read books during vacation? ______
3. Have you read any Japanese literature? ______
4. What do you like about the Japanese culture? ______
5. Have you ever seen a Japanese flower arrangement? ______
6. Is the English teacher fast at correcting essays? ______
7. What is the teacher's first name (下のなまえ)? ______
8. Do you sometime write Japanese in Roman letters? ______
9. Can old people learn a foreign language? ______
10. Do you have any Japanese friends? ______
11. Where were you born? ______
12. Are there many private schools in this city? ______
13. Which do you want to attend, a public university or private university? ______
14. Do you know someone who owns a Honda automobile? ______
15. Have you recently received any handwritten birthday cards? ______
16. Do you write Christmas cards each year? ______

17. Are you afraid of ghosts? ____

____

18. Are western ghosts and Japanese ghosts the same? ______________________________

____

I. Interview Your Partner

Take turns asking the above questions with your partner. Try to answer as fully and appropriately as you can. For best results, you should elaborate on your answers whenever possible.

J. Read and Respond: Letter from a Japanese Friend

The following is a letter from a home stay student named Hanako Yamada who attended your Japanese class last year. You don't have to understand all the Japanese, but try to read her letter and then respond to it in the space below. Be sure to include a greeting and answer her questions as best you can.

日本語クラスのみなさんへ

こんにちは。お元気ですか。私が高校に入学して、もう1ヶ月です。友達がたくさんできたので、学校はとても楽しいです。

私が通っている学校は、山の上にあります。毎日駅から二十分ぐらい歩かなければなりません。大変ですが、山の上からのけしきはすばらしいです。

全校生徒は千二百人で、公立の男女共学です。学校がたてられたのは、六十年前です。とてもれきしがあって、古い学校です。部活動がさかんで、テニス部、サッカー部、水泳部、えんげき部などがあります。制服がありますが、きそくはそんなにきびしくありません。勉強したい生徒が多くて、ほとんどの生徒は卒業した後で、大学に行きます。あなたの学校は、私の高校とちがいますか。にていますか。教えてください。

おへんじを待っています。

山田花子より

93 犬 Dog

一 ナ 大 犬

Four (4) strokes
A dog wagging its tail

■ Trace the gray lines, and then practice on your own.

犬

犬

■ Useful vocabulary: Write the character, and trace the gray ones.

犬	いぬ	**inu**	dog
子犬	こいぬ	**koinu**	puppy
番犬 *	ばんけん	**banken**	watchdog
のら犬	のらいぬ	**norainu**	stray dog

94 鳥 Bird

Stroke order: 11 steps building up to 鳥

Eleven (11) strokes
A small white bird—feathers flowing, four talons outstretched

■ Trace the gray lines, and then practice on your own.

鳥

鳥

■ Useful vocabulary: Write the character, and trace the gray ones.

鳥	とり	**tori**	bird
小鳥	ことり	**kotori**	small bird
白鳥	はくちょう	**hakuchō**	swan
一石二鳥	いっせきにちょう	**isseki nichō**	kill two birds with one stone

* An asterisk denotes vocabulary with kanji that have not yet been introduced.

Reading 10-A

のぼるさんの家族(ぞく)は、マルという犬をかっています。マルはのら犬でしたが、何回かのぼるさんとあそんだ後(あと)で、ある日、のぼるさんの家にもらわれました。マルは人とあそぶのが大好(す)きで、知(し)らない人にもほえません。だから、番犬(ばんけん)にはなれません。近所のねこや鳥をおいかけるマルを見るのはおもしろいです。マルはかわった犬ですが、のぼるさんの家族はマルが大好きです。

ほえる to bark　　おいかける to chase　　かわった strange

Noboru san no kazoku wa, Maru to iu inu o katte imasu. Maru wa norainu deshita ga, nankaika Noboru san to asonda atode, aru hi, Noboru san no ie ni morawaremashita. Maru wa hito to asobu no ga daisuki de, shiranai hito ni mo hoemasen. Dakara, banken niwa naremasen. Kinjo no neko ya tori o oikakeru Maru o miru nowa omoshiroi desu. Maru wa kawatta inu desu ga, Noboru san no kazoku wa Maru ga daisuki desu.

Questions 10-A

1. What kind of pet does Nobori's family have? (A. dog, B. bird, C. cat, D. goldfish)
2. How does Maru behave around strangers? (A. Maru never barks at strangers, B. Maru usually does not bark at strangers, C. Maru occasionally barks at strangers, D. Maru always barks at strangers)
3. How does Maru act around other animals? (A. Maru does not like to chase other animals, B. Maru does not like to chase cats, C. Maru likes to chase cats, D. Maru is often chased by cats and birds)
4. How does Noboru's family feel about Maru? (A. they are happy to have Maru as a pet, B. they want to find another family for Maru, C. they are trying to train Maru, D. they think Maru is too strange to look after him)

95 馬 Horse

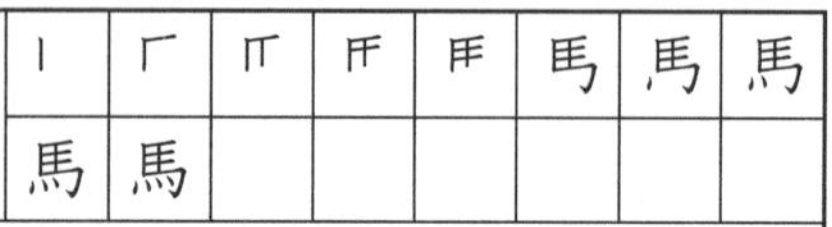

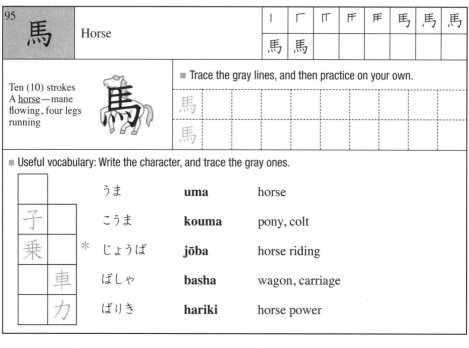

Ten (10) strokes
A horse—mane flowing, four legs running

■ Trace the gray lines, and then practice on your own.

馬
馬

■ Useful vocabulary: Write the character, and trace the gray ones.

□		うま	**uma**	horse
子□		こうま	**kouma**	pony, colt
乗□	*	じょうば	**jōba**	horse riding
□車		ばしゃ	**basha**	wagon, carriage
□力		ばりき	**hariki**	horse power

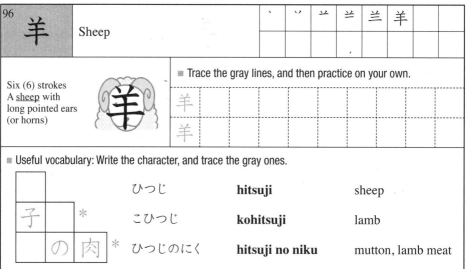

96 羊 Sheep

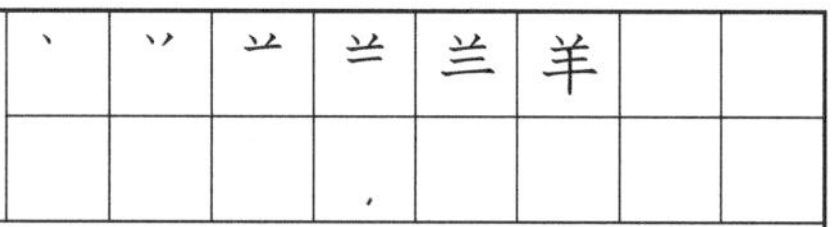

Six (6) strokes
A sheep with long pointed ears (or horns)

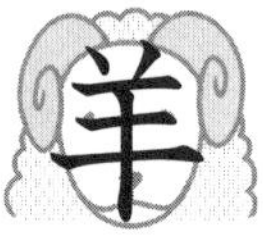

■ Trace the gray lines, and then practice on your own.

羊
羊

■ Useful vocabulary: Write the character, and trace the gray ones.

□		ひつじ	**hitsuji**	sheep
子□	*	こひつじ	**kohitsuji**	lamb
□の肉	*	ひつじのにく	**hitsuji no niku**	mutton, lamb meat

* An asterisk denotes vocabulary with kanji that have not yet been introduced.

Reading 10-B

きみこさんとせいじさんは、毎年学校(がっこう)のあきのバザーがたのしみです。今年、きみこさんは、バーベキューの係(かかり)です。羊の肉をきったり、やいたり、うったりします。ソースがおいしいから、バーベキューはいつもすぐにうりきれます。たくさんのお客(きゃく)さんがきみこさんにソースのレシピを聞きますが、きみこさんはおしえないつもりです。せいじさんはバザーで乗馬(じょうば)のきっぷをうる係です。せいじさんによると、お客さんが少ない時、ただで馬に乗(の)ることが出来(き)るから、乗馬の係になるのが好(す)きだそうです。

係(かかり)	duty, person in charge	うりきれる	to be sold out
～によると	according to ~	ただ	free

Kimiko san to Seiji san wa, maitoshi gakkō no aki no bazā ga tanoshimi desu. Kotoshi, kimiko san wa, bābekyū no kakari desu. Hitsuji no niku o kittari, yaitari, uttari shimasu. Sōsu ga oishii kara, bābekyū wa itsumo sugu ni urikiremasu. Takusan no okyakusan ga Kimiko san ni sōsu no reshipi o kikimasu ga, Kimiko san wa oshienai tsumori desu. Seiji san wa bazā de jōba no kippu o uru kakari desu. Seiji san niyoru to okyakusan ga sukunai toki, tada de uma ni noru koto ga dekiru kara, jōba no kakari ni naru no ga suki da sō desu.

Questions 10-B

1. When is Kimiko and Seiji's school bazaar held? (A. spring, B. summer, C. fall, D. winter)
2. What is Kimiko in charge of this year? (A. the petting park, B. the horse riding booth, C. the balloon stand, D. the barbeque mutton booth)
3. What did many people ask Kimiko? (A. they asked for their money back, B. they asked for directions to the horse riding area, C. they asked her where she was from, D. they asked for the recipe for the barbeque sauce)
4. Why does Seiji like selling tickets at the horse riding area? (A. he gets paid, B. he gets to ride the horses sometimes, C. his girlfriend likes the horses, D. he owns the horses)

97 牛 Cow

Four (4) strokes
A cow with one broken horn

■ Trace the gray lines, and then practice on your own.

牛								
牛								

■ Useful vocabulary: Write the character, and trace the gray ones.

□	うし	**ushi**	cow, cattle
子 □	こうし	**koushi**	calf
□ 肉 *	ぎゅうにく	**gyūniku**	beef

98 魚 Fish

Eleven (11) strokes
A fish—head, scales, tail, and all

■ Trace the gray lines, and then practice on your own.

魚								
魚								

■ Useful vocabulary: Write the character, and trace the gray ones.

□	さかな	**sakana**	fish
□ 屋 *	さかなや	**sakanaya**	fish market
金 □	きんぎょ	**kingyo**	goldfish
人 □	にんぎょ	**ningyo**	mermaid, merman

* An asterisk denotes vocabulary with kanji that have not yet been introduced.

Reading 10-C

てつおさんは、一年間アメリカでホームステイしました。ホストファミリーは、オクラホマしゅうのぼくじょうにすんでいて、牛や馬や羊をかっていました。てつおさんはこんなにたくさんの牛を見たのは、生まれてはじめてでした。てつおさんは、牛にえさをやったり、牛がまい子になったらさがしたりしました。ホストファミリーは、自然(しぜん)が大好きだったので、乗馬を教(おし)えてもらいました。また、てつおさんは、魚つりが上手だったので、時々土曜日に手伝(てつだ)いがおわった後(あと)で、魚つりに行って、つった魚をホストファミリーにりょうりしてあげました。

ぼくじょう	ranch	こんなにたくさん	this many
えさ	animal feed	さがしました	to look for
てつだい	chores		

Tetsuo san wa, ichinenkan amerika de hōmusutei shimashita. Hosuto famirii wa, okurahoma shū no bokujō ni sunde ite, ushi ya uma ya hitsuji o katte imashita. Tetsuo san wa konnani takusan no ushi o mita no wa, umarete hajimete deshita. Tetsuo san wa, ushi ni esa o yattari, ushi ga maigo ni nattara sagashitari, shimashita. Hosuto famirii wa, shizen ga daisuki datta node, jōba o oshiete morai mashita. Mata, Tetsuo san wa, sakana tsuri ga jōzu datta node, tokidoki doyōbi ni tetsudai ga owatta atode, sakana tsuri ni itte, tsutta sakana o hosuto famirii ni ryōri shite agemashita.

Questions 10-C

1. How long did Tetsuo do his home stay in America? (A. one summer, B. one year, C. two years, D. three years)
2. What was one of Tetsuo's chores? (A. milking the cows, B. feeding the sheep, C. watering the animals, D. feeding the cows)
3. What kinds of outdoor activities did Tetsuo's host family do? (A. canoeing and horseback riding, B. horseback riding and fishing, C. fishing and camping, D. camping and canoeing)
4. When did Tetsuo like to go fish? (A. Sundays, B. weekdays, C. Fridays, D. Saturdays)

99 虫	Bug	丶	冂	口	中	虫	虫		

Six (6) strokes
A caterpillar enjoying a bite of a leaf

■ Trace the gray lines, and then practice on your own.

虫									
虫									

■ Useful vocabulary: Write the character, and trace the gray ones.

□	むし	**mushi**	bug, insect
泣き□ *	なきむし	**nakimushi**	crybaby
弱□ *	よわむし	**yowamushi**	coward, weakling
水□	みずむし	**mizumushi**	athlete's foot
本の□	ほんのむし	**hon no mushi**	bookworm (literally and figuratively)

* An asterisk denotes vocabulary with kanji that have not yet been introduced.

Reading 10-D

まりさんは、中学生で、本の虫と言われています。本をよむことが好きで、ほとんど外に出ないからです。でも自分をかえるために、今年のなつ、家族(ぞく)と山で五日間キャンプとハイキングをしました。さいしょの日にハイキングがこわいと言ったら、いもうとに弱虫と言われました。二日目のあさ、まりさんがおきると、テントの中にてんとう虫が一ぴきいました。まりさんが、びっくりして、家にかえりたいとないたので、お父さんに泣き虫だと言われました。まりさんは、来年(らいねん)はキャンプにいかないと言っています。

てんとう虫　　ladybug

Mari san wa, chūgakusei de, hon no mushi to iwarete imasu. Hon o yomu koto ga daisuki de, hotondo soto ni denai kara desu. Demo jibun o kaeru tameni, kotoshi no natsu, kazoku to yama de itsukakan kyanpu to haikingu o shimashita. Saisho no hi ni haikingu ga kowai to ittara, imōto ni yowamushi to iwaremashita. Futsukame no asa, Mari san ga okiru to, tento no naka ni tentōmushi ga ippiki imashita. Mari san ga, bikkuri shite, ie ni kaeritai to naita node, otōsan ni nakimushi da to iwaremashita. Mari san wa, rainen wa kyanpu ni ikanai to itte imasu.

Questions 10-D

1. How long did Mari's family go camping? (A. two days, B. three days, C. four days, D. five days)
2. Why did her little sister call her a weakling? (A. she brought books on the campout, B. she did not like the camp food, C. she cried when she saw a bug, D. she was afraid of hiking)
3. Why did Mari want to go home? (A. her legs became sore, B. she tasted the camp food, C. she saw a ladybug, D. she finished her books)
4. What did Mari's father tell her not to be? (A. a bookworm, B. a weakling, C. a coward, D. a crybaby)

Let's Review

Write the following words with kanji.

1. _____ (dog)	2. _____ _____ (puppy)
3. _____ (bird)	4. _____ _____ (small bird)
5. _____ (horse)	6. _____ _____ (pony, colt)
7. _____ (sheep)	8. _____ _____ (lamb)
9. _____ (cow)	10. _____ _____ (calf)

Lesson 10 Practice

A. Kanji Review

Try writing the kanji for the words below, and then write pronunciation in hiragana below.

 dog	 bird	 horse	 sheep	 cow	 fish	 bug
1.	2.	3.	4.	5.	6.	7.
いぬ						

B. Vocabulary Review

Try writing these words with appropriate kanji and okurigana characters.

1. _____ _____ _____(ほんのむし　bookworm)
2. _____ _____(みずむし　athlete's foot)
3. _____ _____(とりにく　chicken meat)
4. _____ _____(ばりき　horse power)
5. _____ 屋 (さかなや　fish shop)
6. 泣 _____ _____(なきむし　crybaby)
7. _____ _____(ぎゅうにく　beef)
8. _____ _____(きんぎょ　goldfish)
9. 番 _____ (ばんけん　watchdog)
10. 乗 _____(じょうば　riding horses)
11. _____ _____ 肉 (ひつじのにく　mutton)
12. 白 _____(はくちょう　swan)

13. 弱 _____ (よわむし　coward, weakling)

14. _____ 面 _____ (しちめんちょう　turkey)

15. _____ 石 _____ _____ (いっせきにちょう　"Kill two birds with one stone")

16. _____ 車 (ばしゃ　wagon, carriage)

C. Zodiac Animals

Although the kanji characters used for the Zodiac are not all core kanji characters, they are included here for your information, and because Japanese people often ask new friends,「何年(なにどし)（生(う)まれ）ですか」meaning "In what year of the Zodiac were you born?" This is an indirect way to find out someone's age, which is important in knowing the correct register to use when speaking Japanese. Look at the list below and then try to tell the correct year of the Zodiac sign for yourself and four different Zodiac signs of your family or friends. Write the appropriate kanji or hiragana characters.

Example: 校長(こうちょう)先生はたつどし（生(う)まれ）です。(The principal was born in the year of the Dragon.)

わたしは ______________________ です。

______________________ さんは ______________________ です。

______________________ さんは ______________________ です。

______________________ さんは ______________________ です。

______________________ さんは ______________________ です。

1	Mouse	子年	ねずみどし	1960	1972	1984	1996	2008
2	Ox, cow	丑年	うしどし	1961	1973	1985	1997	2009
3	Tiger	寅年	とらどし	1962	1974	1986	1998	2010
4	Rabbit	卯年	うどし	1963	1975	1987	1999	2011
5	Dragon	辰年	たつどし	1964	1976	1988	2000	2012
6	Snake	巳年	へびどし	1965	1977	1989	2001	2013
7	Horse	午年	うまどし	1966	1978	1990	2002	2014
8	Sheep	未年	ひつじどし	1967	1979	1991	2003	2015

9	Monkey	申年	さるどし	1968	1980	1992	2004	2016
10	Rooster	酉年	とりどし	1969	1981	1993	2005	2017
11	Dog	戌年	いぬどし	1970	1982	1994	2006	2018
12	Boar	亥年	いのししどし	1971	1983	1995	2007	2019

D. Japanese Names

Here are more names that include some of the kanji characters we have learned so far. Read the pronunciation, and try to write them in kanji.

1. いぬやま (dog, mountain) _____ _____
2. うしじま (cow, island) _____ 島
3. うしやま (cow, mountain) _____ _____
4. とりやま (bird, mountain) _____ _____

E. Review Questions

Try writing these sentences in Japanese using kanji whenever appropriate. Each sentence has at least one new kanji from this lesson. Then, compare your translations with the answer key at the end of the book.

1. Do you have a pet dog? ______________________________
2. Have you ever owned a goldfish? ______________________________
3. Can you ride horses? ______________________________
4. Are you good at fishing? ______________________________
5. Do you like to eat fish? ______________________________
6. Can you cook meat? ______________________________
7. Do you like beef or chicken? ______________________________
8. Do you know the proverb "Kill two birds with one stone"? ______________
9. Is anyone in your family a bookworm? ______________________________
10. Do you hate bugs? ______________________________
11. Were you a crybaby as a child? ______________________________

F. Interview Your Partner

Take turns asking the above questions with your partner. Try to answer as fully and appropriately as you can. For best results, you should elaborate on your answers whenever possible.

G. Read and Respond: Journal Entry

Tetsuya is staying with a host family in Oklahoma, USA. While there he described their home in his journal. Read his description and answer the questions that follow.

ホストファミリーは、ぼくじょうにすんでいて、木がたくさん生えている。家の左にも大きい木が一本あって、そのうしろに羊がみえる。いつも鳥をおいかけている犬が一ぴきいて、家のうしろに牛が十四とうと馬が二とういる。家の右に川があって、中に魚がたくさんいる。そこで魚をつるのが大好きだ。

ぼくじょう　　farm

1. Around Tetsuya's host family's house there are many________________
2. Where is there one big tree? ________________
3. What is behind the big tree? ________________
4. What does the dog like to chase? ________________
5. What is behind the house? ________________ and ________________
6. What is located to the right of the house? ________________
7. What does Tetsuya like to do there? ________________

100 米 Rice

丶	丷	䒑	半	米	米		

Six (6) strokes
A rice stalk

■ Trace the gray lines, and then practice on your own.

米								
米								

■ Useful vocabulary: Write the character, and trace the gray ones.

［　］	こめ	**kome**	uncooked rice
［　］屋 *	こめや	**komeya**	rice store
［　］国	べいこく	**beikoku**	USA
日［　］	にちべい	**nichibei**	Japan and USA
南［　］	なんべい	**nanbei**	South America

101 来 Come

一	丆	𠂿	亚	平	来	来	

Seven (7) strokes
One (一) and rice (米): Rice harvest comes once each time you plant

■ Trace the gray lines, and then practice on your own.

来								
来								

■ Useful vocabulary: Write the character, and trace the gray ones.

［　］る	くる	**kuru**	come
出［　］る	できる	**dekiru**	can do, be able to do
［　］年	らいねん	**rainen**	next year
［　］月	らいげつ	**raigetsu**	next month

* An asterisk denotes vocabulary with kanji that have not yet been introduced.

Reading 11-A

まゆみさんは学校から帰ると、まず宿題をします。宿題をしていると、毎週月曜日には八百屋さんが野菜やくだものを家に届けに来ます。まゆみさんは、バナナが好きなので、いつも宿題をしながら、届いたばかりのバナナを一本食べます。毎月第二火曜日にはお米屋さんが来ます。今月も十キロ入りのお米を買ったので、一ヵ月くらいは持つでしょう。

届ける (to deliver)　　持つ (to last, have, hold, possess)

Mayumi san wa gakkō kara kaeru to, mazu shukudai o shimasu. Shukudai o shite iru to, maishū getsuyōbi niwa yaoya san ga yasai ya kudamono o ie ni todoke ni kimasu. Mayumi san wa, banana ga suki na node, itsumo shukudai o shinagara, todoita bakari no banana o ippon tabemasu. Maitsuki dai ni kayōbi niwa okomeya san ga kimasu. Kongetsu mo jukkiro iri no okome o katta node, ikkagetsu kurai wa motsu deshō.

Questions 11-A

1. How often does the vegetable stand deliver to Mayumi's house? (A. every day, B. twice per week, C. every week, D. twice per month)
2. When does Mayumi like to eat bananas? (A. while watching TV, B. while doing homework, C. before dinner, D. after dinner)
3. How much rice does the rice deliveryman deliver? (A. 5 kilograms, B. 10 kilograms, C. 15 kilograms, D. 20 kilograms)
4. When will Mayumi's family order rice next? (A. in a week, B. in two weeks, C. in three weeks, D. in four weeks)

102 番

Turn, number

一	𠂉	乊	㓁	平	采	采	釆
番	番	番	番				

Twelve (12) strokes
Cut (ノ), rice (米), and rice field (田): To take one's turn harvesting (cutting) the rice in the fields

■ Trace the gray lines, and then practice on your own.

番

番

■ Useful vocabulary: Write the character, and trace the gray ones.

一	いちばん	**ichiban**	first, most, best
三 線 *	さんばんせん	**sanbansen**	Track No. 3
号 *	ばんごう	**bangō**	number, serial number
テ レ ビ 組 *	テレビばんぐみ	**terebi bangumi**	TV program
当	とうばん	**tōban**	person on duty

103 行

Go

ノ	彡	彳	彳	行	行		

Six (6) strokes
A procession going down the street

■ Trace the gray lines, and then practice on your own.

行

行

■ Useful vocabulary: Write the character, and trace the gray ones.

く	いく	**iku**	to go
う	おこなう	**okonau**	to act, hold an event
旅	りょこう	**ryokō**	travel
事 *	ぎょうじ	**gyōji**	event, function
き 先	いきさき	**ikisaki**	destination

* An asterisk denotes vocabulary with kanji that have not yet been introduced.

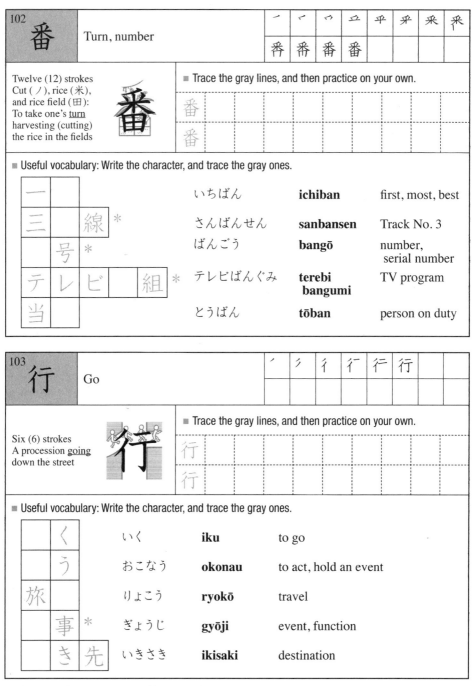

Reading 11-B

よしおさんの一番好きなテレビ番組(ばんぐみ)は金曜(よう)日の午後(ごご)七時から九チャンネルでやっているテニスのアニメです。よしおさんも、友達(だち)も毎週(しゅう)かならず見ています。でも、先週の金曜日、よしおさんの家族(かぞく)は、お父さんの会(かい)社(しゃ)のパーティに行くことになりました。よしおさんは大好きな番組を見ることができなくなって、がっかりしました。ところが、パーティの行われているホテルのロビーにテレビがあったのです！七時になってよしおさんは、こっそりとロビーに行きました。よしおさんはアニメを見ることができました。

がっかりする　to be disappointed　　こっそりと　secretly

Yoshio san no ichiban suki na terebi bangumi wa kinyōbi no gogo shichiji kara kyūchanneru de yatte iru tenisu no anime desu. Yoshio san mo, tomodachi mo maishū kanarazu mite imasu. Demo, senshū no kinyōbi, Yoshio san no kazoku wa, otōsan no kaisha no pātii ni iku koto ni narimashita. Yoshio san wa daisuki na bangumi o miru koto ga dekinakunatte, gakkari shimashita. Tokoro ga, pātii no okonawarete iru hoteru no robii ni terebi ga atta no desu! Shichiji ni natte Yoshio san wa, kossori to robii ni ikimashita. Yoshio san wa anime o miru koto ga dekimashita.

Questions 11-B

1. What is Yoshio's favorite TV program? (A. a sports news program, B. an animated sports program, C. a music video program, D. a comedy program)
2. When does Yoshio watch his favorite TV program? (A. Fridays at 6 p.m., B. Fridays at 7 p.m., C. Saturdays at 6 p.m., D. Saturdays at 7 p.m.)
3. Why couldn't Yoshio watch the TV program last week? (A. because of his father's company party, B. because of his mother's company party, C. because of his big sister's piano recital, D. because of his big brother's piano recital)
4. How was Yoshio able to solve his problem? (A. his parents allowed him to stay home, B. he was able to record the TV program to watch later, C. he watched the TV program that evening, D. his friend recorded the TV program to watch later)

104 待	Wait	ノ	㇒	彳	彳	彳	往	待	待
		待							

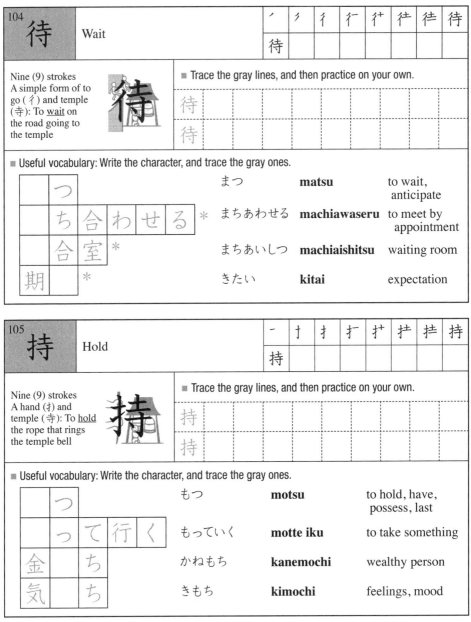

Nine (9) strokes
A simple form of to go (彳) and temple (寺): To <u>wait</u> on the road going to the temple

■ Trace the gray lines, and then practice on your own.

待
待

■ Useful vocabulary: Write the character, and trace the gray ones.

□つ	まつ	**matsu**	to wait, anticipate
□ち合わせる *	まちあわせる	**machiawaseru**	to meet by appointment
□合室 *	まちあいしつ	**machiaishitsu**	waiting room
期□ *	きたい	**kitai**	expectation

105 持	Hold	一	十	扌	扌	扌	拝	挂	持
		持							

Nine (9) strokes
A hand (扌) and temple (寺): To <u>hold</u> the rope that rings the temple bell

■ Trace the gray lines, and then practice on your own.

持
持

■ Useful vocabulary: Write the character, and trace the gray ones.

□つ	もつ	**motsu**	to hold, have, possess, last
□って行く	もっていく	**motte iku**	to take something
金□ち	かねもち	**kanemochi**	wealthy person
気□ち	きもち	**kimochi**	feelings, mood

* An asterisk denotes vocabulary with kanji that have not yet been introduced.

Reading 11-C

今日は大みそかです。えりさんは、夜になったら友達といっしょに、はつもうでへ行くので、駅で待ち合わせることにしました。でも、その前に家族でおじいさんとおばあさんの家へ行って、みんなで食事をすることになっています。えりさんのおばあさんは、お客さんに料理を食べさせるのが大好きです。だから、今晩、えりさんの家族が来るのを楽しみにしています。またいつものように、たくさんのおいしい料理を食べさせてくれるでしょう。みんなで食べるために、えりさんのお母さんは長野のおじさんから送ってもらったおそばを、えりさんは手作りのデザートを持って行くつもりです。

大みそか	New Year's Eve	お客さん	visitors
はつもうで	to pay first visit of the year to shrine or temple		

Kyō wa ōmisoka desu. Eri san wa, yoru ni nattara tomodachi to isshoni, hatsumōde e iku node, eki de machiawaseru koto ni shimashita. Demo, sono mae ni kazoku de ojiisan to obāsan no ie e itte, minna de shokuji o suru koto ni natte imasu. Eri san no obāsan wa, okyaku san ni ryōri o tabesaseru no ga daisuki desu. Dakara, konban, Eri san no kazoku ga kuru no o tanoshimi ni shite imasu. Mata itsumo no yōni, takusan no oishii ryōri o tabesasete kureru deshō. Minna de taberu tameni, Eri san no okāsan wa nagano no ojiisan kara okutte moratta osoba o, Eri san wa tetsukuri no dezāto o motte iku tsumori desu.

Questions 11-C

1. Who is Eri going to visit a shrine with tonight? (A. her family, B. herself, C. her friends, D. her sister)
2. Where will she eat dinner? (A. at home, B. at her grandparents' home, C. at her friend's home, D. at a restaurant near the train station)
3. What does Eri's grandmother enjoy doing? (A. visiting the neighborhood shrine on New Year's Eve, B. visiting a big shrine on New Year's Eve, C. going places with her family, D. cooking for visitors)
4. What does Eri seem to have in common with her grandmother? (A. she likes eating out, B. she likes visiting shrines, C. she likes cooking, D. she likes shopping)

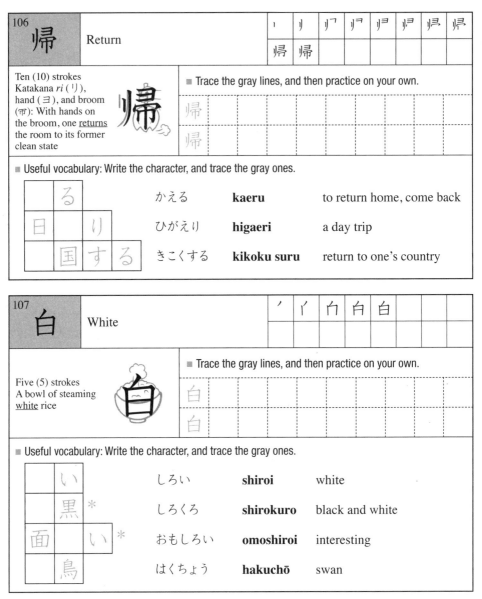

106 帰 Return

Ten (10) strokes
Katakana *ri* (リ), hand (ヨ), and broom (帀): With hands on the broom, one <u>returns</u> the room to its former clean state

■ Trace the gray lines, and then practice on your own.

■ Useful vocabulary: Write the character, and trace the gray ones.

かえる	**kaeru**	to return home, come back
ひがえり	**higaeri**	a day trip
きこくする	**kikoku suru**	return to one's country

107 白 White

Five (5) strokes
A bowl of steaming <u>white</u> rice

■ Trace the gray lines, and then practice on your own.

■ Useful vocabulary: Write the character, and trace the gray ones.

しろい	**shiroi**	white
しろくろ*	**shirokuro**	black and white
おもしろい*	**omoshiroi**	interesting
はくちょう	**hakuchō**	swan

* An asterisk denotes vocabulary with kanji that have not yet been introduced.

Reading 11-D

りくさんは、写真を勉強しています。フィルムのカメラを使っているので、とても面白いそうです。デジタルカメラの方が便利ですが、フィルムのカメラの方がカラーでも白黒でも、芸術的な写真がとれると思っています。来週の週末、りくさんの家族は日帰りで日光へ行きます。りくさんは、カメラを持って行ってたくさん写真をとるつもりです。日光には有名な神社やお寺があるので、よい写真がとれると楽しみにしています。

芸術的な　(artistic)

Riku san wa, shashin o benkyō shite imasu. Firumu no kamera o tsukatte iru node, totemo omoshiroi sō desu. Dejitaru kamera no hō ga benri desu ga, firumu no kamera no hō ga karā demo shirokuro demo, geijutsuteki na shashin ga toreru to omotte imasu. Raishū no shūmatsu, Riku san no kazoku wa higaeri de nikkō e ikimasu. Riku san wa, kamera o motte itte takusan shashin o toru tsumori desu. Nikkō niwa yūmei na jinja ya otera ga aru node, yoi shashin ga toreru to tanoshimi ni shite imasu.

Questions 11-D

1. How does Riku prefer to take pictures? (A. with digital cameras, B. with film cameras and color film, C. with film cameras and black and white film, D. with film cameras and either color or black and white film)
2. When is Riku's family taking a day trip to Nikko? (A. tomorrow, B. this weekend, C. next weekend, D. next month)
3. What does Riku plan to take along on the trip? (A. a friend, B. extra film, C. a film camera, D. a digital camera)
4. Why does Riku think he can take some interesting photos at Nikko? (A. because there is a beach, B. because there is a cable car ride, C. because there are famous shrines and temples, D. because there is a shrine that looks like it is floating in the water)

108 良 Good

Stroke order: 丶 ㇆ ㇕ ㇌ 自 ⾃ 良

Seven (7) strokes
A bowl of steaming white rice on a table with chopsticks—that's good!

■ Trace the gray lines, and then practice on your own.

良
良

■ Useful vocabulary: Write the character, and trace the gray ones.

□い	よい／いい	**yoi/ ii**	good, okay
□さそう	よさそう	**yosasō**	to seem good
□く	よく	**yoku**	well, nicely
不□品 *	ふりょうひん	**furyōhin**	defective product, trash

109 食 Eat

Stroke order: ノ 人 𠆢 今 今 今 食 食 食

Nine (9) strokes
A roof (人) and a steaming bowl of white rice and chopsticks on a table: Time to eat!

■ Trace the gray lines, and then practice on your own.

食
食

■ Useful vocabulary: Write the character, and trace the gray ones.

□べる	たべる	**taberu**	eat
□べ物 *	たべもの	**tabemono**	food
夕□	ゆうしょく	**yūshoku**	dinner
和□ *	わしょく	**washoku**	Japanese-style food
□事 *	しょくじ	**shokuji**	meal, dinner

* An asterisk denotes vocabulary with kanji that have not yet been introduced.

Reading 11-E

去年はるなさんは、留学生として一年間、オーストラリアにいました。ホストファミリーは、はるなさんにオーストラリアの伝統的な料理をたくさん食べさせてくれました。ホストファミリーの作る料理は、とてもおいしかったですが、はるなさんは、時々、和食が食べたくなりました。そこで、ホストファミリーは、はるなさんのお誕生日にはるなさんを和食のレストランへ連れて行って上げることにしました。ひさしぶりの日本の食事はとてもおいしかったので、はるなさんは、最高の誕生日だと思いました。

伝統的な (でんとうてき) traditional

最高 (さいこう) the most, the best

Kyonen Haruna san wa, ryūgakusei toshite ichinenkan, ōsutoraria ni imashita. Hosuto famirii wa, Haruna san ni ōsutoraria no dentōteki na ryōri o takusan tabesasete kure-mashita. Hosuto famirii no tsukuru ryōri wa, totemo oishikatta desu ga, Haruna san wa, tokidoki, washoku ga tabetaku narimashita. Sokode, hosuto famirii wa, Haruna san no otanjōbi ni Haruna san o washoku no resutoran e tsurete itte ageru koto ni shimashita. Hisashiburi no nihon no shokuji wa totemo oishikatta node, Haruna san wa, saikō no tanjōbi da to omoimashita.

Questions 11-E

1. How long did Haruna stay with her host family? (A. one summer, B. one semester, C. one year, D. two years)
2. What kinds of traditional Australian culture did Haruna's host family share with her? (A. music, B. art, C. cooking, C. dance)
3. How often did Haruna eat Japanese food while in Australia? (A. daily, B. regularly, C. sometimes, D. only on special occasions)
4. Why did Haruna think her birthday was the best? (A. because the meal was delicious, B. because Haruna's friends cooked for her, C. because Haruna got to cook a traditional local dish, D. because the host family thought Haruna was a good cook)

110 物	Thing (tangible)	ノ	𠂉	牛	牛	牜	牞	物	物

Eight (8) strokes
The head and body of a cow – a thing of great value

■ Trace the gray lines, and then practice on your own.

物									
物									

■ Useful vocabulary: Write the character, and trace the gray ones.

□語		ものがたり	**monogatari**	story, tale
買い□	*	かいもの	**kaimono**	shopping
荷□	*	にもつ	**nimotsu**	luggage
見□		けんぶつ	**kenbutsu**	sightseeing
動□	*	どうぶつ	**dōbutsu**	animal

* An asterisk denotes vocabulary with kanji that have not yet been introduced.

Reading 11-F

去年(きょ)、みさきさんは友だち三人といっしょにグアムへ行きました。毎日、暖(あたた)かくて良い天気でした。みさきさんは、初(はじ)めてシュノーケリングでたくさんの魚を見ました。また、友達(だち)と買(か)い物に行ってアメリカ製(せい)のかわいい洋服(ようふく)や、家族(ぞく)や学校の友だちへのお土産(みやげ)を買いました。たくさん買ったので、帰りの荷(に)物は、とても重(おも)くなりました。みさきさんたちは、記(き)念公園(ねんこうえん)も見物したかったのですが、時間がなくてできませんでした。次にグアムに行ったら、ぜひ行きたいと思っています。

記念公園(きねんこうえん)　Memorial Park

Kyonen, Misaki san wa tomodachi sannin to isshoni guamu e ikimashita. Mainichi, atatakakute yoi tenki deshita. Misaki san wa, hajimete shunōkeringu de takusan no sakana o mimashita. Mata, tomodachi to kaimono ni itte amerika sei no kawaii yōfuku ya, kazoku ya gakkō no tomodachi eno omiyage o kaimashita. Takusan katta node, kaeri no nimotsu wa, totemo omoku narimashita. Misaki san tachi wa, kinen kōen mo kenbutsu shitakatta no desu ga, jikan ga nakute dekimasen deshita. Tsugi ni guamu ni ittara, zehi ikitai to omotteimasu.

Questions 11-F

1. How was the weather in Guam? (A. a bit rainy, B. a bit cloudy, C. warm and clear, D. very hot)
2. What animal did Misaki and her friends see? (A. birds, B. snakes, C. fish, D. whales)
3. For whom did Misaki buy gifts? (A. family and school friends, B. grandparents, C. boyfriend, D. coworkers)
4. When did Misaki and her friends visit the memorial park? (A. the first day, B. the second day, C. the last day, D. they did not visit it this on trip)

Let's Review

Write the following words with kanji and kana characters.

1. _____ _____ (to come)
2. _____ _____ (to go)
3. _____ _____ (to return)
4. _____ _____ (to wait)
5. _____ _____ (to hold, have)
6. _____ _____ _____ (to eat)
7. _____ (rice)
8. _____ _____ (good)
9. _____ _____ (white—adjective form)
10. _____ (turn, numerical order)
11. _____ (thing that is tangible)

Lesson 11 Practice

A. Kanji Review

Try writing these words in kanji.

 rice	 to come	 numerical order	 to go	 to wait	 to hold
1.	2.	3.	4.	5.	6.
 to return	 white	 good	 to eat	 tangible thing	
7.	8.	9.	10.	11.	

B. Vocabulary Review

Try writing these words with appropriate kanji and okurigana characters.

1. _____ 国 (べいこく　USA – formal)
2. _____ _____ (いちばん　first, most, best)
3. _____ _____ (おこなう　to hold an event)
4. _____ _____ (けんぶつ　sightseeing)
5. _____ _____ _____ (たべもの　food)
6. _____ _____ _____ (ひがえり　a day trip)
7. _____ _____ 合 _____ _____ _____ (まちあわせる　to meet by appointment)
8. _____ _____ (らいねん　next year)

9. 気 _____ _____ (きもち　feelings, mood)

10. 面 _____ _____ (おもしろい　interesting)

11. _____ _____ _____ _____ (よさそう　to seem good)

12. 買 (_____) _____ (かいもの　shopping)

13. _____ _____ _____ _____ 組 (てれびばんぐみ　TV show)

14. _____ 事 (ぎょうじ　event, function)

15. _____ 黒 (しろくろ　black and white)

16. _____ 屋 (こめや　rice store)

17. _____ _____ (らいげつ　next month)

18. _____ 事 (しょくじ　meal, dinner)

19. 南 _____ (なんべい　South America)

20. _____ _____ (よく　well, nicely)

21. 和 _____ (わしょく　Japanese food)

22. _____ _____ _____ (かねもち　wealthy person)

23. 当 _____ (とうばん　person on duty)

24. 不_____ 品 (ふりょうひん　defective product, trash)

25. _____ 客 (らいきゃく　visitor to one's home)

26. 動 _____ (どうぶつ　animal)

27. _____ _____ (ばんけん　watchdog)

28. _____ _____ _____ (できる　can do; not always in kanji)

29. 期 _____ (きたい　expectation)

30. _____ 国 _____ _____ (きこくする　to return to one's country)

31. 旅 _____ (りょこう　travel)

32. 荷 _____ (にもつ　luggage)

33. _____ _____ (にちべい Japan and USA)

34. _____ _____ _____ _____ _____ (もっていく to bring something)

35. _____ _____ _____ (さんばんめ third)

36. _____ _____ (ゆうしょく dinner, evening meal)

37. _____ _____ (ものがたり story, tale)

C. Commonly Mistaken Kanji: Lessons 10 & 11

Which kanji correctly expresses the meaning of the English word? Circle the most appropriate kanji character.

1. cow	午	千	牛	王	年	方
2. to return	持	帰	待	物	対	校
3. white	日	百	母	白	毎	内
4. dog	大	太	六	木	犬	文
5. good	白	食	良	衣	来	先
6. bug, insect	虫	風	公	私	会	母
7. to wait	持	寺	行	何	後	待
8. bird	馬	鳥	白	島	駅	尺
9. tangible thing	牛	場	特	物	持	待
10. to hold	持	指	待	行	物	牛
11. rice	来	未	米	女	半	水
12. horse	黒	駅	島	鳥	馬	悪
13. numerical order	田	米	男	来	思	番
14. fish	黒	魚	思	馬	田	鳥
15. to come	米	羊	未	来	半	牛

16. sheep	羊	牛	未	米	来	木
17. to eat	良	会	食	公	金	今
18. to go	待	来	持	何	行	帰

D. Opposites

Using kanji characters that you have learned so far, write the opposite meaning of the kanji characters below. In some cases there is more than one possible answer.

1. 出 →	2. 行 →	3. 女 →
4. 母 →	5. 内 →	6. 大 →
7. 少 →	8. 下 →	9. 聞 →
10. 開 →	11. 大人 →	12. 左 →

E. Japanese Last Names

Try writing these Japanese last names in kanji.

1. しらかわ (white, river)_____ _____
2. もちだ (hold, rice field)_____ _____
3. しらとり (white, bird)_____ _____
4. しらき (white, tree)_____ _____
5. しらた (white, rice field)_____ _____

F. Verbs, Matching

Match the English phrases on the right with the Japanese phrases on the left. Write the correct number on the line, and then fill in the blank with the appropriate verb using kanji and okurigana (the hiragana following the kanji).

__1__ 友だちの家に（　行く　）	1. to go to a friend's house
____家に（　　　）	2. to eat fish
____じてんしゃで（　　　）	3. to wait for a bus
____ラーメンを（　　　）	4. to return home

___バスを（　　　　　）	5. to come by bicycle
___五百円を（　　　　　）	6. to wait for a friend
___学校に（　　　　　）	7. to have 2 tickets
___お父さんを（　　　　　）	8. to come to school
___牛肉を（　　　　　）	9. to eat ramen
___ケイタイでんわを（　　　　　）	10. to go to a Buddhist temple
___公えんに（　　　　　）	11. to have a cell phone
___きっぷを二まい（　　　　　）	12. to have 500 yen
___お寺に（　　　　　）	13. to wait for your father
___アパートに（　　　　　）	14. to eat beef
___友だちを（　　　　　）	15. to come to the park
___魚を（　　　　　）	16. to return to the apartment
___山に（　　　　　）	17. to go to the mountains

G. Review Questions

Try writing these sentences in Japanese using kanji whenever appropriate. Each sentence has at least one new kanji from this lesson. Then, compare your translations with the answer key at the end of the book.

1. Do you eat Japanese food often? ____________________

   ____

2. Do you make Japanese food sometimes? ____________________

   ____

3. Where can you buy Japanese rice? ____________________

   ____

4. How many times per year do you travel? ____________________

   ____

5. Can you wait for people? ______________________________

____

6. What annual events are held at your school? ______________________________

____

7. Do you think Japanese *anime* is interesting? ______________________________

____

8. Do you understand well what your Japanese teacher says? ______________________________

____

9. Do you plan to study Japanese next year? ______________________________

____

10. What is your favorite TV program? ______________________________

____

11. Have you read an old Japanese story before? ______________________________

____

12. Would like to go sightseeing in Kyoto? ______________________________

____

13. Are you allowed to return home later than usual on weekends? ______________________________

____

H. Interview a Partner

Take turns asking the above questions with your partner. Try to answer as fully and appropriately as you can. For best results, you should elaborate on your answers whenever possible.

111 雨 Rain

一	丆	冂	币	币	雨	雨	雨

Eight (8) strokes
Rain falling on a rice field

■ Trace the gray lines, and then practice on your own.

雨
雨

■ Useful vocabulary: Write the character, and trace the gray ones.

		あめ	**ame**	rain
大		おおあめ	**ōame**	heavy rain
	戸 *	あまど	**amado**	shutter, storm door

112 雪 Snow

一	丆	冖	币	币	雨	雨	雨	雪	雪	雪

Eleven (11) strokes
Snow is the precipitation you have to sweep away.

■ Trace the gray lines, and then practice on your own.

雪
雪

■ Useful vocabulary: Write the character, and trace the gray ones.

		ゆき	**yuki**	snow
	祭り *	ゆきまつり	**yukimatsuri**	snow festival
大		おおゆき	**ōyuki**	heavy snow
初	*	はつゆき	**hatsuyuki**	first snow of a season

* An asterisk denotes vocabulary with kanji that have not yet been introduced.

Reading 12-A

冬休みに、よしえさんは家族で初めて北海道へ行きました。りょかんにとまって、雪まつりを見に行ったり、雪遊びをしたりしました。さっぽろの雪まつりには、雪像がたくさんありましたが、よしえさんは、「雨の中のトトロ」の雪像が一番好きでした。よしえさんはスノーモービルを運転したかったのですが、まだ十五才なのでスノーモービルを運転することができませんでした。でも、お父さんが運転して、よしえさんを後ろに乗せてくれました。東京に帰ると、雨が降りました。寒いのに、雨ばかりで雪は全然ふりませんでした。

雪像（せつぞう） snow sculpture

Fuyu yasumi ni, Yoshie san wa kazoku de hajimete hokkaidō e ikimashita. Ryokan ni tomatte, yuki matsuri o mi ni ittari, yuki asobi o shitari shimashita. Sapporo no yuki matsuri niwa, setsuzō ga takusan arimashita ga, Yoshie san wa, "ame no naka no totoro" no setsuzō ga ichiban suki deshita. Yoshie san wa sunōmōbiru o unten shitakatta desu ga, mada jūgosai na node sunōmōbiru o unten suru koto ga dekimasen deshita. Demo, otōsan ga unten shite, Yoshie san o ushiro ni nosete kuremashita. Tōkyō ni kaeru to, ame ga furimashita. Samui noni, ame bakari de yuki wa zenzen furimasen deshita.

Questions 12-A

1. How many times had Yoshie been to Hokkaido before? (A. she had been to Hokkaido many times, B. she had been to Hokkaido twice before, C. she had been to Hokkaido once before, D. she had never been to Hokkaido before)
2. Which snow sculpture was Yoshie's favorite? (A. Totoro standing in the snow, B. Totoro standing with the Cat Bus, C. Totoro standing with other characters, D. Totoro standing in the rain)
3. Why wasn't Yoshie able to drive the snowmobile? (A. she was not old enough, B. there was not enough snow, C. it was snowing too much, D. the snowmobile was broken)
4. How was the weather in Tokyo when Yoshie's family returned home? (A. it was snowing, B. it was cloudy, C. it was rainy, D. it was clear)

113 電 Electricity

Thirteen (13) strokes
Rain (雨) and lightning in a cloud (申): The electricity in a storm

■ Trace the gray lines, and then practice on your own.

電									
電									

■ Useful vocabulary: Write the character, and trace the gray ones.

	気	*	でんき	**denki**	electricity, electric light
	車		でんしゃ	**densha**	train
	話		でんわ	**denwa**	telephone, phone call
	池	*	でんち	**denchi**	battery

114 風 Wind

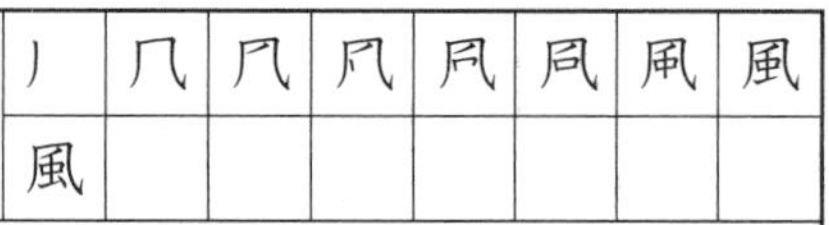

Nine (9) strokes
Simple form of fly (几), wing (㇐), and bug (虫): A winged bug that flies on the wind

■ Trace the gray lines, and then practice on your own.

風									
風									

■ Useful vocabulary: Write the character, and trace the gray ones.

			かぜ	**kaze**	wind
台		*	たいふう	**taifu**	typhoon

* An asterisk denotes vocabulary with kanji that have not yet been introduced.

Reading 12-B

今年の9月のおわりに、大きな台風が来ました。のりおさんの家族はみんな家に帰って来ていて、晩ごはんを食べるところでした。あっという間に、町中の電気が消えてしまいました。でも、のりおさんの家には運良く、かい中電灯と電池があったので、それで部屋を明るくして、ご飯を食べました。のりおさんは、台風の夜にかい中電灯を使って夕食を食べるのは少し変だと思いました。食べ終わった後に、電気がつきました。

かい中電灯　flashlight　　変　strange, weird

Kotoshi no kugatsu no owari ni, ōkina taifū ga kimashita. Norio san no kazoku wa minna ie ni kaette kite ite, bangohan o taberu tokoro deshita. Attoiu ma ni, machijū no denki ga kiete shimai mashita. Demo, Norio san no ie niwa unyoku, kaichūdentō to denchi ga atta node, sore de heya o akaruku shite, gohan o tabemashita. Norio san wa, taifū no yoru ni kaichūdentō o tsukatte yūshoku o taberu no wa sukoshi hen da to omoimashita. Tabe owatta atoni, dengi ga tsukimashita.

Questions 12-B

1. Where were the people in Norio's family when the power went out? (A. no one in Norio's family was home, B. Norio was the only one home, C. everyone in Norio's family was home except Norio, D. everyone in Norio's family was home)
2. Where did the power outage occur? (A. throughout Norio's house, B. throughout Norio's neighborhood, C. throughout Norio's neighborhood, but not at Norio's house, D. throughout the city)
3. What did Norio feel lucky about? (A. that Norio's neighbors had flashlights and batteries, B. that Norio's family had flashlights and batteries, C. that the lights did not go out at Norio's neighbors' houses, D. that the lights did not go out at Norio's house)
4. When did the power come back on? (A. before dinner, B. during dinner, C. after dinner, D. just before they went to bed)

115 元 Origin

一 二 テ 元

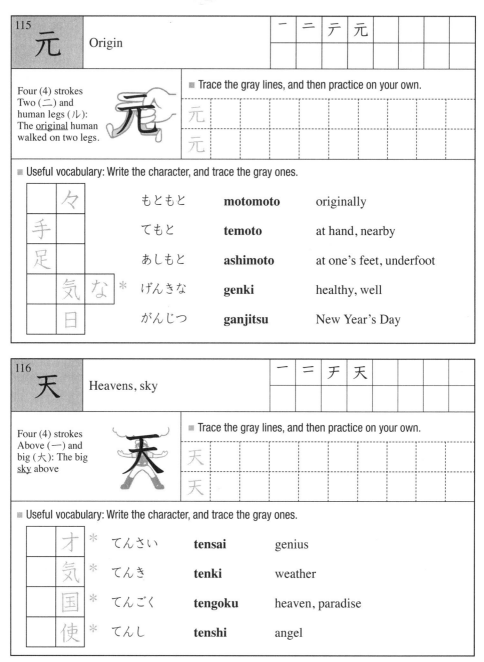

Four (4) strokes
Two (二) and human legs (儿): The original human walked on two legs.

■ Trace the gray lines, and then practice on your own.

元

元

■ Useful vocabulary: Write the character, and trace the gray ones.

元々		もともと	**motomoto**	originally
手元		てもと	**temoto**	at hand, nearby
足元		あしもと	**ashimoto**	at one's feet, underfoot
元気な	*	げんきな	**genki**	healthy, well
元日		がんじつ	**ganjitsu**	New Year's Day

116 天 Heavens, sky

一 二 チ 天

Four (4) strokes
Above (一) and big (大): The big sky above

■ Trace the gray lines, and then practice on your own.

天

天

■ Useful vocabulary: Write the character, and trace the gray ones.

天才	*	てんさい	**tensai**	genius
天気	*	てんき	**tenki**	weather
天国	*	てんごく	**tengoku**	heaven, paradise
天使	*	てんし	**tenshi**	angel

* An asterisk denotes vocabulary with kanji that have not yet been introduced.

Reading 12-C

まゆみさんは、元日に友達(だち)と山へ行く約束(やくそく)をしていました。その日の朝(あさ)、雪がふりました。まゆみさんは元々、雪が大好きなので喜(よろこ)びましたが、友だちがあぶないと言ったので山へ行くのはやめて、近くの公園(こうえん)に出かけました。寒(さむ)い日でしたが、いいお天気でした。雪がたくさん積(つ)もっていたので、坂(さか)をのぼる時は、足元に注意しなければなりませんでした。

約束(やくそく) promise, appointment
喜(よろこ)ぶ be glad, happy

Mayumi san wa, ganjitsu ni tomodachi to yama e iku yakusoku o shite imashita. Sono hi no asa, yuki ga furimashita. Mayumi san wa motomoto yuki ga daisuki na node, yorokobimashita ga, tomodachi ga abunai to itta node yama e iku no wa yamete, chikaku no kōen ni dekakemashita. Samui hi deshita ga, ii o tenki deshita. Yuki ga takusan tumotte ita node, saka o noboru toki wa, ashimoto ni chūi shinakereba narimasen deshita.

Questions 12-C

1. Where did Mayumi and her friends want to go on New Year's Day? (A. to a nearby town, B. to the mountains, C. to the city, C. to the countryside)
2. Why did they have to change their plans? (A. because they could not find enough sleds, B. because one of her friends was not feeling well, C. because Mayumi had to work, D. because there was too much snow)
3. How was the weather? (A. clear and cold, B. cloudy and cold, C. rainy and cold, D. snowy and cold)
4. What happened when climbing the hill? (A. Mayumi's friend slipped and fell, B. Mayumi and her friends had to be careful, C. Mayumi slipped and fell, C. Mayumi's friend was not careful)

117 気	Gas, spirit	ノ	𠂉	𠂉	气	気	気		

Six (6) strokes
An old rice cooker and stove

■ Trace the gray lines, and then practice on your own.

気
気

■ Useful vocabulary: Write the character, and trace the gray ones.

人 _ がある	にんきがある	**ninki ga aru**	popular
_ 持ち	きもち	**kimochi**	feelings
空 _ *	くうき	**kūki**	air
病 _ *	びょうき	**byōki**	illness
_ 付く	きづく	**kizuku**	to notice
_ を付ける	きをつける	**ki o tsukeru**	to take care

* An asterisk denotes vocabulary with kanji that have not yet been introduced.

Reading 12-D

ゆうたさんは、学校でとても人気があります。だれにでも気がるに声(こえ)をかけ、いつもにこにこしているからです。昨日(きのう)、ゆうたさんは、病気(びょうき)で学校を休(やす)みました。友達(だち)は、ゆうたさんが休んだのに気付いていました。

今日(きょう)、学校にもどって来たら、「昨日(きのう)、どうしたの？」ときかれました。「早く元気になってね」とみんなに言われ、ゆうたさんは、うれしかったようです。

声(こえ)をかける　to greet, call out to someone　　気がるに　casually

Yūta san wa, gakkō de totemo ninki ga arimasu. Dare ni demo kigaru ni koe o kake, itsumo nikoniko shite iru kara desu. Kinō, Yūta san wa, byōki de gakkō o yasumimashita. Tomodachi wa, Yūta san ga yasunda no ni kizuite imashita. Kyō, gakkō ni modotte kitara, "kinō, dōshitano?" to kikaremashita. "Hayaku genki ni natte ne" to minnna ni iware, Yūta san wa, ureshikatta yō desu.

Questions 12-D

1. Why is Yūta very popular at school? (A. because he talks to everyone, and he always has a smile, B. because he always has a smile, and he plays football well, C. because he plays football well, and he is good looking, D. because he is good looking, and he talks to everyone)
2. What happened when Yūta missed school? (A. his friends did not notice, B. his friends noticed, C. his friends called him at home, D. his friends visited him at home)
3. What did Yūta's friends say to him? (A. they told him to get well, B. they told him to stay at home until he feels better, C. they told him to take his medicine, D. they told him to get plenty of sleep)
4. What does Yūta probably think about his friends? (A. they give too much advice, B. they are popular students, C. they have much medical knowledge, D. they are good friends)

Let's Review

Write the following words with appropriate kanji or hiragana characters.

1. _____ _____(てんき weather)
2. _____(ゆき snow)
3. _____(あめ rain)
4. _____ (かぜ wind)
5. _____ _____(おおあめ heavy rain)
6. _____ _____ 強 _____(かぜがつよい windy)
7. _____ _____ _____ _____(いいてんき nice weather)
8. 台 _____(たいふう typhoon)

Lesson 12 Practice

A. Kanji Review

Try writing these words in kanji. Use the mnemonic pictures for hints if needed.

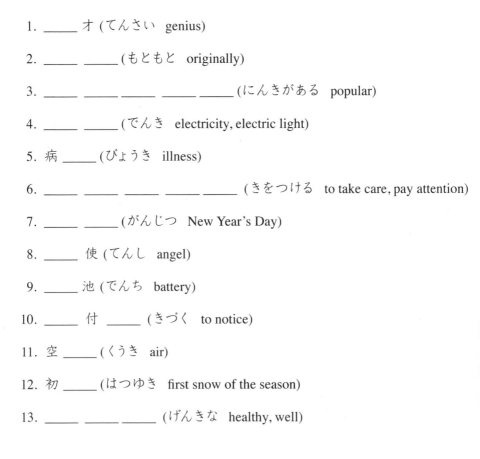

 rain	 snow	 electricity	 wind	 origin	 heaven	 spirit, gas
1.	2.	3.	4.	5.	6.	7.

B. Vocabulary Review

Try writing these words with appropriate kanji and kana characters.

1. _____ 才 (てんさい genius)
2. _____ _____ (もともと originally)
3. _____ _____ _____ _____ _____ (にんきがある popular)
4. _____ _____ (でんき electricity, electric light)
5. 病 _____ (びょうき illness)
6. _____ _____ _____ _____ _____ (きをつける to take care, pay attention)
7. _____ _____ (がんじつ New Year's Day)
8. _____ 使 (てんし angel)
9. _____ 池 (でんち battery)
10. _____ 付 _____ (きづく to notice)
11. 空 _____ (くうき air)
12. 初 _____ (はつゆき first snow of the season)
13. _____ _____ _____ (げんきな healthy, well)

14. _____ _____ (でんわ telephone)

15. 足 _____ (あしもと at one's feet, underfoot)

16. _____ _____ (あまど shutter, storm door)

17. _____ 国 (てんごく heaven)

18. _____ _____ _____ (きもち feelings, mood)

19. _____ _____ (でんしゃ train)

20. _____ _____ _____ _____ (あめあがり just after rainfall)

21. _____ _____ _____ _____ (ゆきまつり snow festival)

22. _____ _____ (てもと at hand, nearby)

C. Japanese Last Names

Try writing these Japanese last names in kanji.

1. やまもと (mountain, origin)_____ _____

2. かざま (wind, among)_____ _____

3. なかもと (middle, origin)_____ _____

4. もとき (origin, tree)_____ _____

D. Weather Broadcast

Read the following weather broadcast and then fill in the chart below in English.

あしたの天気です。明日も全国的(ぜんこくてき)に寒(さむ)いでしょう。さっぽろは雪でしょう。最高気温(さいこうきおん)はマイナス八度(ど)でしょう。にいがたは、くもり時々雪でしょう。最高気温はマイナス二度でしょう。せんだいは、晴(は)れのちくもりでしょう。最高気温は三度でしょう。東京は晴れでしょう。最高気温は九度でしょう。おおさかはくもりでしょう。最高気温は六度でしょう。ひろしまも、くもりでしょう。最高気温は七度でしょう。ふくおかは、くもり時々雨でしょう。最高気温は五度でしょう。おきなわは、くもりのち雨でしょう。最高気温は十四度でしょう。

全国的 (ぜんこくてき)	nationally, around the whole country		
最高気温 (さいこうきおん)	high temperature	八度 (ど)	eight degrees
晴れ (は)	clear weather のち	later	

Sapporo	Snow	High: -8 degrees
Niigata		
Sendai		
Tokyo		
Osaka		
Hiroshima		
Fukuoka		
Okinawa		

E. Review Questions

Try writing these sentences in Japanese using kanji whenever appropriate. Each sentence has at least one new kanji from this lesson. Then, compare your translations with the answer key at the end of the book.

1. Will the weather be fine all day today? ______________________

   ____

2. Does it rain a lot in Okinawa? ______________________

   ____

3. Do you use an umbrella in the rain? ______________________

   ____

4. Have you experienced a typhoon before? ______________________

   ____

5. What do you want to do when it snows? ______________________

   ____

6. Do you ever play in the snow?

7. Have you ridden on a train before?

8. How many hours per day do you talk on the phone?

9. Do your siblings talk on the phone for a long time?

10. Are your grandparents healthy?

11. What does your family do on New Year's Day? Do you have any special customs (特別(とくべつ)なしゅうかん)?

12. Have you ever eaten shrimp tempura before?

13. Was Einstein really a genius?

14. Who is popular at this school?

15. When you get sick, what do you do?

16. Do your teachers notice when students chew gum?

F. Interview a Partner

Take turns asking the above questions with your partner. Try to answer as fully and appropriately as you can. For best results, you should elaborate on your answers whenever possible.

118 石 Stone

Stroke order: 一 ア 不 石 石

Five (5) strokes
A stone in the side of a cliff

■ Trace the gray lines, and then practice on your own.

石
石

■ Useful vocabulary: Write the character, and trace the gray ones.

石	いし	**ishi**	rock, stone
小石	こいし	**koishi**	pebble
化石	かせき	**kaseki**	fossil
石庭*	せきてい	**sekitei**	rock garden
石の上にも三年	石の上にも三年	**ishino uenimo sannen**	"persistence overcomes all things"

119 早 Early

Stroke order: 丨 口 日 日 旦 早

Six (6) strokes
Sun (日) and horizon (一) and pathway up (丨): A sun rising over the horizon, early in the morning. Note that 早い and 速い (fast) are both pronounced はやい.

■ Trace the gray lines, and then practice on your own.

早
早

■ Useful vocabulary: Write the character, and trace the gray ones.

早い	はやい	**hayai**	early
早く	はやく	**hayaku**	early, soon – adverb
早目に	はやめに	**hayameni**	ahead of time
早合点*	はやがてん	**hayagaten**	to jump to a hasty conclusion
早口言葉*	はやくちことば	**hayakuchikotoba**	tongue twister
早速*	さっそく	**sassoku**	immediately

* An asterisk denotes vocabulary with kanji that have not yet been introduced.

Reading 13-A

ゆうすけさんは、小さい時からとても元気な子どもでした。いつも朝早く起きて、家の近くの公園で遊ぶのが大好きでした。ある日、いつものように、ゆうすけさんと友だちは、大きな石の上にのぼって、遊んでいました。楽しかったのですが、服はとてもきたなくなりました。困ったゆうすけさんと友だちは、川で洗うことにしました。でも、きれいにならなくて、ぬれただけです。家に帰ったら、お母さんにすぐ見つかりました。お母さんはおこって、ゆうすけさんをおふろに入れて、「テレビを見ないで、早くねなさい」と言いました。

なる	to become	困る	to be troubled
ぬれる	to get wet	見つかる	(something) is found

Yūsuke san wa, chiisai toki kara totemo genki na kodomo deshita. Itsumo asa hayaku okite, ie no chikaku no kōen de asobu noga daisuki deshita. Aru hi, itsumo no yōni Yūsuke san to tomodachi wa, ōkina ishi noue ni nobotte, asonde imashita. Tanoshikatta no desu ga, fuku wa totemo kitanaku narimashita. Komatta Yūsuke san to tomodachi wa, kawa de arau koto ni shimashita. Demo, kirei ni naranakute, nureta dake desu. Ie ni kaettara, okāsan ni sugu mitsukarimashita. Okāsan wa okotte, Yūsuke san o ofuro ni irete, "terebi o minaide, hayaku nenasai" to iimashita.

Questions 13-A

1. What kind of child was Yūsuke? (A. very smart, B. very active, C. very talented, D. very serious)
2. Where did he climb on a rock? (A. at school, B. at home, C. at a park, D. at the zoo)
3. Why did Yūsuke and his friend go to the river? (A. to swim, B. to go fishing, C. to play in the water, D. to wash their clothes)
4. What did Yūsuke's mother do? (A. she sent him straight to bed, B. she called his father, C. she made him take a bath, D. she sent him to his room)

120 草 Grass

一	⺊	艹	艹	芇	苩	苜	荁
草							

Nine (9) strokes
Grass (艹) and early (早): Grass grows earlier than most other plants

■ Trace the gray lines, and then practice on your own.

草
草

■ Useful vocabulary: Write the character, and trace the gray ones.

草	くさ	**kusa**	grass, weeds
仕草 *	しぐさ	**shigusa**	gesture, mannerism

121 花 Flower

一	⺊	艹	艹	芢	芢	花	

Seven (7) strokes
Grass (艹) and change (化): A flower is a plant (grass) that changes dramatically when it blooms

■ Trace the gray lines, and then practice on your own.

花
花

■ Useful vocabulary: Write the character, and trace the gray ones.

花	はな	**hana**	flower
花見	はなみ	**hanami**	cherry blossom viewing
花火	はなび	**hanabi**	fireworks
生け花	いけばな	**ikebana**	flower arrangement
開花	かいか	**kaika**	blooming
国花	こっか	**kokka**	national flower

* An asterisk denotes vocabulary with kanji that have not yet been introduced.

Reading 13-B

みどりさんは、とてもいそがしいです。高校に入ってから宿題(しゅくだい)がたくさんあるし、バスケットボール部(ぶ)と生(い)け花(ばな)クラブにも入っているからです。みどりさんの家には広(ひろ)い庭(にわ)があって、花の好きなお母さんとみどりさんは、いろいろな花を育(そだ)てています。でも、すぐに草が生(は)えてくるので、お母さんはいつも草をとらなければなりません。だから、みどりさんは、週末(しゅうまつ)にはおかあさんを手伝(つだ)うようにしています。

育(そだ)てる　to raise　　生(は)える　to grow

Midori san wa, totemo isogashii desu. Kōkō ni haitte kara shukudai ga takusan aru shi, basukettobōrubu to ikebana kurabu nimo haitte iru kara desu. Midori san no ie niwa hiroi niwa ga ate, hana no suki na okāsan to Midori san wa, iroiro na hana o sodatete imasu. Demo, sugu ni kusa ga haerte kuru node, okāsan wa itumo kusa o toranakereba narimasen. Dakara, Midori san wa, shūmatsu niwa okāsan o tetsudau yōni shite imasu.

Questions 13-B

1. When did Midori become busy? (A. when she began a part-time job, B. when she began high school, C. in the spring when her family planted a garden, D. when her mother became ill and could not do the weeding)
2. What activities keep Midori busy? (A. homework and school clubs, B. school clubs and a part-time job, C. a part-time job and gardening, D. gardening and homework)
3. Where is the garden? (A. at school, B. at Midori's home, C. at Midori's grandmother's home, D. at Midori's friend's home)
4. Who does most of the work in the garden? (A. Midori, B. Midori's mother, C. Midori's schoolmates, D. Midori's friend Teru)

122 林 Grove

一	十	才	木	木一	村	材	林

Eight (8) strokes
Two trees (木) that represent a grove

■ Trace the gray lines, and then practice on your own.

林

林

■ Useful vocabulary: Write the character, and trace the gray ones.

□	はやし	**hayashi**	woods, grove, forest
熱帯雨□ *	ねったいうりん	**nettaiurin**	rainforest
人工□	じんこうりん	**jinkōrin**	planted forest
□業 *	りんぎょう	**ringyō**	forestry

123 森 Forest

一	十	オ	木	木	木	木	木
森	森	森	森				

Twelve (12) strokes
Three trees (木) that represent a forest

■ Trace the gray lines, and then practice on your own.

森

森

■ Useful vocabulary: Write the character, and trace the gray ones.

□ もり **mori** forest

木を見て□を見ず
きをみてもりをみず
ki o mite mori o mizu
"Cannot see the forest for the trees"

□林 しんりん **shinrin** forest, woods

* An asterisk denotes vocabulary with kanji that have not yet been introduced.

Reading 13-C

よしさんは、小学校三年生の時の楽(たの)しい経験(けいけん)を今でもおぼえています。授業(じゅぎょう)で熱帯雨林(ねったいうりん)について勉強(べんきょう)した後(あと)、森やいろいろな花や動物(どうぶつ)をかいて、かざりました。そして、みんなで教室中(きょうしつじゅう)を熱帯雨林のようにしたのです。そして、お父さんやお母さんに来てもらって、勉強したことを劇(げき)と歌(うた)で発表(はっぴょう)しました。よしさんははずかしがり屋(や)でしたが、とても楽しかったので、いっしょうけんめいやりました。だから、お父さんもお母さんも先生もとてもよろこびました。

かざる	to decorate
発表(はっぴょう)	to give a presentation
はずかしがり屋(や)	shy person

Yoshi san wa shōgakkō sannensei no toki no tanoshii keiken o ima demo oboete imasu. Jugyō de nettaiurin nitsuite benkyō shita atode, mori ya iroiro na hana ya dōbutsu o kaite, kazarimashita. Soshite, minna de kyōshitsujū o nettaiurin no yōni shita no desu. Soshite, otōsan ya okāsan ni kite moratte, benkyō shita koto o geki to uta de happyō shimashita. Yoshi san wa hazukashigariya deshita ga, totemo tanoshikatta node, isshōkenmei yarimashita. Dakara, otōsan mo okāsan mo sensei mo totemo yorokobimashita.

Questions 13-C

1. When did Yoshi learn about the rainforest? (A. as a high school senior, B. as a high school freshman, C. as a sixth grader, D. as a third grader)
2. What did Yoshi and his classmates make to decorate the classroom? (A. a forest, flowers, and animals, B. a forest, river, and animals, C. a river, flowers, and animals, D. a river, mountain, and flowers)
3. What were the parents invited to do? (A. donate money to a rainforest fund, B. purchase books about the rainforest, C. come see a play about the rain forest, D. help their children learn more about the rainforest)
4. Who was very pleased about Yoshi's performance? (A. Yoshi's parents and teacher, B. Yoshi's parents and siblings, C. Yoshi's teacher and siblings, D. Yoshi's siblings)

Lesson 13 Practice

A. Kanji Review

Try writing these words in kanji. Use the mnemonic pictures for hints if needed.

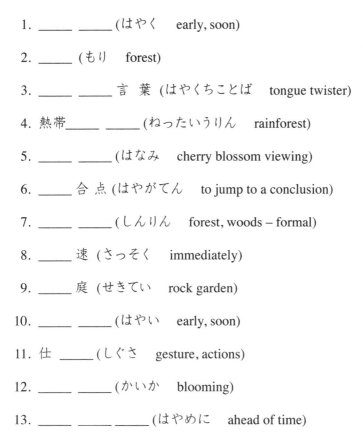

 stone	 early	 grass	 flower	 grove	 forest
1.	2.	3.	4.	5.	6.

B. Vocabulary Review

Try writing these words with appropriate kanji and okurigana characters.

1. _____ _____(はやく early, soon)
2. _____ (もり forest)
3. _____ _____ 言 葉 (はやくちことば tongue twister)
4. 熱帯_____ _____(ねったいうりん rainforest)
5. _____ _____(はなみ cherry blossom viewing)
6. _____ 合 点 (はやがてん to jump to a conclusion)
7. _____ _____(しんりん forest, woods – formal)
8. _____ 速 (さっそく immediately)
9. _____ 庭 (せきてい rock garden)
10. _____ _____(はやい early, soon)
11. 仕 _____(しぐさ gesture, actions)
12. _____ _____(かいか blooming)
13. _____ _____ _____(はやめに ahead of time)

14. _____ (はな　flower)

15. _____ _____ _____ (じんこうりん　planted forest)

16. _____ 業 (りんぎょう　forestry)

17. _____ _____ _____ (いけばな　flower arranging)

18. _____ _____ (はなび　fireworks)

19. _____ _____ _____ _____ (いっせきにちょう　Kill two birds with one stone)

20. _____ _____ _____ _____ _____ _____ _____ _____ (きをみてもりをみず　Not see the forest for the trees)

C. Commonly Mistaken Kanji Characters (Weather and Nature)

Which kanji correctly expresses the meaning of the English word? Circle the most appropriate kanji character.

1. grove	森	村	林	校	木	私
2. rain	風	雪	電	国	雨	内
3. electricity	雨	雲	電	雪	神	石
4. stone	石	若	右	左	有	名
5. snow	雲	電	雨	雪	市	書
6. wind	内	国	肉	門	何	風
7. early	草	早	百	男	白	間
8. origin	見	先	元	九	北	兄
9. forest	林	村	対	校	森	未
10. heaven	元	天	矢	大	木	本
11. flower	化	草	若	花	羊	首
12. spirit, gas	飛	風	教	晩	矢	気
13. grass	花	早	草	茶	黄	若

D. Japanese Last Names

Try writing these Japanese last names in kanji characters.

1. はなだ (flower, rice field)_____ _____
2. くさま (grass, among)_____ _____
3. なかばやし (middle, grove)_____ _____
4. はやしだ (grove, rice field)_____ _____
5. いしかわ (stone, river)_____ _____
6. おおもり (big, forest)_____ _____
7. いしやま (stone, mountain)_____ _____
8. はやかわ (early, river)_____ _____
9. たていし (stand, stone)_____ _____
10. もりした (forest, below)_____ _____
11. もりもと (forest, origin)_____ _____
12. はやし (grove)_____
13. もりやま (forest, mountain)_____ _____
14. おおばやし (big, grove)_____ _____
15. たちばな (stand, flower)_____ _____
16. しらいし (white, stone)_____ _____
17. いしもり (stone, forest)_____ _____
18. もりかわ (forest, river)_____ _____
19. うえばやし (above, grove)_____ _____
20. いまばやし (now, grove)_____ _____
21. もり (forest)_____
22. こばやし (small, grove)_____ _____
23. なかもり (middle, forest)_____ _____

24. いしだ (stone, field)_____ _____

25. おおいし (big, stone)_____ _____

E. Review Questions

Try writing these sentences in Japanese using kanji whenever appropriate. Each sentence has at least one new kanji from this lesson. Then, compare your translations with the answer key at the end of the book.

1. Do you know any Japanese tongue twisters? ____________________

____

2. What does "Kill two birds with one stone" mean? ____________________

____

3. What is an example of "Not seeing the forest for the trees"? ____________________

____

4. Did you study about the rainforest in school? ____________________

____

5. What do you think about Japanese rock gardens? ____________________

____

6. Is the national flower of Japan and the US the same? ____________________

____

7. When do cherry blossoms bloom in Tokyo? (around the beginning of April)

____

8. Do you wake up early in the morning? ____________________

____

9. What are some mannerisms unique (独特(どくとく)) to the Japanese?

____

F. Interview a Partner

Take turns asking the above questions with your partner. Try to answer as fully and appropriately as you can. For best results, you should elaborate on your answers whenever possible.

124 旅 Travel

ˋ	亠	方	方	方	方	方	方
旅	旅						

Ten (10) strokes
Direction (方), flag (𠂉), two people (𧘇): A group of people traveling in the same direction

■ Trace the gray lines, and then practice on your own.

旅
旅

■ Useful vocabulary: Write the character, and trace the gray ones.

旅	たび	**tabi**	journey, trip
旅行	りょこう	**ryokō**	travel, trip
旅館 *	りょかん	**ryokan**	Japanese inn
旅費 *	りょひ	**ryohi**	travel expenses

125 車 Vehicle

一	厂	冂	冃	亘	亘	車	

Seven (7) strokes
Top view of a car and wheels: A rickshaw was a vehicle used like a taxi in old Japan

■ Trace the gray lines, and then practice on your own.

車
車

■ Useful vocabulary: Write the character, and trace the gray ones.

車	くるま	**kuruma**	vehicle, car, wheel
車いす	くるまいす	**kurumaisu**	wheelchair
電車	でんしゃ	**densha**	train
洗車 *	せんしゃ	**sensha**	car wash
自転車 *	じてんしゃ	**jitensha**	bicycle

* An asterisk denotes vocabulary with kanji that have not yet been introduced.

Reading 14-A

かいさんは、１９歳の大学生です。運転免許はありますが、車は持っていません。また、買うつもりもありません。駐車料金もガソリン代も高いからです。東京では、ほとんどの学生は電車で大学へ行きますが、かいさんは自転車で通学しています。自転車は環境にも、健康にも良く、その上経済的なので、友だちにもすすめています。いつか自転車で世界一周旅行をするのが、かいさんの夢です。

運転免許	driver's license	通学	commute to school
世界一周	around the world	夢	dream

Kai san wa, jūkyūsai no daigakusei desu. Untenmenkyo wa arimasu ga, kuruma wa motte imasen. Mata, kau tsumori mo arimasen. Chūsharyōkin mo gasorindai mo takai kara desu. Tōkyō dewa, hotondo no gakusei wa densha de daigaku e ikimasu ga, Kai san wa jitensha de tsugaku shite imasu. Jitensha wa kankyō nimo, kenkō nimo yoku, sonoue keizaiteki na node, tomodachi nimo susumete imasu. Itsuka jitensha de sekaiisshū ryokō o suru no ga, Kai san no yume desu.

Questions 14-A

1. What is Kai's opinion about cars? (A. they are expensive, B. they use too much gas, C. they are convenient, D. they are important for people with disabilities)
2. How does Kai commute to school? (A. by bicycle, B. by car, C. by bus, D. by train)
3. What is Kai's suggestion to his friends? (A. use public transportation, B. ride a bicycle, C. walk, D. drive a car)
4. What is Kai's future dream? (A. to take a cruise around the world, B. to ride his bicycle around the world, C. to take a trip by airplane around the world, D. to travel around the world by hot air balloon)

126 首 Neck, head

丶	丷	䒑	䒑	产	屰	首	首
首							

Nine (9) strokes
A head with tousled hair

■ Trace the gray lines, and then practice on your own.

首									
首									

■ Useful vocabulary: Write the character, and trace the gray ones.

☐		くび	**kubi**	neck, head
手☐		てくび	**tekubi**	wrist
足☐	*	あしくび	**ashikubi**	ankle

127 道 Path

丶	丷	䒑	䒑	产	屰	首	首
首	首	道	道				

Twelve (12) strokes
A path (辶) and neck (首): Tilting one's head to see down the path

■ Trace the gray lines, and then practice on your own.

道									
道									

■ Useful vocabulary: Write the character, and trace the gray ones.

☐		みち	**michi**	path, road, way
山☐		やまみち	**yamamichi**	mountain path
近☐		ちかみち	**chikamichi**	shortcut
柔☐	*	じゅうどう	**jūdō**	judo
神☐	*	しんとう	**shintō**	Shinto, the way of the gods
書☐		しょどう	**shodō**	Japanese calligraphy
華☐	*	かどう	**kadō**	flower arrangement

* An asterisk denotes vocabulary with kanji that have not yet been introduced.

Reading 14-B

みゆさんは、去年は柔道部に入っていました。みゆさんはとても強かったので、県の大会で一番になりました。ところが、練習で山道を走っていた時に、みゆさんは足首をけがしてしまいました。お医者さんに、6か月間走ってはいけない、と言われたので、みゆさんは今年は華道部に入ることにしました。華道も楽しいのですが、柔道部の友達が練習しているのを見ると、いっしょに練習したいと思ってしまいます。

県（けん） prefecture　　けがする to be injured

Miyu san wa, kyonen wa jūdōbu ni haitte imashita. Miyu san wa totemo tsuyokatta node, ken no taikai de ichiban ni narimashita. Tokoroga, renshū de yamamichi o hashitte ita toki ni, Miyu san wa ashikubi o kega shite shimaimashita. Oisha san ni rokkagetsukan hashitte wa ikenai, to iwareta node, Miyu san wa kotoshi wa kadōbu ni hairu koto ni shimashita. Kadō mo tanoshii no desu ga, jūdōbu no tomodachi ga renshū shite iru no o miru to, isshoni renshū shitai to omotte shimaimasu.

Questions 14-B

1. What happened at last year's judo tournament? (A. Miyu injured her leg, B. Miyu injured her arm, C. Miyu took first place, D. Miyu won one match)
2. Where did Miyu injure herself? (A. her wrist, B. her ankle, C. her back, D. her neck)
3. How long did the doctor tell Miyu she could not run? (A. for six days, B. for six weeks, C. for six months, D. until June)
4. When does Miyu find that she misses judo club the most? (A. when she watches judo on TV, B. when she goes to judo tournaments, C. when she reads the sports page in the news, D. when she sees her friends practicing)

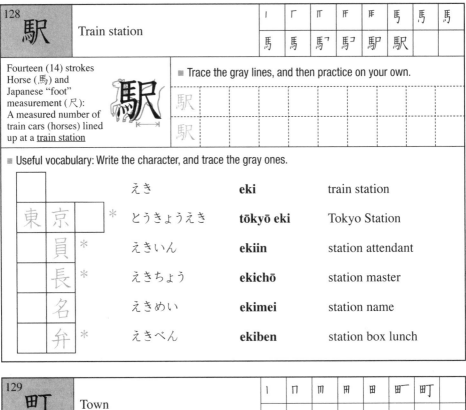

128 駅	Train station							
		丨	厂	冂	幵	馬	馬	馬
		馬	馬	馬	馬	駅	駅	

Fourteen (14) strokes
Horse (馬) and Japanese "foot" measurement (尺):
A measured number of train cars (horses) lined up at a train station

■ Trace the gray lines, and then practice on your own.

駅
駅

■ Useful vocabulary: Write the character, and trace the gray ones.

□		えき	**eki**	train station
東京□	*	とうきょうえき	**tōkyō eki**	Tokyo Station
□員	*	えきいん	**ekiin**	station attendant
□長	*	えきちょう	**ekichō**	station master
□名		えきめい	**ekimei**	station name
□弁	*	えきべん	**ekiben**	station box lunch

129 町	Town							
		丨	冂	冊	田	田	田	町

Seven (7) strokes
Rice field (田) and street (丁):
This is the path to the town.

■ Trace the gray lines, and then practice on your own.

町
町

■ Useful vocabulary: Write the character, and trace the gray ones.

□		まち	**machi**	town, block
□外れ		まちはずれ	**machihazure**	outskirts of town
港□	*	みなとまち	**minatomachi**	harbor town
～□	*	～まち／ちょう	**~machi/chō**	town name suffix
□内会		ちょうないかい	**chōnaikai**	neighborhood association

* An asterisk denotes vocabulary with kanji that have not yet been introduced.

Reading 14-C

こうきさんは、ＪＲ町田駅の近くに住んでいる大学生です。毎日、電車でよこはまの大学へ通っています。こうきさんは、大学でびじゅつをせんこうしています。友達は大学の休みに山や海に行きますが、こうきさんは、ひまな時はいつも絵をかいています。特に、町田駅の前のにぎやかな通りの風景が気に入っています。いつか駅前にアトリエを持ちたいと思っています。人が多い場所なので、絵を見せることもできるかもしれません。

ＪＲ	Japan Railroad company		
せんこう	specialize, major (subject)	にぎやか	bustling, busy
風景	scenery	アトリエ	studio

Kōki san wa, jeiāru machida eki no chikaku ni sunde iru daigakusei desu. Mainichi, densha de yokohama no daigaku e kayotte imasu. Kōki san wa, daigaku de bijutsu o senkō shite imasu. Tomodachi wa daigaku no yasumi ni yama ya umi ni ikimasu ga, Kōki san wa, hima na toki wa itsumo e o kaite imasu. Toku ni, machida eki no mae no nigiyaka na tōri no fūkei ga ki ni itte imasu. Itsuka ekimae ni atorie o mochitai to omotteimasu. Hito ga ōi basho na node, e o miseru koto mo dekiru kamoshiremasen.

Questions 14-C

1. Where does Kōki live? (A. Michida, B. Tamachi, C. Tamichi, D. Machida)
2. How does he commute to school? (A. train, B. bicycle, C. car, D. friend's car)
3. What does Kōki often use for the subject of his paintings? (A. the mountains, B. the sea, C. college campus, D. city streets)
4. Why does he want to open an art studio near the train station? (A. because there are some art stores nearby, B. because the rent is cheap, C. because the view of the ocean is beautiful, D. because there are many people)

130 市 City, market

Five (5) strokes
A merchant in a tent selling his products in the city

■ Trace the gray lines, and then practice on your own.

市

市

■ Useful vocabulary: Write the character, and trace the gray ones.

市	し	**shi**	city
市長*	しちょう	**shichō**	mayor
市立	しりつ	**shiritsu**	municipal, city
市内	しない	**shinai**	within a city
市外電話	しがいでんわ	**shigaidenwa**	long-distance call
市場*	いちば	**ichiba**	marketplace

131 京 Capital

Eight (8) strokes
All roads lead to the capital city

■ Trace the gray lines, and then practice on your own.

京

京

■ Useful vocabulary: Write the character, and trace the gray ones.

京都*	きょうと	**kyōto**	Kyoto
東京	とうきょう	**tōkyō**	Tokyo
東京行き	とうきょうゆき	**tōkyōyuki**	Tokyo bound
北京*	ペキン	**pekin**	Beijing, Peking

* An asterisk denotes vocabulary with kanji that have not yet been introduced.

Reading 14-D

あおいさんは、先月、友達といっしょに中国へ2泊3日「買い物旅行」をしました。市場でたくさんの服を安く買いました。そしてデパートでは色々なアクセサリーも買いました。また北京ダックがおいしそうだったので、2人で食べてみました。日本の中国料理店で食べるのとは少しちがう味で、とてもおいしかったです。京都に帰ったあおいさんは、家族に中国のおみやげをあげたり、自分の買った物を見せたりしました。

2泊3日	にはくみっか	three days and two nights
市場	いちば	marketplace

Aoi san wa, sengetsu, tomodachi to isshoni chūgoku e nihaku mikka "kaimono ryokō" o shimashita. Ichiba de takusan no fuku o yasuku kaimashita. Soshite depāto dewa iroiro na akusesarii mo kaimashita. Mata pekin dakku ga oishisō datta node, futari de tabete mimashita. Nihon no chūgoku ryōriten de taberu no to wa sukoshi chigau aji de, totemo oishikatta desu. Kyōto ni kaetta Aoi san wa, kazoku ni chūgoku no omiyage o agetari, jibun no katta mono o misetari shimashita.

Questions 14-D

1. When did Aoi and her friends travel to China? (A. last year, B. last month, C. winter break, D. spring break)
2. Where did they buy clothes? (A. a marketplace, B. a wholesale outlet, C. a department store, D. a secondhand clothing store)
3. What did Aoi think about the Chinese food? (A. it was a little different, B. it was a little spicy, C. it was cheap, D. the portions were small)
4. What did Aoi do when she returned home? (A. she showed her family some pictures, B. she showed her family a video of her trip, C. she cooked a traditional Chinese meal for her family, D. she gave her family some souvenirs)

132 玉 Ball, Jewel

一 丅 千 王 玉

Five (5) strokes
The king's jewels

■ Trace the gray lines, and then practice on your own.

玉
玉

■ Useful vocabulary: Write the character, and trace the gray ones.

玉	たま	**tama**	jewel, ball
水玉	みずたま	**mizutama**	polka dot
お手玉	おてだま	**otedama**	traditional toy beanbags
お年玉	おとしだま	**otoshidama**	New Year's gift money

133 国 Country

丨 冂 冂 冂 冃 国 国 国

Eight (8) strokes
The walls around the country protect the king's jewels.

■ Trace the gray lines, and then practice on your own.

国
国

■ Useful vocabulary: Write the character, and trace the gray ones.

国	くに	**kuni**	country
中国	ちゅうごく	**chūgoku**	China
国内	こくない	**kokunai**	domestic
外国	がいこく	**gaikoku**	foreign country
国語	こくご	**kokugo**	Japanese language – school subject
母国語	ぼこくご	**bokokugo**	native tongue

* An asterisk denotes vocabulary with kanji that have not yet been introduced.

Reading 14-E

そうたさんは、高校二年生です。今年は、一月一日に家族(ぞく)で北海道(ほっかいどう)のおじいさんとおばあさんの家へ行って、いっしょにお正月を過(す)ごしました。いとこの家族もやってきました。おじさん、おばさん達(たち)から、たくさんお年玉をもらいました。お昼(ひる)におじいさんとおばあさんの家の近くに住んでいる友達(だち)が来たので、いっしょにテレビを見たり、ゲームをしたりしました。少しして雪がたくさん積(つ)もったので、そうたさんは、いとこや友達と外へ出て雪合戦(がっせん)をして遊(あそ)びました。夕方になって外が寒(さむ)くなったので、みんなで家に入って、こたつで手足をあたためました。

雪合戦(がっせん)	snowball fight
あたためる	to warm up (something)

Sōta san wa, kōkō ninensei desu. Kotoshi wa, ichigatsu tsuitachi ni kazoku de hokkaidō no ojiisan to obāsan no ie e itte, isshoni oshōgatsu o sugoshimashita. Itoko no kazoku mo yatte kimashita. Ojisan, obasan tachi kara, takusan otoshidama o moraimashita. Ohiru ni ojiisan to obāan no ie no chikaku ni sunde iru tomodachi ga kita node, isshoni terebi o mitari, gēmu o shitari shimashita. Sukoshi shite yuki ga takusan tsumotta node, Sōta san wa, itoko ya tomodachi to soto e dete yukigassen o shite asobimashita. Yūgata ni natte soto ga samuku natta node, minna de ie ni haitte, kotatsu de teashi o atatamemashita.

Questions 14-E

1. What grade is Sōta in? (A. 2nd grade, B. 8th grade, C. 11th grade, D. college sophomore)
2. Which holiday did Sōta spend with his relatives? (A. Thanksgiving Day, B. Christmas Day, C. New Year's Day, D. Coming-of-Age Day)
3. What did Sōta's relatives give him? (A. gift money, B. toy beanbags, C. candy, D. a game)
4. What did Sōta and his friends do after the snowball fight? (A. they went sledding, B. they ate dinner, C. they watched TV, D. they went indoors)

134 北 North

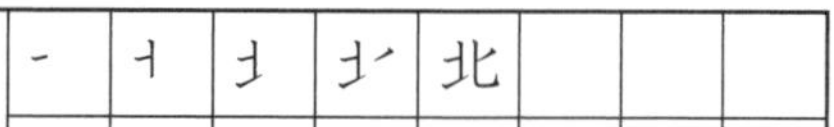

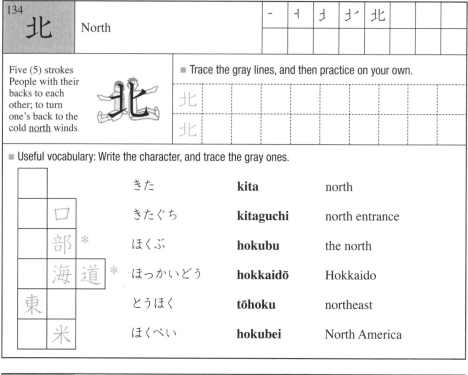

Five (5) strokes
People with their backs to each other; to turn one's back to the cold <u>north</u> winds

■ Trace the gray lines, and then practice on your own.

北
北

■ Useful vocabulary: Write the character, and trace the gray ones.

北	きた	**kita**	north
北口	きたぐち	**kitaguchi**	north entrance
北部 *	ほくぶ	**hokubu**	the north
北海道 *	ほっかいどう	**hokkaidō**	Hokkaido
東北	とうほく	**tōhoku**	northeast
北米	ほくべい	**hokubei**	North America

135 南 South

Nine (9) strokes
Ten (十), sheep, simplified (⺶), and fence (冂): A wealthy family (keeping 10 sheep) who has a <u>southern</u> facing home

■ Trace the gray lines, and then practice on your own.

南
南

■ Useful vocabulary: Write the character, and trace the gray ones.

南	みなみ	**minami**	south
南口	みなみぐち	**minamiguchi**	south entrance
南アメリカ	みなみアメリカ	**minami amerika**	South America
南アフリカ	みなみアフリカ	**minami afurika**	South Africa
南米	なんべい	**nanbei**	South America
南部 *	なんぶ	**nanbu**	the south

* An asterisk denotes vocabulary with kanji that have not yet been introduced.

Reading 14-F

みくさんは、大学で地理学を専攻していて、卒業したら高校の地理の教師になりたいと思っています。みくさんは、海外旅行が好きなので、教師になる前にたくさん旅行をすることにしました。今年の夏休みには、北米に行きました。今度の冬休みには、南米に行くつもりです。みくさんは、あちらこちらから、将来の生徒に見せてあげたい物を集めています。世界の色々な土地の、珍しい物に生徒が興味を持ってくれると、地理の授業も楽しくなるのではないかと思うからです。

地理（ちり）	geography
卒業する（そつぎょうする）	to graduate (from)
将来（しょうらい）	future
専攻する（せんこうする）	to major (in)
教師（きょうし）	teacher

Miku san wa, daigaku de chirigaku o senkō shite ite, sotsugyō shitara kōkō no chiri no kyōshi ni naritai to omotteimasu. Miku san wa, kaigai ryokō ga suki na node, kyōshi ni naru mae ni takusan ryokō o suru koto ni shimashita. Kotoshi no natsu yasumi niwa, beikoku ni ikimashita. Kondo no fuyuyasumi niwa, nanbei ni ikutsumori desu. Miku san wa achira kochira, shōrai no seito ni misete agetai mono o atsumete imasu. Sekai no iroiro na tochi no, mezurashii mono ni seito ga kyōmi o motte kureru to, chiri no jugyō mo tanoshiku naru dewanaika to omou kara desu.

Questions 14-F

1. What does Miku want to do after graduation? (A. study geography in college, B. teach geography in high school, C. teach geography in college, D. become a travel agent)
2. Where did Miku travel this summer? (A. Beijing, B. South America, C. North America, D. South Africa)
3. What did Miku do while she was there? (A. she collected many souvenirs, B. she went shopping, C. she went sightseeing, D. she studied the language)
4. What is the main purpose of Miku's travels? (A. to learn languages, B. to study foreign cultures firsthand, C. to make her classes interesting, D. to sell exotic items)

136 西 West

一	丆	丙	丙	襾	西		

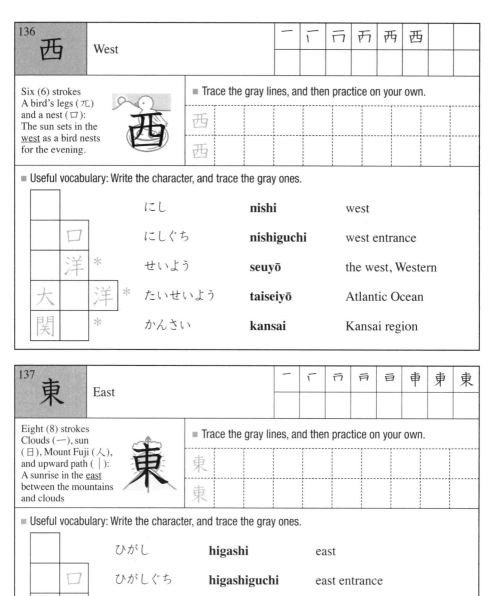

Six (6) strokes
A bird's legs (丌)
and a nest (口):
The sun sets in the west as a bird nests for the evening.

■ Trace the gray lines, and then practice on your own.

西								
西								

■ Useful vocabulary: Write the character, and trace the gray ones.

□	にし	**nishi**	west	
□口	にしぐち	**nishiguchi**	west entrance	
□洋	せいよう	**seuyō**	the west, Western	*
大□洋	たいせいよう	**taiseiyō**	Atlantic Ocean	*
関□	かんさい	**kansai**	Kansai region	*

137 東 East

一	丆	币	両	百	申	東	東

Eight (8) strokes
Clouds (一), sun
(日), Mount Fuji (人),
and upward path (丨):
A sunrise in the east between the mountains and clouds

■ Trace the gray lines, and then practice on your own.

東								
東								

■ Useful vocabulary: Write the character, and trace the gray ones.

□	ひがし	**higashi**	east	
□口	ひがしぐち	**higashiguchi**	east entrance	
中□	ちゅうとう	**chūtō**	Middle East	
□洋	とうよう	**tōyō**	The East, Orient	*
関□	かんとう	**kantō**	northeastern Japan	*

* An asterisk denotes vocabulary with kanji that have not yet been introduced.

Reading 14-G

ひろとさんは関西に住んでいましたが、中学生の時、東京へひっこして来ました。4月に高校1年生になりましたが、今でも時々関西に帰りたいと思うことがあります。今年の夏休みには、大阪のおばあさんの家に泊まりに行きました。そして、いつものように、中学校の時の友達とお好み焼きを食べに行きました。友達の冗談はとてもおかしかったので、2人でずっとわらっていました。大阪には明るくておもしろい人が多いし、食べ物もおいしいので、ひろとさんは、今でも大阪のほうが好きです。ひろとさんは、今度はいつ大阪に遊びに行くことができるか考えています。

泊まる to stay, lodge

冗談 a joke

Hiroto san wa kansai ni sunde imashita ga, chūgakusei no toki, tōkyō e hikkoshi shite kimashita. Shigatsu ni kōkō ichinensei ni narimashita ga, ima demo tokidoki kansai ni kaeritai to omou koto ga arimasu. Kotoshi no natsuyasumi niwa, ōsaka no obāsan no ie ni tomari ni ikimashita. Soshite, itsumo no yōni, chūgakkō no toki no tomodachi to okonomiyaki o tabe ni ikimashita. Tomodachi no jōdan wa totemo okashikatta node, futari de zutto waratte imashita. Ōsaka niwa akarukute omoshiroi hito ga ōi shi, tabemono mo oishii node, hiroto san wa, ima demo ōsaka no hō ga suki desu. Hiroto san wa, kondo wa itsu ōsaka ni asobi ni iku koto ga dekiru ka kangaete imasu.

Questions 14-G

1. Where did Hiroto live when he was small? (A. Hokkaido, B. Kyushu, C. Kanto region, D. Kansai region)
2. When did Hiroto move? (A. in college, B. in high school, C. in middle school, D. in elementary school)
3. What did Hiroto do in Osaka this summer? (A. see a baseball game, B. go shopping, C. visit his grandmother, D. visit his former school)
4. Why does Hiroto prefer Osaka? (A. the cost of living is low, B. the baseball team is good, C. people are nice, D. the college is good)

Lesson 14 Practice

A. Kanji Review

Try writing these words in kanji. Use the mnemonic pictures for hints if needed.

travel	vehicle	neck, head	street, way	train station	town	market
1.	2.	3.	4.	5.	6.	7.

capital	jewels	country	north	south	west	east
8.	9.	10.	11.	12.	13.	14.

B. Commonly Mistaken Kanji

Which kanji correctly expresses the meaning of the English word? Circle the most appropriate kanji character.

1. north	比	花	化	背	死	北
2. travel	坊	族	防	旅	放	方
3. vehicle	事	車	串	書	中	弟
4. south	古	羊	面	南	円	両
5. neck, head	道	苺	首	英	花	買
6. capital	高	東	景	果	少	京
7. street, way	近	進	首	前	道	週
8. west	西	四	酒	見	両	画

9. jewels	王	玉	全	住	国	柱
10. train station	尺	兄	馬	鳥	駅	沢
11. town	田	専	町	丁	庁	冒
12. market	布	帚	帰	市	雪	京
13. country	王	向	玉	困	週	国
14. east	早	東	束	京	木	果

C. Vocabulary Review

Try writing these words with appropriate kanji and okurigana characters.

1. 関 _____ (かんとう northeastern Japan)
2. _____ _____ _____ (くるまいす wheelchair)
3. _____ _____ (てくび wrist)
4. _____ _____ (やまみち mountain trail)
5. _____ _____ _____ (とうきょうえき Tokyo Station)
6. _____ _____ (まちだ city name)
7. _____ 長 (しちょう mayor)
8. _____ 都 (きょうと Kyoto)
9. _____ _____ _____ (じゅうえんだま 10 yen coin)
10. _____ _____ (ちゅうごく China)
11. _____ _____ (きたぐち north entrance)
12. _____ _____ (みなみぐち south entrance)
13. _____ _____ (にしぐち west entrance)
14. _____ _____ (ひがしぐち east entrance)
15. _____ 費 (りょうひ travel expenses)
16. 自転 _____ (じてんしゃ bicycle)
17. 足 _____ (あしくび ankle)

18. _____ _____ (ちかみち shortcut)

19. _____ 員 (えきいん station employee)

20. _____ _____ _____ (まちはずれ outskirts of town)

21. _____ _____ (しりつ municipal, city owned)

22. _____ _____ _____ _____ (とうきょうゆき Tokyo bound)

23. _____ _____ (みずたま polka dot)

24. _____ _____ (こくない domestic)

25. _____ 部 (ほくぶ northern part)

26. _____ _____ _____ _____ _____ (みなみアメリカ South America)

27. _____ _____ (せいよう the west, Western countries)

28. _____ _____ (ちゅうとう Middle East)

29. _____ _____ (りょこう travel, trip)

30. _____ _____ (でんしゃ train)

31. _____ 長 (えきちょう station master)

32. 港 _____ (みなとまち harbor town)

33. _____ _____ _____ _____ (しがいでんわ long-distance phone call)

34. _____ _____ (ペキン Beijing)

35. _____ _____ (しんとう Shinto religion, Way of the Gods)

36. _____ _____ _____ _____ _____ (みなみアフリカ South Africa)

37. _____ _____ 洋 (たいせいよう Atlantic Ocean)

38. _____ 洋 (とうよう the East, Orient)

39. _____ 館 (りょかん travelers' inn)

40. _____ _____ (かざぐるま pinwheel)

41. _____ _____ (えきめい station name)

42. _____ _____ _____ (ちょうないかい neighborhood association)

43. _____ 場 (いちば market)

44. _____ _____ _____ (おてだま beanbags)

45. _____ _____ (こくご Japanese language – school subject)

46. _____ 海 _____ (ほっかいどう Hokkaido)

47. 洗 _____ (せんしゃ car wash)

48. _____ _____ (しょどう calligraphy)

49. _____ _____ _____ (おとしだま New Year's gift money)

50. _____ _____ (てんごく heaven)

51. _____ 部 (なんぶ southern part)

52. _____ _____ _____ (たまねぎ onion)

53. _____ _____ _____ (ぼこくご native tongue)

D. Japanese City Names

You can now write about one tenth of the names of the cities in Japan. Try writing these city names and their populations in kanji below. Of these cities, which five have the greatest populations? Label these one through five in kanji.

1. いちかわし (market, river, city) _____ _____ _____

   (Population: 470,000) _____ _____ _____ _____ _____

2. いぬやまし (dog, mountain, city) _____ _____ _____

   (Population: 80,000) _____ _____ _____

3. うえだし (above, rice field, city) _____ _____ _____

   (Population: 170,000) _____ _____ _____ _____

4. おおつきし (big, moon, city) _____ _____ _____

   (Population: 30,000) _____ _____ _____

5. くにたちし (country, stand, city) _____ _____ _____

   (Population: 70,000) _____ _____ _____

6. こくぶんじし (country, part, temple, city) _____ _____ _____ _____

   (Population: 120,000) _____ _____ _____ _____

7. しもだし (under, rice field, city) _____ _____ _____

   (Population: 30,000) _____ _____ _____

8. たちかわし (to stand, river, city) _____ _____ _____

(Population: 180,000) _____ _____ _____ _____

9. はちおうじし (eight, king, child, city) _____ _____ _____ _____

(Population: 570,000) _____ _____ _____ _____ _____

10. まちだし (town, rice field, city) _____ _____ _____

(Population: 420,000) _____ _____ _____ _____ _____

E. Martial Arts and Hobbies

The names of many martial arts and hobbies include the kanji 道 pronounced どう. This character is often means "the way of the…" or simply "arts." Try writing the names of these martial arts, hobbies, and related words and then match them to the descriptions on the right.

__1__ (Jūdō) じ ゅ う 道		1. The "gentle way" – a martial art that emphasizes self defense
____ (Shodō) _____ _____		2. Japanese tea ceremony, or the "way of the tea"
____ (Kendō) _____ _____ _____		3. Japanese art of archery
____ (Budō) _____ _____		4. Japanese calligraphy
____ (Kyudō) _____ _____ _____ _____		5. Martial arts training place
____ (Sadō) _____ _____		6. Japanese wooden sword fighting
____ (Dōjō) _____ _____ _____ _____		7. The "way of harmonious spirit" – a martial art focused on self defense and attacker safety
____ (Aikidō) _____ _____ _____ _____		8. Martial arts

F. Review Questions

Try writing these sentences in Japanese using kanji whenever appropriate. Each sentence has at least one new kanji from this lesson. Then, compare your translations with the answer key at the end of the book.

1. Do you know a shortcut to the school? ______________________________

____

2. Do you have a bicycle? ________________________________

____

3. Is there a train station near the school? ________________________

____

4. How many times per year do you travel? ______________________

____

5. Do you want to travel to foreign countries? ____________________

____

6. Do you have a souvenir from Japan? _________________________

____

7. Do you like Chinese food? ______________________________

____

8. Have you ever traveled to the Middle East? ____________________

____

9. Have you ever tasted Peking duck? __________________________

____

10. Who is the mayor (市長 [しちょう]) of your city? ____________________

____

11. Do you know what **shodo** is? ____________________________

____

12. What is your native tongue? ______________________________

____

G. Interview a Partner

Take turns asking the above questions with your partner. Try to answer as fully and appropriately as you can. For best results, you should elaborate on your answers whenever possible.

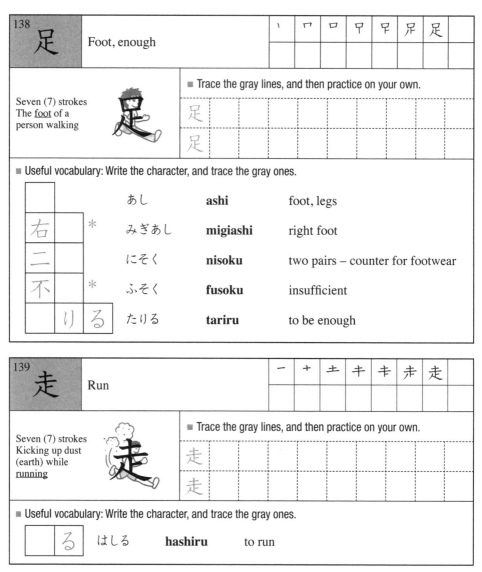

138 足	Foot, enough	丨	冂	口	𠮛	𠯁	𧾷	足	

Seven (7) strokes
The foot of a person walking

■ Trace the gray lines, and then practice on your own.

足
足

■ Useful vocabulary: Write the character, and trace the gray ones.

□		あし	**ashi**	foot, legs
右□	*	みぎあし	**migiashi**	right foot
二□		にそく	**nisoku**	two pairs – counter for footwear
不□	*	ふそく	**fusoku**	insufficient
□りる		たりる	**tariru**	to be enough

139 走	Run	一	十	土	丰	丰	𧺆	走	

Seven (7) strokes
Kicking up dust (earth) while running

■ Trace the gray lines, and then practice on your own.

走
走

■ Useful vocabulary: Write the character, and trace the gray ones.

□る	はしる	**hashiru**	to run

* An asterisk denotes vocabulary with kanji that have not yet been introduced.

Reading 15-A

日本の学校では、毎年運動会が行われます。運動会では、走るだけではなく、おもしろいレースもあります。けんくんは、パン食い競走や借り物競走など、楽しいレースをするのも、見るのも大好きです。今までは、運動会でチームが勝つかどうかは気にしたことがありませんでした。でも、今年は、高校生として最後の運動会だったので、クラスのみんなもけんくんもどうしても勝ちたいと思いました。そこで、クラスのみんなは、毎朝走る練習をすることにしました。そして、運動会でけんくんのクラスはリレーで、二位になりました。

行われる (おこなわれる)	(an event) is held	競走 (きょうそう)	a (foot) race
勝つ (かつ)	to win	二位 (にい)	second place

Nihon no gakkō dewa, maitoshi undōkai ga okonawaremasu. Undōdai dewa, hashiru dake dewanaku, omoshioi rēsu mo arimasu. Ken kun wa, pankui kyōsō ya karimono kyōsō nado, tanoshii rēsu o suru no mo, miru no mo daisuki desu. Ima made wa, undōkai de chiimu ga katsu kadōka wa ki ni shita koto ga arimasen deshita. Demo, kotoshi wa, kōkōsei toshite saigo no undōkai datta node, kurasu no minna mo Ken kun mo dōshitemo kachitai to omoimashita. Sokode, kurasu no minna wa, maiasa hashiru renshū o suru koto ni shimashita. Soshite, undōkai de Ken kun no kurasu wa rirē de, nii ni narimashita.

Questions 15-A

1. What event is mentioned in this passage? (A. city sponsored marathons, B. school swimming meets, C. national track and field tournaments, D. school field days)
2. What does Ken like about this day? (A. participating, B. watching, C. both participating and watching, D. organizing the event)
3. Which of these statements best describes Ken? (A. he is very competitive, B. he is not very competitive, C. he wants to win this year because it is his last, D. he hopes it does not rain and ruin the event).
4. How did Ken's class prepare for the day's events? (A. they practiced running after school, B. they practiced running every morning, C. they practiced swimming daily, D. they took a weight lifting course together)

140 起	Wake up	一	十	土	キ	圭	走	走	起
		起	起						

Ten (10) strokes
The self control to wake up early and go running

■ Trace the gray lines, and then practice on your own.

起									
起									

■ Useful vocabulary: Write the character, and trace the gray ones.

	き	る	おきる	**okiru**	to wake
	立		きりつ	**kiritu**	"Stand"

141 止	Stop	丨	ト	屮	止				

Four (4) strokes
A golfer stops to look for the golf ball

■ Trace the gray lines, and then practice on your own.

止									
止									

■ Useful vocabulary: Write the character, and trace the gray ones.

	め	る			とめる	**tomeru**	to stop something
	ま	る			とまる	**tomaru**	something stops
中		す	る		ちゅうしする	**chūshi suru**	to cancel
雨	が		ん	だ	あめがやんだ	**ame ga yanda**	the rain stopped
行	き		ま	り	いきとまり	**ikitomari**	dead end street

* An asterisk denotes vocabulary with kanji that have not yet been introduced.

Reading 15-B

まいさんは、冬になると、朝、なかなか起きることができません。寒いし、朝はまだくらいからです。それに、高校生は勉強がとてもいそがしいし、クラブ活動をしているとつかれて、何時間ねても足りません。でも、今週は毎日雨がたくさん降ったので、クラブの練習が中止になりました。そこで、まいさんは、できるだけ早く学校の勉強をやって、早くねることにしました。練習がなかったのはざんねんですが、いつもよりのんびりすることができました。

Mai san wa, fuyu ni naru to, asa, nakanaka okiru koto ga dekimasen. Samui shi, asa wa mada kurai kara desu. Sore ni, kōkōsei wa benkyō ga totemo isogashii shi, kurabu katsudō o shite iru to tsukarete, nanjikan netemo tarimasen. Demo, konshū wa mainichi ame ga takusan futta node, kurabu no renshū ga chūshi ni narimashita. Sokode, Mai san wa, dekirudake hayaku gakkō no benkyō o yatte, hayaku neru koto nishimashita. Renshū ga nakatta nowa zannen desu ga, itusmo yori nonbiri suru koto ga dekimashita.

Questions 15-B

1. Why is it difficult for Mai to wake up during the winter? (A. her alarm clock is broken, B. the school year just began, and she is used to the vacation schedule, C. it is winter, and it is dark and cold in the morning, D. she goes to bed late at night)
2. What does Mai feel she does not get enough of? (A. practice, B. study done, C. sleep, D. information)
3. Why did sports practices get canceled? (A. it is too cold outside, B. it is too dark outside, C. it is too rainy, D. it is too snowy)
4. What did Mai decide to do with her extra time? (A. get more sleep, B. spend more time on her homework, C. hang out with her friends, D. take a trip with her family)

142 正 Correct

Stroke order: 一 丅 下 𤴓 正

Five (5) strokes
A golfer stops to observe a hole in one – that's the correct way to do it!

■ Trace the gray lines, and then practice on your own.

正
正

■ Useful vocabulary: Write the character, and trace the gray ones.

___しい	ただしい	**tadashii**	right, correct
お___月	おしょうがつ	**oshōgatsu**	New Year's Day
___門	せいもん	**seimon**	main entry, main gate

143 歩 Walk

Stroke order: 丨 ⺊ 𣥂 止 𣥄 𣥅 𣥆 歩

Eight (8) strokes
A golfer walks a few steps, then stops to take a shot

■ Trace the gray lines, and then practice on your own.

歩
歩

■ Useful vocabulary: Write the character, and trace the gray ones.

___く	あるく	**aruku**	to walk
___いて行く	あるいていく	**aruite iku**	to go by walking

* An asterisk denotes vocabulary with kanji that have not yet been introduced.

Reading 15-C

これから、みなさんに、初詣(はつもうで)について説明(せつめい)します。初詣というのは、その年に初(はじ)めて、神社(じんじゃ)やお寺におまいりに行くことです。たくさんの日本人はお正月の間に初詣をします。歩いて近くの神社やお寺に行く人もいるし、電車やバスに乗(の)って、有名な神社やお寺に行く人もいます。お正月の間は、特別(とくべつ)に夜遅(おそ)くまで電車やバスが走っているから、便利(べんり)です。そして、まず神様(かみさま)に去年(きょねん)までのお礼(れい)を言ってから、今年もよろしくお願いしますとお祈(いの)りをします。その後で、お守(まも)りを買(か)ったり、おみくじをひいたりする人もいます。とても特別(とくべつ)で、伝統的(でんとうてき)な行事(ぎょうじ)です。これで発表(はっぴょう)を終(お)わります。

祈(いの)り	prayer	お守(まも)り	a charm
おみくじ	a written fortune		

Kore kara, minasan ni, hatsumōde nitsuite setsumei shimasu. Hatsumōde toiu no wa, sono toshi ni hajimete, jinja ya otera ni omairi ni iku koto desu. Takusan no nihonjin wa oshōgatsu no aida ni hatsumōde o shimasu. Aruite chikaku no jinja ya otera ni iku hito mo iru shi, densha ya basu ni notte, yūmei na jinja ya otera ni iku hito mo imasu. Oshōgatsu no aida wa, tokubetsu ni yoru osoku made densha ya basu ga hashitte iru kara, benri desu. Soshite, mazu kamisama ni kyonen made no orei o itte kara, kotoshimo yoroshiku onegaishimasu to oinori o shimasu. Sono atode, omamori o kattari, omikuji o hiitari suru hito mo imasu. Totemo tokubetsu de, dentōteki na gyōji desu. Kore de happyō o owarimasu.

Questions 15-C

1. What is this presentation about? (A. one's first visit of the year to a shrine or temple, B. summer festivals on the grounds of shrines and temples, C. field day events on the grounds of a shrine or temple, D. visiting a shrine or temple the year one becomes 3, 5, or 7 years old)
2. According to the speaker, how do people travel to the shrines and temples? (A. by walking, B. by public transportation, C. by both walking and public transportation, D. by car)
3. What does the speaker say is convenient? (A. there is generous public parking at shrines and temples, B. famous shrines and temples are located within walking distance to most homes, C. public transportation has extended operating hours during the New Year holiday, D. many people own their own cars)
4. What does the speaker say one should do first during "Hatsumode"? (A. purchase a charm, B. select a written fortune, C. pray for future health and happiness, D. give thanks for the blessings of the past year)

144 休 Rest

Stroke order: ノ 亻 仁 什 休 休

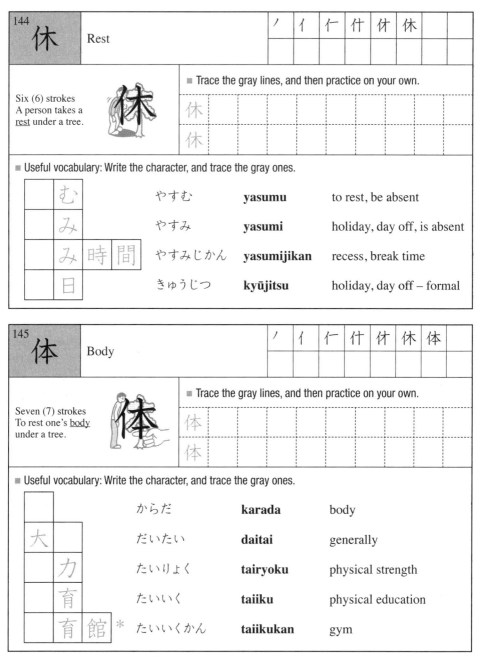

Six (6) strokes
A person takes a rest under a tree.

■ Trace the gray lines, and then practice on your own.

休

休

■ Useful vocabulary: Write the character, and trace the gray ones.

休む	やすむ	**yasumu**	to rest, be absent
休み	やすみ	**yasumi**	holiday, day off, is absent
休み時間	やすみじかん	**yasumijikan**	recess, break time
休日	きゅうじつ	**kyūjitsu**	holiday, day off – formal

145 体 Body

Stroke order: ノ 亻 仁 什 休 休 体

Seven (7) strokes
To rest one's body under a tree.

■ Trace the gray lines, and then practice on your own.

体

体

■ Useful vocabulary: Write the character, and trace the gray ones.

体	からだ	**karada**	body
大体	だいたい	**daitai**	generally
体力	たいりょく	**tairyoku**	physical strength
体育	たいいく	**taiiku**	physical education
体育館 *	たいいくかん	**taiikukan**	gym

* An asterisk denotes vocabulary with kanji that have not yet been introduced.

Reading 15-D

ゆきさんの家族は、長い休みには、いつも旅行をすることにしています。いつもは、色々な町に行きますが、今回は、おきなわにあるきれいな家を二週間、借りることにしました。その家からは海が見えて、歩いても海まで十分もかかりません。その上、あまり人がいないので、とてもしずかで、のんびりすることができます。ゆきさんもお兄さんも毎日海で泳いだので、体力がつきました。それに黒くなったので、ひさしぶりに会った人がびっくりしていました。とても楽しかったので、来年も同じ所に行きたいと思っています。

Yuki san no kazoku wa, nagai yasumi niwa, itsumo ryokō o suru koto ni shite imasu. Itsumo wa, iroiro na machi ni ikimasu ga, konkai wa, Okinawa ni aru kirei na ie o nishūkan, kariru koto ni shimashita. Sono ie kara umi ga miete, aruitemo umi made juppun mo kakarimasen. Sono ue, amari hito ga inai node, totemo shizuka de, nonbiri suru koto ga dekimasu. Yuki san mo oniisan mo mainichi umi de oyoida node, tairyoku ga tsukimashita. Sore ni kuroku natta node, hisashiburi ni atta hito ga bikkuri shite imashita. Totemo tanoshikatta node, rainen mo onaji tokoro ni ikitai to omotteimasu.

Questions 15-D

1. What does Yuki's family do during vacations? (A. visit relatives, B. travel, C. vacation in the countryside, D. stay at home)
2. What will they do this year? (A. stay at a rental house for two weeks, B. stay at their summer home, C. finish building their summer home, D. visit their relatives for two weeks)
3. How long does it take to get to the beach? (A. 10 minutes by bus, B. 10 minutes by walking, C. 10 minutes by car, D. 10 minutes by train)
4. What do they like about this place? (A. they can see the stars at night, B. the city is conveniently nearby, C. it is quiet and relaxing, D. the people in the area are kind)

146 指

Finger, point

一	十	扌	扌	扌	扌	指	指
指							

Nine (9) strokes
A person pointing to the sun with his or her finger

■ Trace the gray lines, and then practice on your own.

指									
指									

■ Useful vocabulary: Write the character, and trace the gray ones.

□	ゆび	**yubi**	finger, toe
□す	さす	**sasu**	to point
目□す	めざす	**mezasu**	to aim
□名する	しめいする	**shimei suru**	to nominate

147 背

Back, stature

一	𠃌	十	北	北	北	背	背
背							

Nine (9) strokes
Two people standing back to back to see who is the tallest

■ Trace the gray lines, and then practice on your own.

背									
背									

■ Useful vocabulary: Write the character, and trace the gray ones.

□	せ／せい	**se/ sei**	height
□が高い	せがたかい	**segatakai**	is tall
□中	せなか	**senaka**	person's back

* An asterisk denotes vocabulary with kanji that have not yet been introduced.

Reading 15-E

しょうくんは、背が高くて、かっこいいだけではありません。スポーツもできるし、頭(あたま)も良くて、歌(うた)と踊(おど)りにも興味(きょうみ)があります。そこで、将来(しょうらい)は、できれば有名な歌手(かしゅ)か俳優(はいゆう)になりたいと思っています。俳優を目指すために、今、学校の後で、ボイストレーニングをしたり、踊り方を習ったりしています。色々(いろいろ)なことができたら、色々な役(やく)もできるからです。友達(だち)も家族(ぞく)も、いつも「がんばって」と言ってくれます。

俳優(はいゆう) actor

役(やく) role

Shō kun wa, segatakakakute, kakkoii dake dewa arimasen. Supōtsu mo dekiru shi, atama mo yokute, uta to odori nimo kyōmi ga arimasu. Sokode, shōrai wa dekireba yūmei na kashu ka haiyū ni naritai to omotte imasu. Haiyū o mezasu tameni, ima, gakkō no atode, boisutorēningu o shitari, odorikata o narattari shite imasu. Iroiro na koto ga dekitara, iroiro na yaku mo dekiru kara desu. Tomodachi mo kazoku mo, itsumo "ganbatte" to itte kuremasu.

Questions 15-E

1. What kind of person is Shō? (A. talkative and funny, B. short, but good at sports, C. tall and a bit awkward, D. tall and athletic)
2. What is Shō interested in? (A. singing and playing music, B. playing and writing songs, C. singing and dancing, D. making people laugh)
3. Why is Shō taking voice lessons? (A. he is interested in many things, B. he wants to be able to act out various roles, C. it is a requirement for acting school, D. his parents encourage him)
4. How does Shō's family feel about his choices? (A. they wish he would be more committed to his sport team, B. they wish he would study harder, C. they do not understand him, D. they support him wholeheartedly)

148 自 Oneself

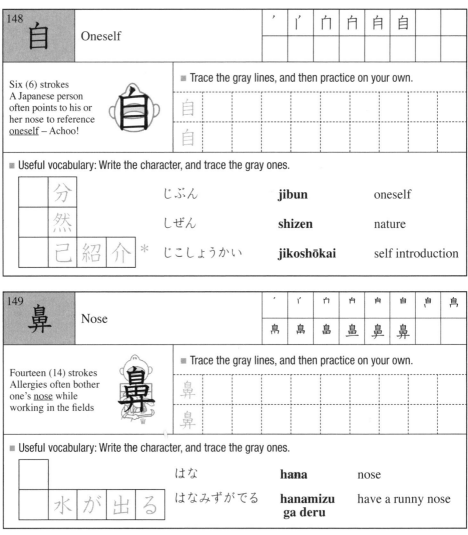

Six (6) strokes
A Japanese person often points to his or her nose to reference oneself – Achoo!

■ Trace the gray lines, and then practice on your own.

自
自

■ Useful vocabulary: Write the character, and trace the gray ones.

□分		じぶん	**jibun**	oneself
□然		しぜん	**shizen**	nature
□己紹介	*	じこしょうかい	**jikoshōkai**	self introduction

149 鼻 Nose

Fourteen (14) strokes
Allergies often bother one's nose while working in the fields

■ Trace the gray lines, and then practice on your own.

鼻
鼻

■ Useful vocabulary: Write the character, and trace the gray ones.

□	はな	**hana**	nose
□水が出る	はなみずがでる	**hanamizu ga deru**	have a runny nose

* An asterisk denotes vocabulary with kanji that have not yet been introduced.

Reading 15-F

この前、日本語のクラスに日本から高校生が十人来てくれました。その中にかわった自己紹介をした生徒がいました。日本人の名前はおぼえにくいのですが、その人は、「私の名前は、豊田せい子です。豊田は、有名な車の会社の名前で、せい子もセイコーという日本の時計の会社の名前と発音が似ています。会社の名前を聞いたことがある人は、私の名前をおぼえやすいでしょう。」と言ったのです。だから、クラスのみんなは、すぐにせい子さんの名前をおぼえました。せい子さんは、自然が大好きで、よく山にのぼったり、ハイキングをしたりするそうです。でも、時々、山に行くと、アレルギーのために、鼻水が止まらなくなるので、こまるそうです。

はつおん
発音　pronunciation

に
似ている　similar

Kono mae, nihongo no kurasu ni nihon kara kōkōsei ga jūnin kite kuremashita. Sono naka ni kawatta jikoshōkai o shita seito ga imashita. Nihonjin no namae wa oboenikui desu ga, sono hito wa, "watashi no namae wa, Toyota Seiko desu. Toyota wa yūmei na kuruma no kaisha no namae de, Seiko mo seikō toiu nihon no tokei no kaisha no namae to hatsuon ga nite imasu. Kaisha no namae o kiita koto ga aru hito wa, watashi no namae o oboeyasui desho" to itta no desu. Dakara, kurasu no minna wa, sugu ni Seiko san no namae o oboemashita. Seiko san wa, shizen ga daisuki de, yoku yama ni nobottari, haikingu o shitari suru sō desu. Demo, tokidoki, yama ni iku to arerugii no tame ni hanamizu ga tomaranaku naru node, komaru sō desu.

Questions 15-F

1. What is this passage about? (A. a foreign student who visited a Japanese school, B. someone who gave an interesting self-introduction, C. someone from the Toyota auto company who visited a school, D. a class that visited the Seiko watch company)
2. Why was it easy for the class to remember the person's name? (A. it is similar to the names of two famous companies, B. it is similar to a famous actor's, C. it is short, D. it does not sound Japanese)
3. What is something this person enjoys doing? (A. swimming, B. eating out, C. hiking, D. traveling)
4. What is this person troubled about? (A. adjusting to the new time zone, B. adjusting to the high altitude, C. spring allergies, D. the flu season)

150 寝	Sleep, lie down	

Thirteen (13) strokes
One sleeps in the house on a bed mat, with the covers pulled up

■ Trace the gray lines, and then practice on your own.

寝
寝

■ Useful vocabulary: Write the character, and trace the gray ones.

	る				ねる	**neru**	to sleep, lie down
	る	時	間		ねるじかん	**neru jikan**	bed time
早		早	起	き	はやねはやおき	**hayane hayaoki**	early to bed, early to rise

* An asterisk denotes vocabulary with kanji that have not yet been introduced.

Reading 15-G

みなさんは、何時に寝ますか。そして、一日に何時間ぐらい寝ていますか。新聞(しんぶん)によると、成績(せいせき)がいい人は、だいたい八時間ぐらい寝ているそうです。そこで、あるアメリカの大学では、大学生三千人にアンケートをとりました。その結果(けっか)、80%の学生が毎日八時間から九時間寝ていることがわかりました。しかし、日本人の学生の寝る時間は、毎年、みじかくなってきているようです。夜(よる)おそくまで勉強(べんきょう)をしているからかもしれません。また、夜中(よなか)におもしろいテレビを見ているのかもしれません。インターネットをしたり、友達(だち)とチャットをしているからかもしれません。

結果(けっか) result

夜中(よなか) midnight

Minasan wa, nanji ni nemasu ka. Soshite, ichinichi ni nanjikan gurai nete imasu ka. Shinbun niyoru to, seiseki ga ii hito wa, daitai hachijikan gurai nete iru sō desu. Sokode, aru amerika no daigaku dewa, daigakusei sanzennin ni ankēto o torimashita. Sono kekka, hachijū pāsento no gakusei ga mainichi hachijikan kara kujikan nete iru koto ga wakarimashita. Shikashi, nihonjin no gakusei no nerujikan wa, maitoshi, mijikakunatte kite iru yō desu. Yoru osoku made benkyō oshiteiru kara kamoshiremasen. Mata, yonaka ni omoshiroi terebi o mite iru no kamoshiremasen. Intānetto o shitari, tomodachi to chatto o shite iru kara kamoshiremasen.

Questions 15-G

1. What source does the speaker quote in the passage? (A. a science magazine, B. a newspaper article, C. a research journal, D. a national health organization)
2. According to the article, what is one of the benefits of getting about eight hours of sleep? (A. better grades, B. better relationships with friends, C. fewer traffic accidents, D. better attitudes about school)
3. Which demographic group is said to get about eight hours of sleep? (A. US high school students, B. Japanese high school students, C. US university students, D. Japanese university students)
4. What is the main cause of Japanese youth not getting enough sleep? (A. studying late at night, B. watching TV at midnight, C. using the internet, and chatting with friends, D. there is no main cause given in the research)

Lesson 15 Practice

A. Kanji Review

Write these kanji. Use the mnemonic picture if needed.

 foot	 run	 wake up	 stop	 correct	 walk	 rest
1.	2.	3.	4.	5.	6.	7.
 body	 finger	 back	 oneself	 nose	 sleep	
8.	9.	10.	11.	12.	13.	

B. Commonly Mistaken Kanji

Which kanji correctly expresses the meaning of the English word? Circle the most appropriate kanji character.

1. sleep	受	夜	寝	漫	背	将
2. stop	上	止	仕	士	土	正
3. nose	自	界	夏	鼻	専	息
4. wake up	歩	記	走	徒	強	起
5. back	背	育	北	比	皆	階
6. walk	少	止	小	武	歩	歳
7. foot	走	定	足	使	起	庭

8. finger	持	指	掃	背	明	昨
9. rest	本	林	体	代	休	守
10. run	起	定	徒	走	足	遠
11. body	代	本	休	林	守	体
12. correct	止	上	正	士	王	土
13. oneself	目	自	白	百	田	由

C. Vocabulary Review

Write these words and phrases in Japanese. You may use the word bank below for hints.

1. two pairs of shoes	2. correct answer	3. to wake up at 6:30
4. to walk slowly	5. the rain stopped	6. (one's) finger hurts
7. is tall	8. aim for an A	9. the train stopped
10. to cancel a sports game	11. right foot	12. recess, break time
13. New Year's	14. to walk to school	15. one's back
16. oneself	17. to point to the answer	18. 5000 yen is enough
19. strong body	20. to stop the car	21. early to bed, early to rise
22. to run five kilometers	23. bed time	24. holiday, day off, absent

25. to sleep well	26. to be absent from school	27. to have a runny nose
28. dead end, blind alley	29. approximately 60 years old	30. Stop!

右足	二足のくつ	五千円で足りる	五キロを走る
六時半に起きる	止まれ！	車を止める	電車が止まった
しあいを中止する	雨が止んだ	行き止まり	正しいこたえ
お正月	ゆっくり歩く	がっこうに歩いて行く	がっこうを休む
休み	休み時間	つよい体	大体六十才
指がいたい	こたえを指す	Aを目指す	背がたかい
背中	自分	鼻水が出る	よく寝る
寝る時間	早寝早起き		

D. Vocabulary Writing – Parts of the Body

Use kanji to label the body parts.

E. Vocabulary Writing – Daily Routine

Write 田中さん's school day routine in Japanese.

1. Tanaka san wakes up at 6:30. ______________________________
2. (He) eats breakfast at 7:00. ______________________________
3. (He) walks to school at 7:30. ______________________________
4. (He) goes to the library at 11:00. ______________________________
5. (He) plays soccer at 4:00 ______________________________
6. (He) returns to home at 6:00. ______________________________
7. (He) eats dinner at 6:30. ______________________________
8. (He) watches TV at 7:00. ______________________________
9. (He) does homework at 7:30. ______________________________
10. (He) goes to bed at 10:00. ______________________________

F. Review Questions

Try writing these sentences in Japanese using kanji whenever appropriate. Each sentence has at least one new kanji from this lesson. Then, compare your translations with the answer key at the end of the book.

1. Is $3000 dollars enough to travel to Japan for two weeks? ______________

   ____

2. Do you like to run? ______________________________________

   ____

3. Does a bus stop near your house? _____________________________

   ____

4. Do you walk to school sometimes? ______________________

____

5. Who is absent today? ______________________

____

6. What do you plan to do on your next holiday? ______________________

____

7. What kind of person are you interested in (aiming for)? ______________________

____

8. Do you go to bed early and get up early? ______________________

____

G. Interview Your Partner

Take turns asking the above questions with your partner. Try to answer as fully and appropriately as you can. For best results, you should elaborate on your answers whenever possible.

H. Read and Respond

Suppose you are writing a Japanese pen pal, Makiko, and she has sent you an email describing to you her boyfriend. Read the email below and respond to it. Begin with an appropriate greeting, be sure to answer her questions, and ask her one or two questions.

こんにちは！お元気ですか。私は元気です。こちらは、さむくなりました。そちらの天気はどうですか。

先しゅうの土曜日に私は、ボーイフレンドとアイススケートに行きました。すごくたのしかったです。かれは、あまりアイススケートが上手じゃないけれど、話がおもしろいし、やさしい人だからです。

ボーイフレンドのなまえは山田たかしくんで、十七才の高校三年生です。かれは、学校のクロスカントリーのチームに入っています。足がながくて、走るのがとてもはやいです。

そして、山田くんは、鼻がとても高くて、少しえいがのスターににています。

あなたは、好きな人がいますか。どんな人とつきあってみたいですか。やさしい人と、かっこいい人と、おもしろい人では、どんな人がいいですか。

では、また。おへんじ待っています。

まきこより

151 新 New

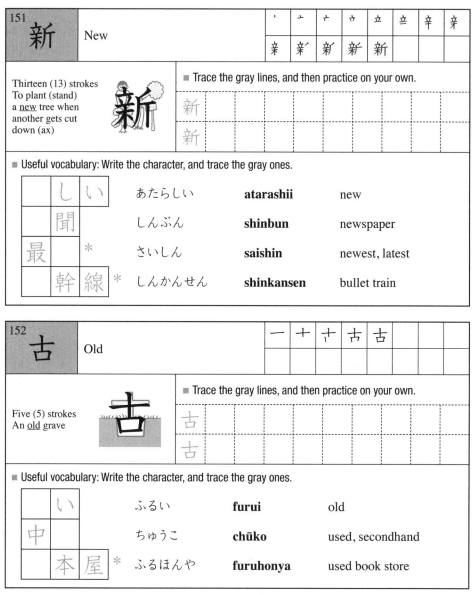

Thirteen (13) strokes
To plant (stand) a new tree when another gets cut down (ax)

■ Trace the gray lines, and then practice on your own.

新

新

■ Useful vocabulary: Write the character, and trace the gray ones.

□しい	あたらしい	**atarashii**	new
□聞	しんぶん	**shinbun**	newspaper
最□ *	さいしん	**saishin**	newest, latest
□幹線 *	しんかんせん	**shinkansen**	bullet train

152 古 Old

Five (5) strokes
An old grave

■ Trace the gray lines, and then practice on your own.

古

古

■ Useful vocabulary: Write the character, and trace the gray ones.

□い	ふるい	**furui**	old
中□	ちゅうこ	**chūko**	used, secondhand
□本屋 *	ふるほんや	**furuhonya**	used book store

* An asterisk denotes vocabulary with kanji that have not yet been introduced.

Reading 16-A

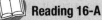

最近(さいきん)、日本で、新しいスタイルの古本屋がふえているそうです。今までの古本屋は、古い本しかない店というイメージが強(つよ)かったのですが、最近の古本屋には、新しい本の古本や音楽のCDやコンピューターゲームのソフトを売っている店もあります。もちろん、本を読んだ後、その本を古本屋に持って行って、売ることもできます。あまり高くは売れませんが、お金をもらえないよりいいと思う人が多いようです。それに、その本を読みたいと思う人にとって、本が安く買えるからいいです。でも、出版社(しゅっぱんしゃ)はあまりうれしくないようです。新しい本を買う人が少なくなるからです。みなさんはどう思いますか。

最近(さいきん) recently　　出版社(しゅっぱんしゃ) publishing company

Saikin, nihon de, atarashii sutairu no furuyonya ga fuete iru sō desu. Ima made no furuyonya wa, furui hon shika nai mise toiu imēji ga tsuyokatta no desu ga, saikin no furuyonya niwa, atarashii hon no furuyon ya ongaku no shiidii ya konpyūtāgēmu no sofuto o utte iru mise mo arimasu. Mochiron, hon o yonda ato, sono hon o furuhonya ni motte itte, uru koto mo dekimasu. Amari takaku wa uremasen ga, okane o moraenai yori ii to omou hito ga ōi yō desu. Sore ni, sono hon o yomitai to omou hito nitotte, hon ga yasuku kaeru kara ii desu. Demo, shuppansha wa amari ureshikunai yō desu. Atarashii hon o kau hito ga sukunaku naru kara desu. Minasan wad dō omoimasu ka.

Questions 16-A

1. What is the main topic of this article? (A. newspapers, B. current events, C. secondhand book stores, D. books vs. video games)
2. How have used bookstores changed? (A. Now they sell very old books, B. Now they sell used copies of newly published books, C. Now they sell computer software, D. Now they sell soft ice cream)
3. What is one good thing about used bookstores? (A. they buy books from customers, B. they discount their books once a month, C. they give book vouchers instead of money, D. they trade books with customers)
4. How do publishing companies view these used bookstores? (A. they are happy that many people are reading books, B. they are happy because more people are buying books, C. they are not happy because not many people are reading books, D. they are not happy because fewer people are buying new books)

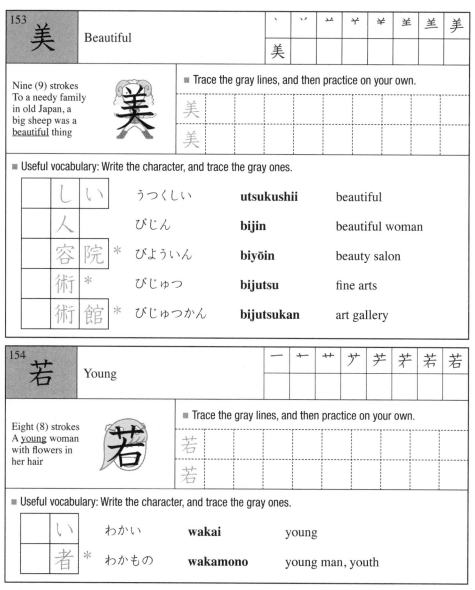

153 美 Beautiful

丶	丷	䒑	䒑	𦍌	𦍌	𦍌	美
美							

Nine (9) strokes
To a needy family in old Japan, a big sheep was a <u>beautiful</u> thing

■ Trace the gray lines, and then practice on your own.

美
美

■ Useful vocabulary: Write the character, and trace the gray ones.

美しい	うつくしい	**utsukushii**	beautiful
美人	びじん	**bijin**	beautiful woman
美容院 *	びよういん	**biyōin**	beauty salon
美術 *	びじゅつ	**bijutsu**	fine arts
美術館 *	びじゅつかん	**bijutsukan**	art gallery

154 若 Young

一	十	艹	𦫳	苎	若	若	若

Eight (8) strokes
A <u>young</u> woman with flowers in her hair

■ Trace the gray lines, and then practice on your own.

若
若

■ Useful vocabulary: Write the character, and trace the gray ones.

若い	わかい	**wakai**	young
若者 *	わかもの	**wakamono**	young man, youth

* An asterisk denotes vocabulary with kanji that have not yet been introduced.

Reading 16-B

最近、今までの美術館とは少し違う美術館ができました。とても人気があるので、週末は、美術館に入るまで一時間待つこともあるそうです。そして、お年よりだけでなく、若い人や小さい子もたくさん来ます。人気の理由はたくさんあります。まず、ふつう、美術館は入り口が一つですが、この美術館には、四つの入り口があります。美術館に来る人が好きな所から入れるようにするためです。また、美術館の中のかべは白で、ガラスがたくさん使われていて、とても明るいです。みどりの庭や、まわりの木や自然もとてもきれいです。最後に、この美術館では、美術にさわったり、遊んだりすることができるそうです。だから、来た人は美術はおもしろいと思うのです。これから人気の理由なんですね。

違う (ちが) different　　理由 (りゆう) reason

Saikin, ima made no bijutsukan towa sukoshi chigau bijutsukan ga dekimashita. Totemo ninki ga aru node, shūmatsu wa, bijutsukan ni hairu made ichijikan matsu koto mo aru sō desu. Soshite, otoshiyori dake denaku, wakai hito ya chiisai ko mo takusan kimasu. Ninki no riyū wa takusan arimasu. Mazu, futsū, bijutsukan wa iriguchi ga hitotsu desu ga, kono bijutsukan niwa, yottsu no iriguchi ga arimasu. Bijutsukan ni kuru hito ga suki na tokoro kara hairu yōni suru tame desu. Mata, bijutsukan no naka no kabe wa shiro de, garasu ga takusan tsukawarete ite, totemo akarui desu. Midori no niwa ya, mawari no ki ya shizen mo totemo kirei desu. Saigo ni, kono bijutsukan dewa, bijutsu ni sawattari, asondari suru koto ga dekiru sō desu. Dakara, kita hito wa bijutsu wa omoshiroi to omou no desu. Kore kara ninki no riyū nan desu ne.

Questions 16-B

1. What is one of the results of the museum's popularity? (A. people travel for more than one hour to see it, B. people often wait for one hour to get in, C. four TV news crews recently did reports on it, D. the presidents from four world countries recently visited it)
2. Why are there four entries to the museum? (A. because it is so popular that more entrances are needed, B. there are four train stations nearby, C. there are four themes and four sections, D. so that people can enter the museum from anywhere they want)
3. What is a reason why the museum is popular (A. the museum theme is endangered species, B. the rock garden is very big, C. the inside of the museum is bright with natural lighting, D. people who work there are cheerful)
4. What else is appealing to museum visitors? (A. you may go to different exhibits every month, B. you may touch and play with some of the exhibits, C. you may plant a tree or shrub, D. you may make an piece of art and bring it home)

155 長	Long								
		丨	𠂆	⼘	𠂒	𠀍	镸	𨱗	長

Eight (8) strokes
A Japanese elder's
long hair and
flowing robes

■ Trace the gray lines, and then practice on your own.

長								
長								

■ Useful vocabulary: Write the character, and trace the gray ones.

い	ながい	**nagai**	long
さ	ながさ	**nagasa**	length
市	しちょう	**shichō**	mayor
会	かいちょう	**kaichō**	president of a society
男	ちょうなん	**chōnan**	eldest son
女	ちょうじょ	**chōjo**	eldest daughter
校	こうちょう	**kōchō**	school principal

156 太	Fat								
		一	ナ	大	太				

Four (4) strokes
A sumo wrestler
with a *mawasshi* belt

■ Trace the gray lines, and then practice on your own.

太								
太								

■ Useful vocabulary: Write the character, and trace the gray ones.

い	ふとい	**futoi**	fat, thick
っている	ふとっている	**futotte iru**	to be fat, heavy

* An asterisk denotes vocabulary with kanji that have not yet been introduced.

Reading 16-C

若い女の子の中で、自分は太っていると思っている人が多いようです。自分の足は太すぎると思っているのに、制服のスカートの長さを短くする生徒が多いようです。理由は、短いスカートの方がかわいいし、はやっているからだそうです。しかし、見つかると、校長先生におこられるので、学校の外にいる時だけ、スカートを短くする高校生もたくさんいるそうです。あなたの学校には制服の規則がありますか。

制服 (せいふく) uniform　はやる be in fashion　規則 (きそく) rules

Wakai onna no ko no naka de, jibun wa futotte iru to omotte iru hito ga ōi yō desu. Jibun no ashi wa futosugiru to omotte iru noni, seifuku no sukāto no nagasa o michikaku suru seito ga ōi yō desu. Riyū wa, mijikai sukāto no hō ga kawaii shi, hayatte iru kara da sō desu. Shikashi, mitsukaru to kōchō sensei ni okorareru node, gakkō no soto ni iru toki dake, sukāto o mijikaku suru kōkōsei mo takusan iru sō desu. Anata no gakkō niwa seifuku no kisoku ga arimasu ka.

Questions 16-C

1. What attitude does this article describe among Japanese school girls? (A. many think that fashion is not as important as school, B. many love their school uniforms, C. many think their legs are fat, D. many do not like the school uniforms)
2. What do some Japanese schoolgirls do to their uniforms? (A. they shorten the skirt, B. they lengthen the skirt, C. they do not change their uniform skirt length, D. they do not care)
3. What is the current fashion trend? (A. long skirts are popular, B. non-uniform clothing is popular, C. short skirts are popular, D. wearing the school uniform is popular even at schools that do not have a uniform).
4. What do students do so they will not get in trouble? (A. they wear their school uniform properly, B. they do not shorten their skirt length, C. they cut their uniform skirt short, but not so it is obvious, D. they make the skirt length short when they are outside of school)

157 高 — Tall, expensive

Stroke order: 丶 亠 亠 亣 亩 产 亭 高 高 高

Ten (10) strokes
A tall, many-storied building

■ Trace the gray lines, and then practice on your own.

高
高

■ Useful vocabulary: Write the character, and trace the gray ones.

☐い	たかい	**takai**	high, high-priced, tall
☐さ	たかさ	**takasa**	height
☐校	こうこう	**kōkō**	high school

158 安 — Peace, cheap

Stroke order: 丶 丶 宀 宊 安 安

Six (6) strokes
A peaceful girl in a house

■ Trace the gray lines, and then practice on your own.

安
安

■ Useful vocabulary: Write the character, and trace the gray ones.

☐い	やすい	**yasui**	inexpensive, peaceful
☐心する	あんしんする	**anshin suru**	to be relieved
☐全*	あんぜん	**anzen**	safety, safe

* An asterisk denotes vocabulary with kanji that have not yet been introduced.

Reading 16-D

日本語クラスのみなさんへ

　こんにちは。みなさんが日本に来る前に、私たちの高校について、少し説明（せつめい）したいと思います。森田高校は東京の西にあって、七十年前にたてられました。東京というと、人が多くて、大きい町だと思うでしょう。でも、森田高校がある町は、東京から電車で一時間ぐらいかかります。まわりに緑(みどり)がたくさんあって、晴(は)れた日には富士山(ふじさん)が見えます。近くに大きな川もあるんですよ。

みなさんがホームステイをするのは、春(はる)なので、近くの山に山登(のぼ)りに行くことができます。富士山を見たり、ピクニックをしたりしましょう。とてもおもしろいですよ。

ホストファミリーの家は、ぜんぶ、高校の近くにあります。この町の人はみんな、とてもやさしいし、一人で歩いても安全なので、安心してください。

それでは、私たちの高校に来てくれるのを楽しみにしています。

森田高校　生徒会(せいとかい)より

生徒会(せいとかい)　student council

Nihongo kurasu no minasan e

Konnichiwa. Minisan ga nihon ni kuru mae ni, watashi tachi no kōkō nitsuite, sukoshi setsumei shitai to omoimasu. Morita kōkō wa Tōkyō no nishi ni ate, nanajūnen mae ni tateraremashita. Tōkyō to iu to, hito ga ōkute, ōkii machi da to omou deshō. Demo, morita kōkō ga aru machi wa, Tōkyō kara densha de ichijikan gurai kakarimasu. Mawari ni midori ga takusan ate, hareta hi niwa fujisan ga miemasu. Chikaku ni ōkina kawa mo aru n desu yo.

Minasan ga hōmusutei o suru no wa, haru na node, chikaku no yama ni yamanobori ni iku koto ga dekimasu. Fujisan o mitari, pikunikku o shitari shimashō. Totemo omoshiroi desu yo.

Hosutofamirii no ie wa, zenbu, kōkō no chikaku ni arimasu. Kono machi no hito wa minna, totemo yasashii, hitori de aruitemo anzen na node, anshin shite kudasai.

Sore dewa, watashi tachi no kōkō ni kite kureru no o tanoshimi ni shite imasu.

Morita kōkō seitokai yori

Questions 16-D

1. Who is this letter from, and who is it addressed to? (A. It is from host a family to a student, B. It is from a high school in U.S. to high school in Japan, C. It is from a student in U.S. to students in Japan, D. It is from a high school in Japan to students in U.S.)
2. Where is the high school located? (A. in a busy and big town, B. in a historical town, C. in the city center, D. near the mountains)
3. What activities are recommended in the spring? (A. mountain climbing, B. camping, C. going to museums, D. shopping at electronics stores)
4. How is the safety of the city described? (A. there are many police officers, B. you can walk alone, C. everyone knows one another, D. crimes are punished severely)

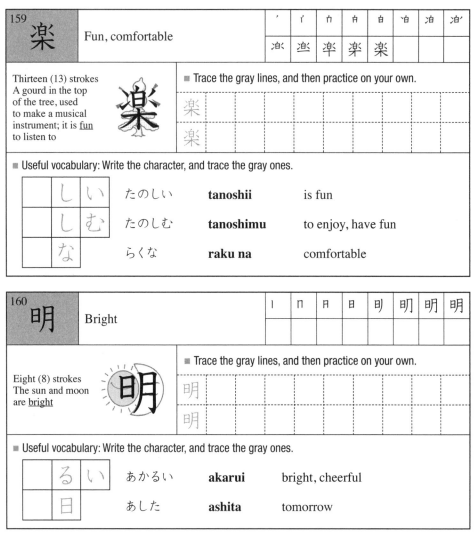

159 楽	Fun, comfortable	′	亻	巾	白	白	ˋ白	冫白	冫白′
		冫白く	冫白冫	楽	楽	楽			

Thirteen (13) strokes
A gourd in the top of the tree, used to make a musical instrument; it is fun to listen to

■ Trace the gray lines, and then practice on your own.

楽
楽

■ Useful vocabulary: Write the character, and trace the gray ones.

しい	たのしい	**tanoshii**	is fun
しむ	たのしむ	**tanoshimu**	to enjoy, have fun
な	らくな	**raku na**	comfortable

160 明	Bright	丨	冂	月	日	日丿	明	明	明

Eight (8) strokes
The sun and moon are bright

■ Trace the gray lines, and then practice on your own.

明
明

■ Useful vocabulary: Write the character, and trace the gray ones.

るい	あかるい	**akarui**	bright, cheerful
日	あした	**ashita**	tomorrow

* An asterisk denotes vocabulary with kanji that have not yet been introduced.

Reading 16-E

色々な性格(せいかく)の人がいますが、楽しくて明るい人は、人気があります。私は、それは、色々なことを楽しむことができる人のことだと思います。たとえば、日本に行った時に、大好きなアメリカンフットボールをすることができなくても、日本でやっているスポーツを楽しんでやってみようと思う人です。つまり、前(まえ)向(む)きな人のことですね。それから、楽しくて明るい人は、よく笑(わら)う人のことだと思います。前向きでよく笑う人がまわりにいると、私達(たち)も楽しくなりますよね。みなさんも、自分のことを考えてみてください。あなたは、楽しくて明るい人ですか？

性格	せいかく	personality
前(まえ)向(む)き	まえむき	positive, forward looking

Iroiro na seikaku no hito ga imasu ga, tanoshikute akarui hito wa, ninki ga arimasu. Watashi wa, sore wa, iroiro na koto o tanoshimu koto ga dekiru hito no koto da to omoimasu. Tatoeba, nihon ni itta toki ni, daisuki na amerikan futtobōru o suru koto ga dekinakutemo, nihon de yatte iru supōtsu o tanoshinde yatte miyō to omou hito desu. Tsumari, maemuki na hito no koto desu ne. Sore kara, tanoshikute akarui hito wa, yoku warau hito no koto da to omoimasu. Maemuki de yoku warau hito ga mawari ni iru to, watashi tachi mo tanoshiku narimasu yo ne. Minasan mo, jibun no koto o kangaete mite kudasai. Anata wa, tanoshikute akarui hito desu ka.

Questions 16-E

1. How does this passage describe people who tend to be popular? (A. fun and cheerful, B. smart, C. athletic, D. easygoing)
2. What example is given of such a person? (A. someone who plays American Football, B. someone who knows about American Football, C. someone who is willing to teach others how to play American Football, D. someone who shows a willingness to try out new sports)
3. What kind of people does the author say are more enjoyable to be around? (A. people who are talkative, B. people who appear happy, C. people who are considerate of others, D. people who are knowledgeable about know about athletics)
4. What is the author's main message? (A. being popular is about looks, B. people should be more athletic, C. people who appear happy tend to be well liked, D. people who appear sophisticated tend to be most popular)

161 広	Wide, spacious	丶 亠 广 広 広

Five (5) strokes
To gather things into one spacious house

■ Trace the gray lines, and then practice on your own.

広
広

■ Useful vocabulary: Write the character, and trace the gray ones.

広い	ひろい	**hiroi**	wide, spacious
広さ	ひろさ	**hirosa**	width
広大な	こうだいな	**kōdai na**	vast

162 有	Have, exist	ノ ナ 冇 有 有 有

Six (6) strokes
To hold (have) a meal of thin sliced beef (i.e., shabushabu or sukiyaki)

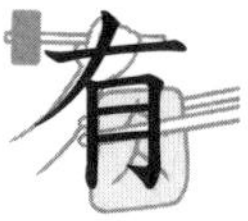

■ Trace the gray lines, and then practice on your own.

有
有

■ Useful vocabulary: Write the character, and trace the gray ones.

有名な*	ゆうめいな	**yūmei na**	famous

* An asterisk denotes vocabulary with kanji that have not yet been introduced.

Reading 16-F

大阪や広島のお好み焼きはとてもおいしくて有名です。では、お好み焼きのルーツを知っていますか。それは、今から四百年ぐらい前の江戸時代の茶道の時に食べられていた「みそのクレープ」のような食べ物です。クレープというのは、フランス語で、うすいパンケーキのことです。

　さて、その後、お好み焼きは、子どものおやつになったのですが、今では肉や魚、そして野菜をたくさん入れて、昼ご飯や晩ご飯に食べるようになりました。ところで、広島のお好み焼きにキャベツが多いのは、戦争の後で、お米や小麦粉が不足した時に、畑からキャベツをとって来て、おなかがいっぱいになるようにしたからだそうです。

戦争 (せんそう)	war	小麦粉 (こむぎこ)	flour	畑 (はたけ)	field, farm

Ōsaka ya Hiroshima no okonomiyaki wa totemo oishikute yūmei desu. Dewa, okonomiyaki no rūtsu o shitte imasu ka. Sore wa, ima kara yonhyakunen gurai mae no edojidai no sadō no toki ni taberarete ita "miso kurēpu" no yōna tabemono desu. Kurēpu to iu no wa, furansugo de, usui pankēki no koto desu.

Sate, sono ato, okonomiyaki wa, kodomo no oyastu ni natta no desu ga, ima dewa niku ya sakana, soshite yasai o takusan irete, hirugohan ya bangohan ni taberu yōni narimashita. Tokorode, Hiroshima no okonomiyaki ni kyabetsu ga ōi no wa, sensō no atode, okome ya komugiko ga fuzoku shita toki ni, hatake kara kyabetsu o totte kite, onaka ga ippai ni naru yōni shita kara da sō desu.

Questions 16-F

1. When did people begin eating okonomiyaki? (A. in the Heian period, B. during World War II, C. in the Edo period, D. during the Korean War)
2. Who ate okonomiyaki at first? (A. foreigners, B. tea ceremonies' participants, C. soldiers, D. festival-goers)
3. For a time, which segment of society was most associated with okonomiyaki? (A. children, B. fishermen, C. construction workers, D. the elderly)
4. Why is cabbage a main ingredient in Hiroshima okonomiyaki? (A. because it was the only vegetable you were allowed to eat during the war, B. because after the war, there was a shortage of rice and flour, C. because cabbage is considered a sacred food, D. because cabbage is considered lucky)

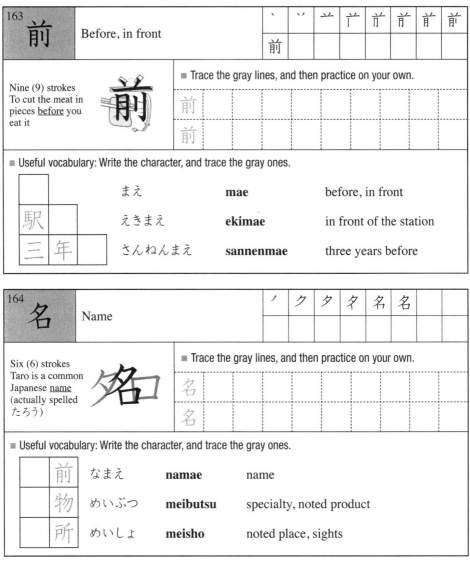

163 前 Before, in front

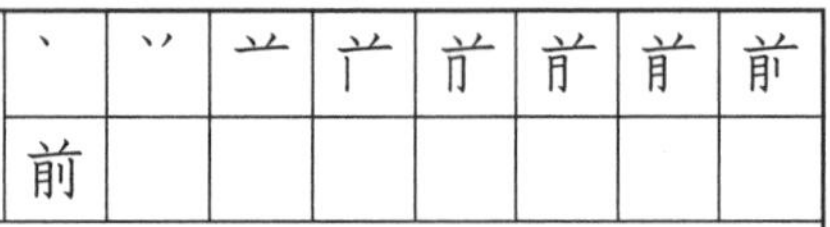

Nine (9) strokes
To cut the meat in pieces before you eat it

■ Trace the gray lines, and then practice on your own.

前

前

■ Useful vocabulary: Write the character, and trace the gray ones.

[ ]	まえ	**mae**	before, in front
駅 [ ]	えきまえ	**ekimae**	in front of the station
三 年 [ ]	さんねんまえ	**sannenmae**	three years before

164 名 Name

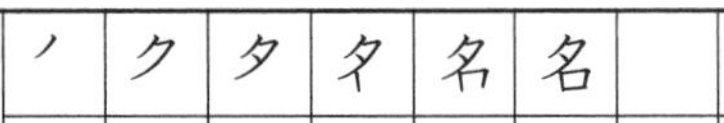

Six (6) strokes
Taro is a common Japanese name (actually spelled たろう)

■ Trace the gray lines, and then practice on your own.

名

名

■ Useful vocabulary: Write the character, and trace the gray ones.

[ ] 前	なまえ	**namae**	name
[ ] 物	めいぶつ	**meibutsu**	specialty, noted product
[ ] 所	めいしょ	**meisho**	noted place, sights

* An asterisk denotes vocabulary with kanji that have not yet been introduced.

Reading 16-G

日本には色々な名所があります。東京で一番古いお寺や、京都の有名な神社、兵庫県にある美しいお城、広島の宮島などはとてもすばらしいので、行くといいです。でも、最近、東京では新しい名所が人気だそうです。その中の一つが、渋谷にあるスクランブル交差点です。ここは、ハリウッド映画にも出たので、とても有名になりました。よく外国から来た観光客が一度に交差点をわたるたくさんの人たちの写真を撮っています。交差点の前には、有名なコーヒー屋さんもあるので、そこでコーヒーを買って飲みながら、交差点を歩く人を見ることもできます。日本に行ったら、行ってみてください。

一度 one time, once　　観光客 tourists

Nihon niwa iroiro na meisho ga arimasu. Tōkyō de ichiban furui otera ya, kyōto no yūmei na jinja, hyōgoken ni aru utsukushii oshiro, Hiroshima no miyajima nado wa totemo subarashii node, iku to ii desu. Demo, saikin, tōkyō dewa atarashii meisho ga ninki da sō desu. Sono naka no hitotsu ga, shibuya ni aru sukuranburu kōsaten desu. Koko wa, hari-uddo eiga nimo deta node, totemo yūmei ni narimashita. Yoku gaikoku kara kita kankōkyaku ga ichido ni kōsaten o wataru takusan no hito tachi no shashin o totte imasu. Kōsaten no mae niwa, yūmei na kōhiiya san mo aru node, soko de kōhii o katte nomina-gara, kōsaten o aruku hito o miru koto mo dekimasu. Nihon ni ittara, itte mite kudasai.

Questions 16-G

1. Which sightseeing place does the writer mention? (A. the biggest temple in Tokyo, B. a famous temple in Kyoto, C. a beautiful castle in Hyogo, D. a big island in Miyajima)
2. Which new place is highlighted in the passage? (A. a shrine in Tokyo, B. a restaurant famous for scrambled eggs, C. a hot springs resort n Kyoto, D. an intersection in Shibuya)
3. Why did this place become popular? (A. there are beautiful views of Mount Fuji, B. it has been depicted in movies, C. the owners advertise well, D. the commercials are funny)
4. What do many tourists do there? (A. get a picture taken with a famous actor or actress, B. watch the crowds of people, C. buy a good luck charm, D. have their fortunes told)

165 後	After, behind	ノ	ク	彳	彳'	彳丝	彳幺	後	後
		後							

Nine (9) strokes
To drag one's feet and fall <u>behind</u>

■ Trace the gray lines, and then practice on your own.

後								
後								

■ Useful vocabulary: Write the character, and trace the gray ones.

□(で)	あと(で)	**atode**	after, later
□ろ	うしろ	**ushiro**	behind
十年□	じゅうねんご	**jūnengo**	ten years later

* An asterisk denotes vocabulary with kanji that have not yet been introduced.

Reading 16-H

みなさんは、「後で」という言葉(ことば)をよく使いますか？私は、「後で勉強する」、「後でそうじする」など、あまりやりたくない時に「後で」という言葉を使います。ところで、最近、「あとで新聞」という新聞ができました。これは、「あとで読む」という言葉から生まれた新聞です。ウェブサイトに行くと、読みたい人が多い記事(きじ)が読めるそうです。しかし、問題点(もんだいてん)もあります。このサイトは、一日に一回しか新しくならないので、少し古いニュースしか読めないこともあるそうです。でも、一日前のニュースを読むためには、いいサイトでしょう。

記事(きじ) newspaper article　　問題点(もんだいてん) problems, the point at issue

Minasan wa, "atode" to iu kotoba o yoku tsukaimasu ka. Watashi wa, "atode benkyō suru," "atode sōji suru," nado, amari yaritakunai toki ni "atode" to iu kotoba o tsukaimasu. Tokorode, saikin, "atode shinbun" to iu shinbun ga dekimashita. Kore wa, "atode yomu" to iu kotoba kara umareta shinbun desu. Uebusaito ni iku to, yomitai hito ga ōi kiji ga yomeru sō desu. Shikashi, mondaiten mo arimasu. Kono saito wa, ichinichi ni ikkai shika atarashiku naranai node, sukoshi furui nyūsu shika yomenai koto mo aru sō desu. Demo, ichinichi mae no nyūsu o yomu tame niwa, ii saito deshō.

Questions 16-H

1. What does the word "later" refer to? (A. things the writer does not want to do, B. things the writer wants someone else to do, C. things the writer does not have to do now, D. things the writer wants to do now, but doesn't have time for)
2. Where did the name "Atode Newspaper" come from? (A. news articles that people wanted to read later, B. news articles that people saved for future reference, C. the practice of saving newspapers for historical purposes, D. stories that will be written about in newspapers later)
3. What kinds of online articles does the writer mention? (A. articles that not many people want to read, B. articles that many people want to read, C. articles on which more than one writer collaborated, D. the articles with some problems to be fixed later)
4. What is the main drawback of these online articles? (A. the top news may not be important news, B. you may have to read the news not many people want to read, C. you can only read unusual news, D. the site is not updated many times per day)

Lesson 16 Practice

A. Kanji Review

Write the 15 "description" kanji characters in this lesson. Use the mnemonic pictures if needed.

new	old	beautiful	young	long	fat	high, tall	inex-pensive, peace
1.	2.	3.	4.	5.	6.	7.	8.
				タロ		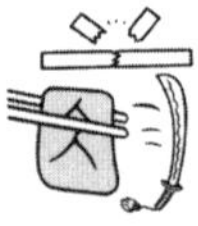	
fun	bright	wide	have	name (actually spelled たろう)		before	after
9.	10.	11.	12.	13.		14.	15.

B. Commonly Mistaken Kanji

Which kanji correctly expresses the meaning of the English word? Circle the most appropriate kanji character.

1. have	右	式	有	左	在	存
2. fat	犬	大	夫	太	人	入
3. fun	薬	楽	柔	葉	課	果
4. high, tall	呂	宮	京	商	高	売
5. bright	昨	的	明	有	泊	消
6. new	親	近	所	現	部	新

7. wide	店	台	去	広	公	反
8. inexpensive, peace	家	字	安	完	空	守
9. old	仕	吉	赤	土	古	占
10. name	外	名	右	多	夕	台
11. young	花	石	芋	英	右	若
12. before	首	側	例	前	判	道
13. beautiful	美	洋	羊	業	様	着
14. after	行	待	術	終	後	降
15. long	走	表	長	衣	馬	鳥

C. Vocabulary Review

Write these vocabulary and phrases using the appropriate kanji and kana characters. The number in the parentheses represents how many kanji you should write. An asterisk (*) indicates you should use okurigana (the hiragana part of kanji words). You may select from the word bank below.

1. long legs (2)*	2. mayor (2)
3. inexpensive car (2)*	4. to be relieved (2)*
5. old book (2)*	6. newspaper (2)
7. eldest son (2)	8. fun class (1)*
9. high school (2)	10. young teacher (3)*
11. new friend (2)*	12. to enjoy soccer (1)*
13. bright room (1)*	14. eldest daughter (2)

15. length (1)*	16. tomorrow (2)
17. comfortable chair (1)*	18. used, secondhand (2)
19. expensive shoes (1)*	20. spacious house (2)*
21. beautiful picture (1)*	22. fat dog (2)*
23. famous place (2)	24. ten years later (3)
25. my name (3)*	26. famous person (3)*
27. after school (3)*	28. before class (1)*
29. three years before (3)	

新しい友だち　新聞　古い本　中古　美しいえ　若い先生　長い足
長さ　市長　長男　長女　高いくつ　高校　安い車　安心する
楽しいじゅぎょう　サッカーを楽しむ　楽ないす　明るいへや　明日
広い家　名所　有名な人　私の名前　じゅぎょうの前　三年前
学校の後で　十年後　太っている犬

D. Opposites

Write the kanji which means the opposite of the words below.

1. せまい	2. やせています	3. たかい
4. つまらない	5. みにくい	6. ふるい
7. あと	8. あたらしい	9. みじかい
10. せがひくい	11. まえ	12. 年をとっています

E. Common Japanese Last Names

Match these common Japanese last names in kanji with their pronunciations and meanings.

前田 ______ ______	1. たかぎ	A. (fat/great, rice field)
高木 ______ ______	2. ふるかわ	B. (before, rice field)
広田 ______ ______	3. おおた	C. (tall, tree)
古川 ______ ______	4. わかばやし	D. (young, small forest)
若林 ______ ______	5. ひろた	E. (old, river)
太田 ______ ______	6. まえだ	F. (wide, rice field)

F. Review Questions

Try writing these sentences in Japanese using kanji whenever appropriate. Each sentence has at least one new kanji from this lesson. Then, compare your translations with the answer key at the end of the book.

1. Have you made any new friends this year? ______________________
2. How many times per week do you read the newspaper? ______________________
3. Is your English textbook old? ______________________
4. Do you drive a used car? ______________________
5. What kinds of paintings do you think are beautiful? ______________________
6. Are your grandparents young? ______________________
7. Do you like long hair? ______________________
8. Is it good to be born the oldest son/daughter in the family? ______________________
9. Are there many fat people? ______________________
10. Were your shoes expensive? ______________________
11. When did you come to this high school? ______________________
12. Do you want a cheap car? ______________________

13. Is your math class fun? ______________________________

14. Who is the most cheerful person in class? ______________________________

15. Is your house spacious? ______________________________

16. Who is more famous, Hayao Mizaki or Akira Kurosawa? ______________________________

17. Do you know how to write your name in kanji? ______________________________

18. What do you usually do after school? ______________________________

G. Interview Your Partner

Take turns asking the above questions with your partner. Try to answer as fully and appropriately as you can. For best results, you should elaborate on your answers whenever possible.

H. Read and Respond

Imagine you are a student named Alex, who has just received the following email from the Morita family. Reply to the email in the space provided. You should give reasons for your choice.

アレックスさん

こんにちは。はじめまして。
来月、私たちの家にホームステイに来るんですね。楽しみにしています。
さて、私たちの家の近所には、おもしろい所がたくさんあります。

たとえば、歩いて30分ぐらいの所に勉強の神様で有名な神社があります。途中(とちゅう)に日本の伝統的な家がたくさんあるので、さんぽをしながら行くと楽しいですよ。また、自転車で20分ぐらい行くと、日本のまんがやアニメのDVDがたくさんある図書館(としょかん)もあります。ここもとてもおもしろいです。そして、電車で1時間ぐらいの所に、小さいお城(しろ)があります。お城のまわりにたくさんお店があって、おみやげを買うこともできます。お城の近くの公園(こうえん)で、ピクニックをすることもできますよ。

アレックスさんが私たちの家に来ている間に、一日、自由(じゆう)時間がありますね。時間がないので、全部(ぜんぶ)に行くことはできませんから、来る前に、どんな所に行きたいか考(かんが)えて、私たちに教えてください。

返事(へんじ)を待っています。

森田

途中(とちゅう)	on the way	自由(じゆう)	free
全部(ぜんぶ)	all	返事(へんじ)	reply

166 族

Family, tribe

丶	亠	方	方	方'	方𠂉	方𠂉	方𠂉
方𠂉	方𠂉	族					

Eleven (11) strokes
A tribe that hunts together in the same direction

■ Trace the gray lines, and then practice on your own.

族									
族									

■ Useful vocabulary: Write the character, and trace the gray ones.

家		かぞく	**kazoku**	family
民		* みんぞく	**minzoku**	race

167 様

Formal title, Mr./Mrs./Ms./Miss

一	十	才	木	木'	木''	木⺷	木⺷
木⺷	样	样	样	様	様		

Fourteen (14) strokes
A pleasant picture of sheep watering near a forest. This kanji is a pleasant mode of address that shows politeness toward others.

■ Trace the gray lines, and then practice on your own.

様									
様									

■ Useful vocabulary: Write the character, and trace the gray ones.

田	中			たなかさま	**tanaka sama**	Mr./Mrs./Ms./Miss Tanaka
	々	な		さまざまな	**samazama na**	various
	子			ようす	**yōsu**	situation, status, appearance
こ	の		に	このように	**kono yōni**	in this way

* An asterisk denotes vocabulary with kanji that have not yet been introduced.

Reading 17-A

テレビをつけると、毎日、たくさんのおもしろい番組(ばんぐみ)を見ることができます。その中でも、とても人気があるものの一つが、「家族」という番組です。毎回、日本の様々な所に行って、そこに住んでいる色々(いろいろ)な家族と話をするのです。この番組では、それぞれの家族の色々な話が聞けます。また、そこに住んでいる人がやっているしごとについておしえてもらったり、そこでしか見られないけしきを見たり、そこでしか食べられない物を食べたりします。家族のおもしろい話も、かなしい話も、すごい話も作られたものではありません。ぜんぶ本当(ほんとう)なので、この番組は人気があるそうです。

Terebi o tsukeru to, mainichi, takusan no omoshiroi bangumi o miru koto ga dekimasu. Sono naka demo, totemo ninki ga aru mono no hitotsu ga, "kazoku" to iu bangumi desu. Maikai, nihon no samazama na tokoro ni itte, soko ni sunde iru iroiro na kazoku to hanashi o suru no desu. Kono bangumi dewa, sorezore no kazoku no iroiro na hanashi ga kikemasu. Mata, soko ni sunde iru hito ga yatte iru shigoto nitsuite oshiete morattari, soko de shika mirarenai keshiki o mitari, soko de shika taberarenai mono o tabetari shimasu. Kazoku no omoshiroi hanashi mo, kanashii hanashi mo, sugoi hanashi mo tsukurareta mono dewa arimasen. Zenbu hontō na node, kono bangumi wa ninki ga aru sō desu.

Questions 17-A

1. What kind of TV program is "The Family"? (A. drama, B. sitcom, C. documentary, D. cartoon)
2. What is "The Family" about? (A. a typical Japanese family, B. a foreign family, C. families from various places in Japan, D. the royal family of Japan)
3. What do viewers learn about from "The Family"? (A. traditional Japanese customs, B. the cultures of different countries, C. how to get along with various personality types, D. the jobs of various Japanese families)
4. Why is "The Family" popular? (A. because is it funny, B. because it is clever, C. because it teaches traditional values, D. because it is based on actual events)

168 主 Master

Stroke order: 丶 亠 亍 丰 主

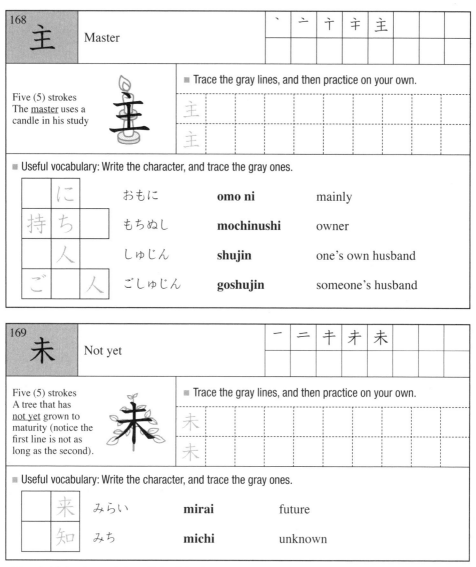

Five (5) strokes
The <u>master</u> uses a candle in his study

■ Trace the gray lines, and then practice on your own.

主
主

■ Useful vocabulary: Write the character, and trace the gray ones.

［ ］に	おもに	**omo ni**	mainly
持ち［ ］	もちぬし	**mochinushi**	owner
［ ］人	しゅじん	**shujin**	one's own husband
ご［ ］人	ごしゅじん	**goshujin**	someone's husband

169 未 Not yet

Stroke order: 一 二 キ 未 未

Five (5) strokes
A tree that has <u>not yet</u> grown to maturity (notice the first line is not as long as the second).

■ Trace the gray lines, and then practice on your own.

未
未

■ Useful vocabulary: Write the character, and trace the gray ones.

［ ］来	みらい	**mirai**	future
［ ］知	みち	**michi**	unknown

* An asterisk denotes vocabulary with kanji that have not yet been introduced.

Reading 17-B

二十年前に私たちの会社では「未来の電話コンテスト」をしました。その時にある子どもが小さくて、持って歩くことができる電話の絵(え)をかきました。それは、今のけいたい電話とおなじような電話だったのです。子どものゆめが、二十年後にはたくさんの人が使っている物になりました。

そこで、私たちの会社では、今年も子どもたちに未来の絵をかいてもらって、大人にも未来についてかんがえてもらうことにしました。テーマは「未来の生活(せいかつ)」です。「ぼくはこうしているだろう」とか「私はこんな物がほしい」と思うことを絵にかいてください。いつか、その絵にかいてあることが、本当(ほんとう)になるかもしれません。コンピューターでかいても、手でかいてもいいです。小学一年生から高校三年生の人はぜひさんかしてください。

ゆめ	dream	本当(ほんとう)	real, truth, fact
さんか	to participate		

Nijūnen mae ni watashi tachi no kaisha dewa "mirai no denwa kontesuto" o shimashita. Sono toki ni aru kodomo ga chiisakute, motte aruku koto ga dekiru denwa no e o kakimashita. Sore wa, ima no keitai denwa to onaji yō na denwa datta no desu. Kodomo no yume ga, nijūnengo niwa takusan no hito ga tsukatte iru mono ni narimashita.

Soko de, watashi tachi no kaisha dewa, kotoshi mo kodomo tachi ni shōrai no e o kaite moratte, otona nimo shōrai nitsuite kangaete morau koto ni shimashita. Tēma wa "mirai no seikatsu" desu. "Boku wa kō shite iru darō" toka "watashi wa konna mono ga hoshii" to omou koto o e ni kaite kudasai. Itsuka, sono e ni kaite aru koto ga hontō ni naru kamoshiremasen. Konpyūtā de kaitemo, te de kaitemo ii desu. Shōgaku ichinensei kara kōkō sannensei no hito wa zehi sanka shite kudasai.

Questions 17-B

1. What is the purpose of this passage? (A. to announce the contest winners, B. to encourage contest participation, C. to describe the contest rules, D. to notify people that the contest has been cancelled)
2. What surprised the company? (A. the accuracy of a child's dream, B. the popularity of the cell phone, C. the complaints of the customers, D. the shopping trends of the customers)
3. What is the new theme mentioned in the passage? (A. telephones of the future, B. schools of the future, C. life in the future, D. homes of the future)
4. What are participants invited to do? (A. draw on the computer, B. enter the contest online, C. enter the contest by phone, D. get their application fee refunded)

170 姉 Big sister

く	女	女	女'	女亠	女	女	姉

Eight (8) strokes
Big sister goes to the market

■ Trace the gray lines, and then practice on your own.

姉
姉

■ Useful vocabulary: Write the character, and trace the gray ones.

□	あね	**ane**	one's older sister
お□さん	おねえさん	**onēsan**	older sister

171 妹 Little sister

く	女	女	女一	女二	女	女	妹

Eight (8) strokes
Little sister is not yet a woman

■ Trace the gray lines, and then practice on your own.

妹
妹

■ Useful vocabulary: Write the character, and trace the gray ones.

□	いもうと	**imōto**	little sister
姉□	しまい	**shimai**	sisters
姉□校	しまいこう	**shimaikō**	sister school
姉□都市 *	しまいとし	**shimaitoshi**	sister city

* An asterisk denotes vocabulary with kanji that have not yet been introduced.

Reading 17-C

アナさんは、ある日新聞で姉妹都市についてのきじを読みました。アナさんの住んでいる町には、日本やドイツに姉妹都市があります。その新聞によると、その姉妹都市に住んでいる人たちの交流(こうりゅう)のために、日本かドイツに行きたい人をさがしているそうです。日本やドイツの文化にきょうみがある高校生か大学生で、来年の七月に二週間、その国に行ける人です。飛行機代(ひこうきだい)は、町がはらってくれるそうです。くわしいことは、町の姉妹都市センターに聞かなければなりません。アナさんは、大学で日本語を勉強しているので、夏(なつ)休みにぜひ日本に行きたいと思いました。

きじ article　　交流(こうりゅう) exchange

Ana san wa, aru hi shinbun de shimaitoshi nitsuite no kiji o yomimashita. Ana san no sunde iru machi niwa, nihon ya doitsu ni shimaitoshi ga arimasu. Sono shinbun niyoru to, sono shimaitoshi ni sunde iru hito tachi no kōryū no tame ni, nihon ka doitsu ni ikitai hito o sagashite iru sō desu. Nihon ya doitsu no bunka ni kyōmi ga aru kōkōsei ka daigakusei de, rainen no shichigatsu ni nishūkan, sono kuni ni ikeru hito desu. Hikōkidai wa, machi ga haratte kureru sō desu. Kuwashii koto wa, machi no shimaitoshi sentā ni kikanakereba narimasen. Ana san wa, daigaku nihongo o benkyō shite iru node, natsu yasumi ni zehi nihon ni ikitai to omoimashita.

Questions 17-C

1. Where did Anna find the information? (A. a magazine article, B. a newspaper article, C. a town office, D. a university)
2. What is the town looking for? (A. people interested in working in the sister cities, B. students interested in visiting the sister cities, C. someone to advertise the sister cities, D. someone to work for the town's sister city center)
3. What is the town willing to do to support the participants? (A. pay for the airfare, B. purchase luggage, C. let students organize a trip, D. invite people from the sister cities)
4. What will Anna most likely do next? (A. go to Germany next February, B. find a part time job, C. contact the center, D. wait to hear from the town)

172 兄 Older brother

Stroke order: 丨 ⼌ 口 尸 兄

Five (5) strokes
Big brother has long legs and a big mouth

■ Trace the gray lines, and then practice on your own.

兄
兄

■ Useful vocabulary: Write the character, and trace the gray ones.

□	あに	**ani**	one's older brother
お□さん	おにいさん	**oniisan**	older brother
父□	ふけい	**fukei**	parents and guardians

173 弟 Younger brother

Stroke order: 丶 丷 䒑 当 弓 弟 弟

Seven (7) strokes
Little brother gets into mischief with his bow and arrow

■ Trace the gray lines, and then practice on your own.

弟
弟

■ Useful vocabulary: Write the character, and trace the gray ones.

□	おとうと	**otōto**	little brother
□子	でし	**deshi**	disciple
兄□	きょうだい	**kyōdai**	siblings, brothers

* An asterisk denotes vocabulary with kanji that have not yet been introduced.

Reading 17-D

プロ野球(やきゅう)の選手(せんしゅ)になった兄弟がいます。弟が今年、高校を卒業(そつぎょう)する前に、プロ野球のチームに入ることがきまりました。インタビューによると、弟は、「兄とちがうチームに入りたかったです。兄と試合(しあい)をして、かちたかったからです。」と言ったそうです。でも、兄は、「弟といっしょのチームでよかったです。ぼくが色々(いろいろ)なことを教えてあげられるからです。それに、弟にまけないように、がんばろうと思えるからです。」と言いました。二人を小学生のころ教えていたリトルリーグのコーチは、「プロ野球はとてもきびしい。二人ともがんばって練習をして、いい選手になってほしい。」と言いました。

Puro yakyū no senshu ni natta kyōdai ga imasu. Otōto ga kotoshi, kōkō o sotsugyō suru mae ni, puro yakyū no chiimu ni hairu koto ga kimarimashita. Intabyū niyoru to, otōto wa, "Ani to chigau chiimu ni hairitakatta desu. Ani to shiai o shite, kachitakatta desu" to itta sō desu. Demo, ani wa, "Otōto to issho no chiimu de yokatta desu. Boku ga iroiro na koto o oshiete agerareru kara desu. Sore ni, otōto ni makenai yōni, ganbarō to omoeru kara desu." to iimashita. Futari o shōgakusei no koro oshiete ita ritoruriigu no kōchi wa, "Puro yakyū wa totemo kibishii. Futari tomo ganbatte renshū o shite, ii senshu ni natte hoshii." to iimashita.

Questions 17-D

1. What is this passage about? (A. two brothers who play on the same high school baseball team, B. two brothers who play on the same professional baseball team, C. two brothers who play on different professional baseball teams, D. two brothers who coach professional baseball)
2. What is the younger brother's personality? (A. competitive, B. thoughtful, C. timid, D. stubborn)
3. What is the older brother's opinion? (A. the same as the younger brother's, B. different from his younger brother's, C. neutral, D. has same as the coach)
4. The coach in the passage used to: (A. attend the brothers' school, B. coach the brothers in high school, C. be a professional baseball player, D. coach the brothers in elementary school)

Lesson 17 Practice

A. Kanji Review

Try writing these words in kanji. Use the mnemonic pictures for hints if needed.

 tribe, group	 formal title	 main	 not yet
1.	2.	3.	4.
 older sister	 little sister	 older brother	 little brother
5.	6.	7.	8.

B. Commonly Mistaken Kanji

Which kanji correctly expresses the meaning of the English word? Circle the most appropriate kanji character.

1.	little brother	兄	弟	引	弓	剃	張
2.	formal title	洋	遅	様	美	着	業
3.	older sister	布	柿	帚	妹	姉	好
4.	main	住	王	柱	主	全	任
5.	tribe, group	訪	旅	防	族	坊	放
6.	older brother	元	只	弟	見	尺	兄

7.	little sister	姉	妹	好	安	味	柿
8.	not yet	味	末	未	米	来	春

C. Vocabulary Review

Write these vocabulary and phrases with the appropriate kanji and kana when needed. The number in the parentheses indicates the number of kanji, and an asterisk tells if there are any kana. You may choose from the word bank below.

1. owner (2)*	2. older sister – polite form (1)*
3. little brother (1)	4. Mr./Mrs./Ms./Miss Tanaka – formal (3)
5. Various (2)	6. my older brother (1)
7. future (2)	8. one's own husband (2)
9. older brother – polite form (1)*	10. my older sister (1)
11. family (2)	12. siblings, brothers (2)
13. little sister (1)	14. situation, appearance (2)
15. sisters (2)	16. disciple (2)
17. in this way (1)*	18. parents and guardians (2)
19. unknown (2)	20. mainly (1)*
21. sister school (3)	22. husband – polite form (2)*

家族	田中様	様々	様子	この様に	主に
持ち主	主人	ご主人	未来	未知	妹
姉	お姉さん	姉妹	姉妹校	弟	弟子
兄	お兄さん	兄弟	父兄		

D. Vocabulary Writing – Describe Your Family

Suppose that Tanaka Kei, your email pen pal in Japan, asked you to tell about your family. Give a brief description of your family, including names, ages, and grades or occupations. Be sure to use the informal family terms.

E. Review Questions

Try writing these sentences in Japanese using kanji whenever appropriate. Each sentence has at least one new kanji from this lesson. Then, compare your translations with the answer key at the end of the book.

1. How many people are in your family? ______________________________

2. Is there a Mr. Tanaka here? ______________________________

3. Can you eat with chopsticks like the Japanese? ______________________________

4. What do you mainly want to study in college? ______________________________

5. Who was the previous owner of your house? ______________________________

6. Does Mrs. Tanaka's husband speak English? ______________________________

7. Do you think the car of the future will run on electricity? ______________________________

8. Do you want to travel to unknown places? ______________________________

9. Does your little sister borrow your music books? ______________________________

10. Does your older sister sometimes cook for you? ______________________________

11. What kind of gift should we give to our sister school? ______________________

____

12. Is your little brother fast at running? ______________________

____

13. Is your older brother married? ______________________

____

14. Do you quarrel with your siblings? ______________________

____

F. Interview Your Partner

Take turns asking the above questions with your partner. Try to answer as fully and appropriately as you can. For best results, you should elaborate on your answers whenever possible.

G. Read and Respond

Read the following school notice that came in the mail. Then answer the questions that follow.

お知らせ

日本にある大学に行きたいと思っている生徒さんのための集会が行われます。校長やカウンセラーの話を聞いたり、入学願書の書き方を教えてもらったり、卒業生からのアドバイスをもらったりすることができます。高校二、三年生や父兄の皆様は、ぜひいらして下さい。質問があったら、学校までお電話ください。

日時：11月23日(水) 七時から八時半まで
場所：103号室
よろしくおねがいします。

願書 application　　　号室 room number

1. What is the subject of this notice? ____________________
2. What date will the event be held? ____________________
3. What day of the week? ____________________
4. What time? ____________________
5. Where will it be held? ____________________
6. What types of information will there be? ____________________
7. Who will be speaking? ____________________
8. Who is invited? ____________________
9. Why is the phone number given? ____________________

174 住

Live, reside

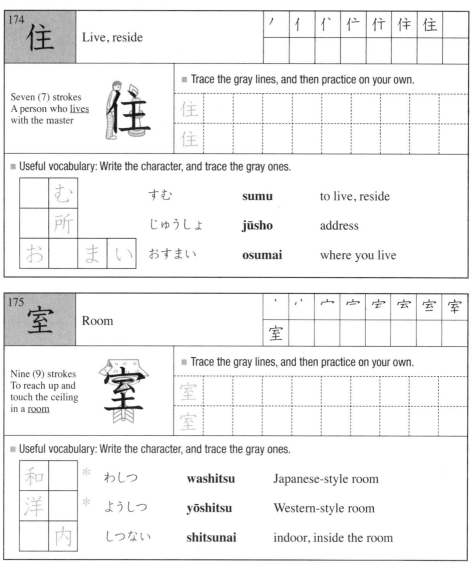

Seven (7) strokes
A person who lives with the master

■ Trace the gray lines, and then practice on your own.

住
住

■ Useful vocabulary: Write the character, and trace the gray ones.

すむ	**sumu**	to live, reside	[ ]む
じゅうしょ	**jūsho**	address	[ ]所
おすまい	**osumai**	where you live	お[ ]まい

175 室

Room

室

Nine (9) strokes
To reach up and touch the ceiling in a room

■ Trace the gray lines, and then practice on your own.

室
室

■ Useful vocabulary: Write the character, and trace the gray ones.

和[ ] *	わしつ	**washitsu**	Japanese-style room
洋[ ] *	ようしつ	**yōshitsu**	Western-style room
[ ]内	しつない	**shitsunai**	indoor, inside the room

* An asterisk denotes vocabulary with kanji that have not yet been introduced.

Reading 18-A

みんなが住んでいる家で、自分のためにも地球（ちきゅう）のためにもいい、エコなことができます。それを家（うち）でできるエコ、つまり「うちエコ」といいます。「うちエコ」は様々なやり方がありますが、今回は服（ふく）と食べ物について話します。

まず、服は、冬のさむい時にもう1まいセーターを着たり、あたたかい冬用の下着をはいたりするといいです。ヒーターの温度（おんど）を上げなくてもいいからです。また、食事でも「うちエコ」ができます。たとえば、あたたかい物やからい物を食べると体があたたまります。その中でも、冬の日本料理の「なべ」はとてもいいそうです。なべをすると、室内だけでなく、体もあたたかくなるからです。

みなさんも「うちエコ」で地球にいいことを始めてみませんか。一人では何も変（か）わらないかもしれないけれど、みんなの力を合（あ）わせれば、きっと何か変わると思いますよ！

地球（ちきゅう）	earth	あたたまる	(something) warms up

Minna ga sunde iru ie de, jibun no tame nimo chikyū no tame ni mo ii, eko na koto ga dekimasu. Sore o uchi de dekiru eko, tsumari "uchi eko" to iimasu. "Uchi eko" wa samazama na yari kata ga arimasu ga, konkai wa fuku to tabemono nitsuite hanashimasu.

Mazu, fuku wa, fuyu no samui toki ni mō ichimai sētā o kitari, atatakai fuyu yō no shitagi o haitari suru to ii desu. Hiitā no ondo o agenakutemo ii kara desu. Mata, shokuji demo "uchi eko" ga dekimasu. Tatoeba, atatakai mono ya karai mono o taberu to karada ga atatamarimasu. Sono naka demo, fuyu no nihon ryōri no "nabe" wa totemo ii sō desu. Nabe o suru to, shitsunai dake denaku, karada mo atatakaku naru kara desu.

Minasan mo "uchi eko" de chikyū ni ii koto o hajimete mimasen ka. Hitori dewa nanimo kawaranai kamoshirenai keredo, minna no chikara o awasereba, kitto nanika kawaru to omoimasu yo!

Questions 18-A

1. What does the word "**eko**" mean in this passage? (A. economy, B. echo, C. *e. coli*, D. ecology)
2. How many clothing suggestions are there? (A. two, B. three, C. four, D. five)
3. Which of the following suggestions is given in the passage? (A. to eat in a heated room, B. to wash your food, C. to eat reasonably priced food, D. to eat spicy food)
4. Why should people eat the Japanese food called **nabe**? (A. because it is tasty, B. because it is cheap, C. because it makes both the room and body warm, D. because it keeps fresh for a long time)

176 部 Section

Eleven (11) strokes
A person standing on a stone, building a section of a stone wall

■ Trace the gray lines, and then practice on your own.

部
部

■ Useful vocabulary: Write the character, and trace the gray ones.

	屋	へや	**heya**	room
一		いちぶ	**ichibu**	one part
	分	ぶぶん	**bubun**	part

177 屋 Roof, shop

Nine (9) strokes
To reach up and touch the ceiling of a shop

■ Trace the gray lines, and then practice on your own.

屋
屋

■ Useful vocabulary: Write the character, and trace the gray ones.

本		ほんや	**honya**	bookstore
魚		さかなや	**sakanaya**	fish market
	上	おくじょう	**okujō**	rooftop
	外	おくがい	**okugai**	outdoors

* An asterisk denotes vocabulary with kanji that have not yet been introduced.

Reading 18-B (18-A continued)

毎日の生活(せいかつ)の中で、みんなが少し気をつけて何かを変えると、エネルギーを使いすぎなくてもいいです。「うちエコ」のもう一つのポイントは、部屋です。たとえば、エアコンやヒーターのフィルターを1ヶ月に1回そうじすると、使うエネルギーをへらすことができます。それに、みんなでおなじ部屋にいることも大切(たいせつ)だそうです。たとえば、家族五人がちがう部屋にいると、たくさん電気やエネルギーを使います。でも、みんなが一つの部屋にいると、電気やエアコンやヒーターも一つしか使わなくていいです。今日からみなさんも「うちエコ」をしませんか。一人では何もできなくても、みんなでやれば何かが変(か)わるかもしれませんよ！

生活(せいかつ) life　　　へらす to reduce

Mainichi no seikatsu no naka de, minna ga sukoshi ki o tsukete nanika o kaeru to, enerugii o tsukai suginakutemo ii desu. “Uchi eko” no mō hitotsu no pointo wa, heya desu. Tatoeba, eakon ya hiitā o ikkagetsu ni ikkai sōji suru to, tsukau enerugii o herasu koto ga dekimasu. Sore ni, minna de onaji heya ni iru koto mo taisetsu da sō desu. Tatoeba, kazoku gonin ga chigau heya ni iru to, takusan denki ya enerugii o tsukaimasu. Demo, minna ga hitotsu no heya ni iru to, denki ya eakon ya hiitā mo hitotsu shika tsukawanakute ii kara desu. Kyō kara minasan mo “uchi eko” o shimasen ka. Hitori dewa nanimo dekinakutemo, minna de yareba nanika ga kawaru kamoshiremasen yo!

Questions 18-B

1. How does this passage suggest conserving fuel? (A. by walking more, B. by eating more raw foods, C. by changing simple daily routines, D. by giving community service)
2. How often should air conditioner filters be cleaned? (A. every year, B. twice a year, C. once a month, D. once a week)
3. What can families do to minimize fuel use? (A. talk about conservation, B. share room use, C. help neighbors learn about conservation, D. take turns preparing meals)
4. When does the writer suggest turning the heating/cooling off? (A. when sleeping at night, B. when no one is using the room, C. when cooking, D. when wearing extra layers of clothing)

178 和

Harmony, Japanese style

Eight (8) strokes
When all the mouths are fed (grain) there is more harmony

■ Trace the gray lines, and then practice on your own.

和
和

■ Useful vocabulary: Write the character, and trace the gray ones.

		わ	**wa**	harmony
食		わしょく	**washoku**	Japanese-style food
服	*	わふく	**wafuku**	Japanese clothing, kimono
牛		わぎゅう	**wagyū**	Japanese beef

179 洋

Ocean, Western style

Nine (9) strokes
The waves on the ocean appear to be a flock of sheep

■ Trace the gray lines, and then practice on your own.

洋
洋

■ Useful vocabulary: Write the character, and trace the gray ones.

西		せいよう	**seiyō**	the West
東		とうよう	**tōyō**	the East
食		ようしょく	**yōshoku**	Western-style food
大西		たいせいよう	**taiseiyō**	Atlantic Ocean
太平	*	たいへいよう	**taiheiyō**	Pacific Ocean

* An asterisk denotes vocabulary with kanji that have not yet been introduced.

Reading 18-C

グルメタウンへようこそ

グルメタウンは、デパートの11階(かい)にあって、和食、洋食、中国りょうり、エスニックなど様々な食事(しょくじ)が楽しめます。今月、おすすめのお店(みせ)をしょうかいします。

みさき屋：おさしみやおすしや天ぷらなどが食べられる和食のレストランです。魚がおいしいので有名です。夜(よる)はけしきがきれいですから、ロマンチックな食事ができます。

ミラノのあさ：スパゲッティやピザだけでなく、おいしいワインやイタリアのデザートもあります。明るくて楽しくて、ふんいきがいいお店です。とても広いので、たくさんの人とパーティができます。ケーキセットは大人気です。

ロータス：ベトナムのりょうりを食べたことがありますか。やさいをたくさん食べたかったら、ぜひロータスへ。とてもやさしい味(あじ)です。一回食べたら、わすれられないでしょう。一人でもだいじょうぶです。ぜひ来てください。

ふんいき　atmosphere　　味(あじ)　taste, flavor

Gurume taun e yōkoso

Gurume taun wa, depāto no jūikkai ni ate, washoku, yōshoku, chūgoku ryōri, esunikku nado samazama na shokuji ga tanoshimemasu. Kongetsu, osusume no omise o shōkai shimasu.

Misakiya: Osashimi ya osushi ya tenpura nado ga taberareru washoku no resutoran desu. Sakana ga oishii node yūmei desu. Yoru wa keshiki ga kirei desu kara, romanchikku na shokuji ga dekimasu.

Mirano no asa: Supagetti ya piza dake dewanaku, oishii wain ya itariya no dezāto mo arimasu. Akarukute tanoshikute, funiki ga ii omise desu. Totemo hiroi node, takusan no hito to pātii ga dekimasu. Kēki setto wa daininki desu.

Rōtasu: betonamu no ryōri o tabeta koto ga arimasu ka. Yasai o takusan tabetakattara, zehi rōtasu e. Totemo yasashii aji desu. Ikkai tabetara, wasurerarenai deshō. Hitori demo daijōjbu desu. Zehi kite kudasai.

Questions 18-C

1. What is this advertisement about? (A. a floating restaurant on the river, B. several new restaurants, C. an all-organic restaurant, D. several recommended restaurants)
2. Where might you go if you wanted dinner with a pleasant view? (A. the Japanese restaurant, B. the western food restaurant, C. the ethnic food restaurant, D. the Chinese restaurant)
3. The most popular menu item at Milan's Morning is (A. the spaghetti, B. the pizza, C. the salad, D. the dessert)
4. Where might you go to eat alone? (A. the Japanese restaurant, B. the western restaurant, C. the Vietnamese restaurant, D. the Chinese restaurant)

Lesson 18 Practice

A. Kanji Review

Try writing these words in kanji. Use the mnemonic pictures for hints if needed.

 live, reside	 room	 harmony, Japan	 Ocean, Western	 section	 roof, shop
1.	2.	3.	4.	5.	6.

B. Commonly Mistaken Kanji

Which kanji correctly expresses the meaning of the English word? Circle the most appropriate kanji character.

1. harmony, Japan	知	私	和	利	秋	科
2. roof, shop	遅	室	所	宝	屋	至
3. live, reside	主	住	柱	注	王	宝
4. section	院	都	倍	部	限	暗
5. room	宝	至	屋	空	客	室
6. ocean, Western	洋	注	様	法	羊	泣

C. Vocabulary Review

Write these vocabulary and phrases with the appropriate kanji and kana when needed. The number in the parentheses indicates the number of kanji, and an asterisk tells if there are any kana. You may choose from the word bank below.

1. Japanese-style food (2)	2. my address (3)*

3. western-style room (2)	4. the East, Eastern (2)
5. Atlantic Ocean (3)	6. my room (3)*
7. living in Japan (3)*	8. where the teacher lives (3)*
9. western-style food (2)	10. roof of the department store (2)*
11. outdoor pool (2)*	12. the West, Western (2)
13. Japanese-style room (2)	14. fish market (2)
15. bookstore (2)	16. computer parts (2)*
17. part of the cake (2)*	18. indoors, inside the room

日本に住んでいる　私の住所　先生のお住まい　和室　洋室　室内
和食　西洋　東洋　大西洋　洋食　私の部屋　コンピューターの部分
ケーキの一部　本屋　魚屋　デパートの屋上　屋外プール

D. Application: Types of Rooms and Types of Stores

Match the various types of rooms and stores listed below with their most appropriate Japanese counterparts. Write the matching Japanese word in the blanks.

1. bakery	________________	肉屋
2. classroom	________________	花屋
3. room	________________	パン屋
4. florist	________________	和菓子(がし)屋
5. pharmacist	________________	靴(くつ)屋
6. principal's office	________________	薬(くすり)屋

7. butcher shop ____________________ 八百屋

8. guest room ____________________ 教室（きょう）

9. library (room) ____________________ 校長室

10. Japanese sweets shop ____________________ 図書室（としょ）

11. bedroom ____________________ 保健室（ほけん）

12. vegetable stand ____________________ 部室

13. shoe store ____________________ 客室（きゃく）

14. nurse's office ____________________ 寝室

E. Japanese Last Names

Match these Japanese last names with the their meaning and common pronunciation. Note that many Japanese last names have multiple pronunciations, and those below are only one of several possible pronunciations.

和田 ________________ a. (harmony, song, mountain) わかやま

安部 ________________ b. (river, section) かわべ

川部 ________________ c. (middle, shop) なかや

中屋 ________________ d. (harmony, field) わだ

土屋 ________________ e. (earth, roof/shop) つちや

和歌山 ________________ f. (inexpensive/peace, part) あべ

F. Review Questions

Try writing these sentences in Japanese using kanji whenever appropriate. Each sentence has at least one new kanji from this lesson. Then, compare your translations with the answer key at the end of the book.

1. Do you like Japanese-style food? ________________________________

____

2. Do you think Japanese people often eat Western-style food? ______________

____

3. Have you sat in a Japanese-style room before? ______________

____

4. Where is the chemistry classroom? ______________

____

5. What is the address of our school? ______________

____

6. Where do you live? ______________

____

7. Do you have a TV in your room? ______________

____

8. Let's go to the bookstore today. ______________

____

G. Interview Your Partner

Take turns asking the above questions with your partner. Try to answer as fully and appropriately as you can. For best results, you should elaborate on your answers whenever possible.

H. Read and Respond

Suppose your class has been invited to respond to a discussion board sponsored by your sister school in Japan. The discussion board topic is comparing Japanese homes and Western homes. Read the discussion board prompt below, and respond as fully as possible.

日本に行ったことがある人、これから日本へ行こうと思っている人、日本語を勉強している人へ

日本フォーラムに参加（さんか）しませんか。このフォーラムでは、日本の文化や日本語について、みんなで考えます。

さて、今回のテーマは、「日本の家と西洋の家」です。

どんな違（ちが）いがありますか。考えて、三つの違いを書いてみましょう！

また、もっと書きたい人は、どうしてそれらの違いがあるかも考えて書いてください。

みなさんのポストを待っています。

日本語フォーラム
小林

180 知 To know

ノ	𠂉	𠂒	𠂒	矢	矢	知	知

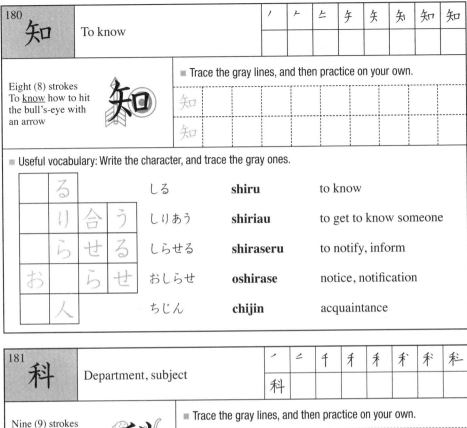

Eight (8) strokes
To know how to hit the bull's-eye with an arrow

■ Trace the gray lines, and then practice on your own.

知
知

■ Useful vocabulary: Write the character, and trace the gray ones.

知る	しる	**shiru**	to know
知り合う	しりあう	**shiriau**	to get to know someone
知らせる	しらせる	**shiraseru**	to notify, inform
お知らせ	おしらせ	**oshirase**	notice, notification
知人	ちじん	**chijin**	acquaintance

181 科 Department, subject

ノ	ニ	千	禾	禾	禾	禾	禾	科

Nine (9) strokes
A measurement of grain is a metaphor for the divisions of school departments

■ Trace the gray lines, and then practice on your own.

科
科

■ Useful vocabulary: Write the character, and trace the gray ones.

科目	かもく	**kamoku**	subject
教科書	きょうかしょ	**kyōkasho**	textbook
科学	かがく	**kagaku**	science

Reading 19-A

日本科学館(かん)は、子どもから大人まで楽しめる科学が好きな人のための国(こく)立(りつ)の博物館(はくぶつかん)です。新しい科学をたくさんの人に知ってもらうために作(つく)られました。色々(いろいろ)な科学者(しゃ)の見方がわかると、みなさんの世界(せかい)の見方もかわります。

開館時間：十時〜十七時
休館日　：毎週火曜日
入館料　：大人六百円、小学生〜高校生二百円

お知らせ1
今月のイベント

- 「おいしいよ。ヨーグルトのひみつ」
  毎週木曜日の十一時と二時（四十五分間）
- 「ロボットのふしぎ」
  第三土曜日の一時半から（一時間）
- 「サイエンス・ミニ・トーク」
  毎週月曜日の十一時、一時、三時（二十分間）

お知らせ2
科学館でボランティアをしませんか。ボランティアをすると、科学についてもっとよくわかります。また、色々な人と知り会って、新しい自分を知ることができます。今月は、科学館のツアーとサービスカウンターのボランティアをさがしています。

館(かん) building	博物館(はくぶつかん) museum

Nihon kagakukan wa, kodomo kara otona made tanoshimeru kagaku ga suki na hito no tame no kokuritsu no hakubutsukan desu. Atarashii kagaku o takusan no hito ni shitte morau tame ni tsukuraremashita. Iroiro na kagakusha no mikata ga wakaru to, minasan no sekai no mikata mo kawarimasu.

Kaikan jikan : jūji ~ jūshichiji
Kyūkanbi : maishū kayōbi
Nyūkanryō : otona roppyakuen, shōgakusei ~ kōkōsei nihyakuen

Oshirase 1
Kongetsu no ibento

- **"Oishii yo. Yōguruto no himitsu" – Maishū mokuyōbi no jūichiji (yonjūgofunkan)**
- **"Robotto no fushigi" – Dai san doyōbi no ichiji han kara (ichijikan)**
- **"Saiensu mini tōku" – Maishū getsuyōbi no jūichiji, ichiji, sanji (nijuppunkan)**

Oshirase 2
Kagakukan de borantia o shimasen ka. Borantia o suru to, kagaku nitsuite motto yoku wakarimasu. Mata, iroiro na hito to shiriatte, atarashii jibun o shiru koto ga dekimasu. Kongetsu wa, kagakukan no tsuā to sābisukauntā no borantia o sagashiteimasu.

Questions 19-A

1. What is the focus of the museum? (A. new science technology, B. physics, C. scientists, D. history of science development).
2. How much do college students pay for admission? (A. 200 yen, B. 400 yen, C. 600 yen, D. 800 yen)
3. What time does the event about robots finish? (A. 1:30, B. 2:00, C. 2:30, D. 3:00)
4. What is one of the benefits of being a volunteer at the museum? (A. free movie tickets, B. possible job opportunity in the future, C. meeting famous scientists, D. learning more about oneself)

182 教	Teach	一	十	土	耂	耂	孝	孝	孝
		孝	教	教					

Eleven (11) strokes
An older person guides the teaching of a younger person

■ Trace the gray lines, and then practice on your own.

教									
教									

■ Useful vocabulary: Write the character, and trace the gray ones.

[ ]える	おしえる	**oshieru**	to teach
[ ]室	きょうしつ	**kyōshitsu**	classroom, class, lesson
[ ]会	きょうかい	**kyōkai**	church

183 枚	Counter of sheets of things	一	十	才	木	木	杧	枚	枚

Eight (8) strokes
Tree pulp is pressed into sheets of paper

■ Trace the gray lines, and then practice on your own.

枚									
枚									

■ Useful vocabulary: Write the character, and trace the gray ones.

一[ ]の紙	いちまいのかみ	**ichimai no kami**	one sheet of paper

Reading 19-B

一枚の紙を通して環境問題について考えるための教室があります。この教室は、環境問題や紙の大切さを子どもたちに教えるために始まりました。ふつう紙をつくるためには、こうぞという木をつかいます。でも、こうぞは、一本の木が大きくなるまでにたくさんの時間がかかります。

そこでこの教室では、すぐに大きくなる竹をつかって紙をつくります。竹の紙は少しざらざらしていますが、とてもすてきです。それに自分で紙をつくると、みんな大切につかおうと思います。この教室を始めた人は、竹で紙を作った後環境を大切にしようと思う子どもがふえるのがうれしいそうです。

環境 (かんきょう)	environment	問題 (もんだい)	issue
竹 (たけ)	bamboo	ざらざら	rough

Ichimai no kami o tōshite, kankyō mondai nitsuite kangaeru tame no kyōshitsu o hiraite iru hito ga imasu. Kono kyōshitsu wa kankyō mondai ya kami no taisetsusa o kodomo tachi ni oshieru tame ni hajimarimashita. Futsū kami o tsukuru tame niwa, kōzo to iu ki o tsukaimasu. Demo, kōzo wa, ippon no ki ga ōkiku naru made ni takusan no jikan ga kakarimasu.

Soko de kono kyōshitsu dewa, sugu ni ōkiku naru take o tsukatte kami o tsukurimasu. Take no kami wa sukoshi zarazara shite imasu ga, totemo suteki desu. Jibun de kami o tsukuru to, minna taisetsu ni tsukaō to omoimasu. Kono kyōshitsu o hajimeta hito wa, take de kami o tsukutta ato, kankyō o taisetsu ni shiyō to omou kodomo ga fueru no ga ureshisō desu.

Questions 19-B

1. What is the objective of the class? (A. to teach about how newspapers are made, B. to teach how to wrap a present, C. to teach how to print on paper, D. to teach about environmental issues)
2. What is a **kōzo**? (A. a type of tree, B. a child who bullies others, C. another name for paper, D. the name of an environmental issue)
3. Why is bamboo used? (A. because the color is beautiful, B. because it is more traditional, C. because it is rough, D. because it grows quickly)
4. Why does the writer seem happy? (A. because many children attend the lessons, B. because the lessons will be advertised on TV, C. because many children care for the environment, D. because the environmental club membership has grown every year)

184 英

England, English, splendid

一	十	艹	艹	芇	苩	茟	英

Eight (8) strokes
The center of a flower (grass) is splendid

■ Trace the gray lines, and then practice on your own.

英
英

■ Useful vocabulary: Write the character, and trace the gray ones.

語	えいご	**eigo**	English
会話	えいかいわ	**eikaiwa**	English conversation
国	えいこく	**eikoku**	England, Great Britain

185 音

Sound

'	亠	亠	立	立	产	音	音
音							

Nine (9) strokes
The sound of a rooster as the sun come up

■ Trace the gray lines, and then practice on your own.

音
音

■ Useful vocabulary: Write the character, and trace the gray ones.

	おと	**oto**	sound
楽	おんがく	**ongaku**	music
楽家	おんがくか	**ongakuka**	musician
読み	おんよみ	**onyomi**	Chinese reading of kanji

Reading 19-C

あつ子さんは、英語が大好きで、英会話の教室に行っている。その教室では、新聞を読んだり、テレビを見たりした後で、そのトピックについて英語で話をする。あつ子さんは毎週英会話の教室に行くのを首(くび)を長くして待つほど大好きだが、とくに、今日のレッスンはとてもおもしろいと思った。それは、英語である音楽グループについての記事(きじ)を読んだからだ。あつ子さんはそのグループの音楽を聞いたことがあったが、だれが歌(うた)っているのか知らなかった。今日、そのグループがその歌を作った時のことについて習(なら)ったので、もっとその音楽が好きになった。来週は英会話の教室でその歌を歌うことになった。今週の宿題はその歌を英語で歌えるようになることだ。あつ子さんは英会話の教室でクラスメートと歌を歌うことをとても楽しみにしている。

首(くび)を長くして待つほど expression: "(She) can't wait."
(lit. (She) is waiting with a stretched out neck)

Atsuko san wa, eigo ga daisuki de, eikaiwa no kyōshitsu ni itte iru. Sono kyōshitsu dewa, shinbun o yondari, terebi o mitari shita atode, sono topikku nitsuite eigo de hanashi o suru. Atsuko san wa maishū eikaiwa no kyōshitsu ni iku no o kubi o nagaku shite matsu hodo daisuki da ga, tokuni, kyō no ressun wa totemo omoshiroi to omotta. Sore wa, eigo de aru ongaku gurūpu nitsuite no kiji o yonda kara da. Atsuko san wa sono gurūpu no ongaku o kiita koto ga atta ga, dare ga utatte iru no ka shiranakatta. Kyō, sono gurūpu ga sono uta o tsukutta toki no koto nitsuite naratta node, motto ongaku ga suki ni natta. Raishū wa eikaiwa no kyōshitsu de sono uta o utau koto ni natta. Konshū no shukudai wa sono uta o eigo de utaeru yōni naru koto da. Atsuko san wa eikaiwa no kyōshitsu de kurasumēto to uta o utau koto o totemo tanoshimi ni shite iru.

Questions 19-C

1. What do the students do after they read an article or watch a TV clip? (A. they write a summary in Japanese, B. they write a newspaper article in English, C. they discuss the topic in English, D. they talk about the topic in Japanese.)
2. How does Atsuko like attending the English class? (A. her parents make her attend the English class, B. she loves attending the English class, C. she only attends to get a good grade on her exams, D. she is a volunteer at the class, helping students with their English).
3. What did Atsuko know about the musical band her class studied? (A. she knew they were from England, B. she had heard the song before, but did not know who wrote it, C. she has met the members of the band, D. she knows the manager of the band)
4. What is Atsuko going to do next week? (A. learn about the musicians, B. start the English class, C. meet the musicians, D. sing the song in class)

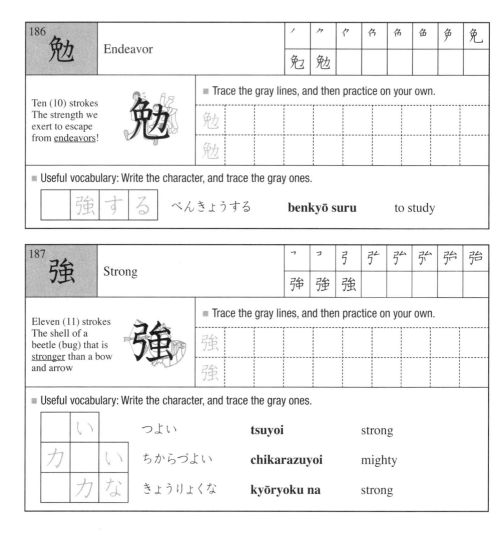

186 勉 Endeavor

Ten (10) strokes
The strength we exert to escape from <u>endeavors</u>!

■ Trace the gray lines, and then practice on your own.

勉
勉

■ Useful vocabulary: Write the character, and trace the gray ones.

	強	す	る	べんきょうする	**benkyō suru**	to study

187 強 Strong

Eleven (11) strokes
The shell of a beetle (bug) that is <u>stronger</u> than a bow and arrow

■ Trace the gray lines, and then practice on your own.

強
強

■ Useful vocabulary: Write the character, and trace the gray ones.

	い		つよい	**tsuyoi**	strong
力		い	ちからづよい	**chikarazuyoi**	mighty
	力	な	きょうりょくな	**kyōryoku na**	strong

Reading 19-D

みなさんは、勉強のし方について考(かんが)えたことがありますか。たとえば、日本語を勉強する時に、漢字(かんじ)はとても大切です。では、みなさんは、漢字をどうやって勉強していますか。漢字を見ておぼえる人、何回も書く人、おぼえやすくするために漢字の形(かたち)から話を作る人など、色々(いろいろ)いるでしょう。大切(たいせつ)なのは、自分に合(あ)った勉強のし方がわかっているかどうかです。日本語のクラスにいる人や先生と、勉強のし方について話し合ってみたらどうでしょうか。今まで知らなかった新しい勉強のし方を見つけることができるかもしれません。

形(かたち) shape

Minasan wa, benkyō no shikata nitsuite kangaeta koto ga arimasu ka. Tatoeba, nihongo o benkyō suru toki ni, kanji wa totemo taisetsu desu. Dewa, minasan wa, kanji o dōyatte benkyō shite imasu ka. Kanji o mite oboeru hito, nankaimo kaku hito, oboeyasuku suru tameni kanji no katachi kara hanashi o tsukuru hito nado, iroiro iru deshō. Taisetsu na no wa, jibun ni atta benkyō no shikata ga wakatteiru kadōka desu. Nihongo no kurasu ni iru hito ya sensei to benkyō no shikata nitsuite hanashiatte mitara dō deshō ka. Ima made shiranakatta atarashii benkyō no shikata o mitsukeru koto ga dekiru kamoshiremasen.

Questions 19-D

1. What does this passage state is important to Japanese studies? (A. pronunciation, B. kanji, C. grammar, D. vocabulary)
2. According to the passage, how do some people learn kanji? (A. they make up a story about the shape of the kanji, B. they use flash cards, C. they use computer programs, D. they teach kanji to others)
3. What is the main point of this passage? (A. to try various study methods, B. to not be overly concerned about your study, C. to write kanji repeatedly, D. to teach the best way of studying)
4. Why does the passage suggest talking with classmates and the teacher? (A. because you may learn new ways of teaching, B. because you may not know the newest techniques, C. because you might learn new ways of studying, D. because they might be better than you at studying kanji)

188 漢

Han Dynasty

Thirteen (13) strokes
During the Han Dynasty, China uses advanced irrigation techniques to feed its many (two) people

■ Trace the gray lines, and then practice on your own.

漢
漢

■ Useful vocabulary: Write the character, and trace the gray ones.

字	かんじ	**kanji**	kanji characters
文	かんぶん	**kanbun**	classical Chinese literature

189 紙

Paper

Ten (10) strokes
One's family names are written on a scroll of paper

■ Trace the gray lines, and then practice on your own.

紙
紙

■ Useful vocabulary: Write the character, and trace the gray ones.

	かみ	**kami**	paper
手	てがみ	**tegami**	letter
和	わし	**washi**	Japanese paper

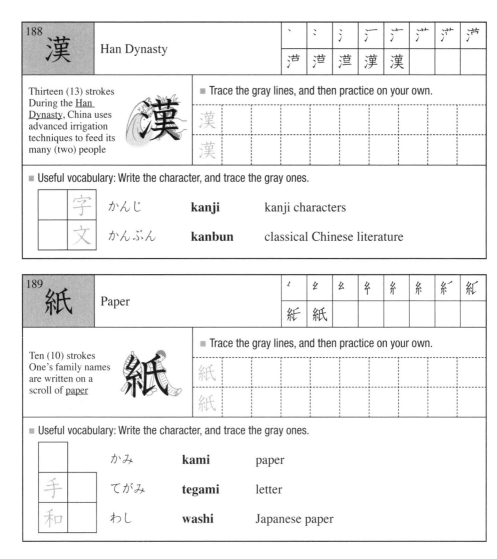

Reading 19-E

十二月十二日は漢字の日です。その日に京都(きょうと)のお寺で「今年の漢字」を発表(はっぴょう)します。毎年、十万人ぐらいの人がその年を表(あらわ)す漢字をえらびます。そして、一番多かった漢字を、そのお寺のおぼうさんが大きな和紙に大きなふでで書くのです。食べ物のもんだいがたくさんあった年は「食」、オリンピックで金メダルが多かった年には「金」など、毎年その年に何があったかわかる漢字がえらばれます。また、1900年代(だい)のさいごの1999年には「末」が一番多かったです。「末」は「まつ」と「すえ」と読みます。週末のまつで、おわりといういみと、これから先はよくなるという末広(すえひろ)がりのいみもあります。今年はどんな漢字がえらばれるでしょうか。

表(あらわ)す	to express, show	えらぶ	to select, to choose
発表(はっぴょう)	announce, release	(お)ぼうさん	a monk

Jūnigatsu jūninichi wa kanji no hi desu. Sono hi ni kyōto no otera de "kotoshi no kanji" o happyō shimasu. Maitoshi, jūmannin gurai no hito ga sono toshi o arawasu kanji o erabimasu. Soshite, ichiban ōkatta kanji o, sono otera no obōsan ga ōkina washi ni ōkina fude de kaku no desu. Tabemono no mondai ga takusan atta toshi wa "shoku", orinpikku de kin medaru ga ōkatta toshi niwa "kin" nado, maitoshi sono toshi ni nani ga attaka wakaru kanji ga erabaremasu. Mata, senkyūhyaku nendai no saigo no senkyūhyaku kyūjūkyūnen niwa "matsu" ga ichiban ōkatta desu. "Matsu" wa "matsu" to "sue" to yomimasu. Shūmatsu no matsu de, owari toiu imi to, korekara saki wa yoku naru toiu suehirogari no imi mo arimasu. Kotoshi wa donna kanji ga erabareru deshō ka.

Questions 19-E

1. What is announced on "kanji day"? (A. the winner of the national calligraphy contest, B. the kanji of the year, C. the new kanji to be added to the dictionary, D. the kanji that have been simplified in number of strokes)
2. How is the kanji chosen? (A. popular vote, B. temple monks, C. ministry of education, D. national board of education)
3. What does the kanji represent? (A. how many people named their baby using the kanji, B. which kanji the monks felt were most important, C. the name of the most popular temple, D. the things that people remember about the year)
4. Why was the kanji "**matsu/sue**" chosen? (A. because it had the most strokes, B. because it was the most often-used kanji among publishing companies, C. because it was the end of one century and the beginning of another, D. because Japan earned many gold medals in that year's Olympic games)

190 絵	Picture	㇛	㇜	幺	糸	糸	糸	糸	紒
		紒	紒	絵	絵				

Twelve (12) strokes
A picture is a collection (meeting) of lines on paper

■ Trace the gray lines, and then practice on your own.

絵
絵

■ Useful vocabulary: Write the character, and trace the gray ones.

☐	え	**e**	picture
☐はがき	えはがき	**ehagaki**	picture postcard

Reading 19-F

絵はがき教室

心のこもった絵はがきをかけるようになります。

はがきに自分で好きな絵をかくと、特別なものになります。

季節(きせつ)の絵や庭(にわ)にある花、魚やペットなどの動物をかいて、
だれかにはがきを送(おく)ってみませんか。

メールはすぐに届(とど)きます。でも、そんな時代(じだい)だからこそ、
絵はがきをもらった人はきっともっとよろこぶでしょう。

中学生からおじいさん、おばあさんまで、
色々(いろいろ)な人がさんかしている教室です。

絵はがきはむずかしくないです。ぜひ挑戦(ちょうせん)してみてください。

月、木、土の10時半、1時、3時半、6時から
5回のコース
15,000円（はがきなど材料(ざいりょう)とお茶代(だい)こみ）
木下カルチャーセンターで受付(うけつけ)をしてください。

挑戦(ちょうせん)	try, challenge	材料(ざいりょう)	materials, ingredients
こみ	included		

Ehagaki kyōshitsu

Kokoro no komotta ehagaki o kakeru yōni narimasu.

Hagaki ni jibun de suki na e o kaku to, tokubetsu na mono ni narimasu.

Kisetsu no e ya niwa ni aru hana, sakana ya petto nado no dōbutsu o kaite, darekani hagaki o okutte mimasen ka.

Mēru wa suguni todokimasu. Demo, sonna jidai dakara koso, ehagaki o moratta hito wa kitto motto yorokobu deshō.

Chūgakusei kara ojiisan, obāsan made, iroiro na hito ga sanka shite iru kyōshitsu desu.

Ehagaki wa muzukashikunai desu. Zehi chōsen shite mitekudasai.

Getsu, moku, do no jūjihan, ichiji, sanjihan, rokuji kara
Gokai kōsu
Ichiman gosen en (hagaki nado zairyō to ochadai komi)
Kinoshita karuchāsentā de uketsuke o shite kudasai.

Questions 19-F

1. What kind of writing is this? (A. a letter, B. an advertisement, C. a newspaper article, D. the script of a speech)
2. According to the passage, why are people happy to receive a picture postcard? (A. because some people do not have an email address, B. because postcards are cheap, C. because hand-written postcards are more heartfelt, D. because people love pictures)
3. Who attends the class mentioned in the passage? (A. middle school students, B. high school students, C. old people only, D. people of various ages)
4. What is the 15,000 yen used for? (A. five lessons, postcards, materials, and tea, B. pictures, flowers and fish, C. five drawing lessons, D. picture postcards of famous paintings)

Lesson 19 Practice

A. Kanji Review

Try writing these words in kanji. Use the mnemonic pictures for hints if needed.

 to know	 department, subject	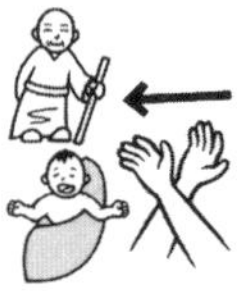 to teach	 counter for flat objects	 England, splendid	 sound
1.	2.	3.	4.	5.	6.
 endeavor	 strong	 Han Dynasty	 paper	 picture	
7.	8.	9.	10.	11.	

B. Commonly Mistaken Kanji

Which kanji correctly expresses the meaning of the English word? Circle the most appropriate kanji character.

1. strong	弟	風	第	虫	弱	強
2. counter for flat objects	教	村	枚	放	林	妹
3. Han Dynasty	難	洋	活	漢	注	洗
4. to teach	枚	教	者	暑	都	政
5. England, splendid	央	映	決	茶	英	前
6. picture	絵	紙	係	孫	糸	約

7. department, subject	私	移	和	斜	料	科
8. sound	部	暗	音	立	泣	新
9. paper	係	絵	糸	紙	孫	氏
10. endeavor	免	晩	娩	逸	勉	挽
11. to know	和	知	族	私	旅	味

C. Vocabulary Review

Write these vocabulary and phrases with the appropriate kanji and kana when needed. The number in the parentheses indicates the number of kanji, and an asterisk tells if there are any kana. You may choose from the word bank below.

1. one piece of paper (3)*	2. strange music (2)*
3. England (2)	4. my father's acquaintance (3)*
5. I don't know (1)*	6. favorite school subject (4)*
7. to study kanji (4)*	8. loud sound (1)*
9. church (2)	10. washi (Japanese paper) (2)
11. powerful way of writing (4)*	12. to inform the teacher (3)*
13. white paper (2)*	14. beautiful painting/picture (2)*
15. textbook (3)	16. English (2)

17. to teach Japanese (4)*	18. a letter to a friend (3)*
19. strong team (1)*	20. science classroom (4)*

知りません　先生に知らせる　父の知人　大好きな科目　教科書
科学の教室　日本語を教える　教会　一枚の紙　英語　英国
うるさい音　へんな音楽　漢字を勉強する　強いチーム
力強い書き方　白い紙　友だちへの手紙　和紙　美しい絵

D. Education and Medicine Related Terms

You may not understand all of the vocabulary below, but use the kanji to guess their meanings. Match the various education and medical related terms below with their appropriate Japanese counterparts. Write the katakana character of the matching Japanese word in the blanks.

1. Pediatrics	________	ア. 家庭(てい)科
2. Ear, Nose, Throat (ENT)	________	イ. 工学科
3. home economics	________	ウ. 英文科
4. internal medicine	________	エ. 国語科
5. engineering department	________	オ. 小児(しょうに)科
6. surgery	________	カ. 漢方薬(かんぽうやく)
7. English department	________	キ. 耳鼻咽喉(じびいんこう)科
8. Chinese herbal medicine	________	ク. 外(げ)科
9. Department of Japanese (as a school subject)	________	ケ. 内科

E. Counters Review

Match the phrases listed below with their most appropriate Japanese counterparts. Write the matching Japanese word in the blanks.

1. 300 yen	______________	二年（間）
2. two times, twice	______________	三分（間）
3. $3,000 dollars	______________	二回
4. one hour	______________	二日間
5. (for) two years	______________	一番
6. two pairs (shoes)	______________	二足
7. two days	______________	一か月
8. 10,000 yen	______________	三枚
9. (for) three minutes	______________	一時間
10. three sheets (e.g. paper)	______________	三百円
11. number one	______________	三千ドル
12. one month	______________	一万円

F. Review Questions

Try writing these sentences in Japanese using kanji whenever appropriate. Each sentence has at least one new kanji from this lesson. Then, compare your translations with the answer key at the end of the book.

1. What is your favorite school subject? ______________

____

2. Is your science classroom spacious? ______________

____

3. Are your school textbooks heavy? ______________

____

4. Do you think kanji characters are difficult to read? ____________________

____

5. Do you study Japanese every day? ____________________

____

6. Do you notify your teachers when you are going to be absent?

____

7. Do you submit English reports on paper or do you submit them by email?

____

8. What kind of music do you like? ____________________

____

9. Are you good at drawing pictures? ____________________

____

10. Do you know your state governor's name? ____________________

____

G. Interview Your Partner

Take turns asking the above questions with your partner. Try to answer as fully and appropriately as you can. For best results, you should elaborate on your answers whenever possible.

H. Read and Respond

Suppose your classmates in Japanese class have conducted interviews of Japanese immigrants to your country, and then posted the summaries of their interviews on the class website. Read the following summary and answer the questions in English.

生徒(と)：はじめまして。名前は、マイクです。どうぞよろしくお願(ねが)いします。

和田(わだ)：どうぞよろしく。

生徒：お名前は、何ですか。

和田：和田まりこです。

生徒：いつアメリカに来られましたか。

和田：二十年前に来ました。

生徒：ご主人とどこで会われましたか。

和田：珍(めずら)しいかもしれないけれど、私は、手紙で主人と知り合いました。

生徒：そうですか。アメリカに来られた時に困(こま)ったことがありましたか。

和田：英語があまりよく話せなかったので、いろいろなことに困(こま)りました。

生徒：子どもさんが、いらっしゃいますか。

和田：はい、息子(むすこ)が二人います。一人は、二年前に高校を卒業(そつぎょう)して、今、大学で科学を勉強しています。そしてもう一人は、高校三年生です。

生徒：でもお子さんのためにもがんばったんですね。今日はお忙(いそが)しい所、ありがとうございました。

珍(めずら)しい　unusual, rare　　　困(こま)る　to be troubled

1. What is the name of the person the student interviewed (hiragana or romaji)?

____

2. When did she come to America?

____

3. How did she meet her husband?

____

4. What kinds of troubles did she encounter when she first came to America?

____

5. How many children does she have?

____

6. What is her oldest son studying?

____

191 肉 Meat, flesh

丨	冂	内	内	肉	肉		

Six (6) strokes
A thin slice of meat

■ Trace the gray lines, and then practice on your own.

肉
肉

■ Useful vocabulary: Write the character, and trace the gray ones.

肉	にく	**niku**	flesh, meat
牛肉	ぎゅうにく	**gyūniku**	beef
肉体	にくたい	**nikutai**	physical body
肉親 *	にくしん	**nikushin**	blood relative

192 反 Against

一	厂	万	反				

Four (4) strokes
A person climbing a cliff who appears to be fighting against it

■ Trace the gray lines, and then practice on your own.

反
反

■ Useful vocabulary: Write the character, and trace the gray ones.

反対する	はんたいする	**hantai suru**	to be opposed
反対語	はんたいご	**hantaigo**	antonym
反対側 *	はんたいがわ	**hantai gawa**	opposite side, i.e., street
違反 *	いはん	**ihan**	violation

* An asterisk denotes vocabulary with kanji that have not yet been introduced.

Reading 20-A

しょうたさんは肉が好きです。とり肉、ぶた肉、牛肉など、肉なら何(なん)でも好きです。しかし、お母さんはしょうたさんにもっとやさいを食(た)べてほしいと思(おも)っています。肉よりやさいのほうが体によいからです。でも、しょうたさんはお母さんの言(い)うことを聞(き)かないで、肉ばかり食べています。お母さんがどんなに強く反対しても、しょうたさんは、話を聞くだけで、なかなかやさいを食べません。お母さんは、しょうたさんがあこがれている近所のお兄さんに、けんこうと食べ物についてしょうたさんに話をしてもらおうと思っています。

あこがれる　　to admire, aspire

Shōta san wa niku ga suki desu. Toriniku, butaniku, gyūniku nado, niku nara nandemo suki desu. Shikashi, okāsan wa Shōta san ni motto yasai o tabete hoshii to omotte imasu. Niku yori yasai no hō ga karada ni yoi kara desu. Demo, Shōta san wa okāsan no iu koto o kikanaide, niku bakari tabete imasu. Okāsan ga donna ni tsuyoku hantai shitemo, Shōta san wa, hanashi o kiku dake de, nakanaka yasai o tabemasen. Okāsan wa, Shōta ga akogarete iru kinjo no oniisan ni, kenkō to tabemono nitsuite Shōta san ni hanashi o shite moraō to omotte imasu.

Questions 20-A

1. What does Shōta like to eat? (A. meat, B. sweets, C. any kind of food, D. he does not like to eat)
2. What does Shōta's mother wish? (A. that he would finish his food, B. that he was not so picky, C. that he ate fewer sweets, D. that he ate more vegetables)
3. What is Shōta's main problem, according to his mother? (A. he only eats meat, B. he often overeats, C. he eats too many sweets, D. he does not eat enough)
4. What was Shōta's response when his mother gave him advice about eating? (A. he gladly did what she asked, B. he did what she asked, but complained about it, C. he listened, but did what he wanted anyway, D. he argued with her)

193 飯	Meal, cooked rice	ノ	𠆢	亽	今	今	刍	食	食
		飠	飣	飯	飯				

Twelve (12) strokes
A measure of cooked rice for a meal

■ Trace the gray lines, and then practice on your own.

飯
飯

■ Useful vocabulary: Write the character, and trace the gray ones.

ご□		ごはん	**gohan**	food, meal, cooked rice
朝ご□	*	あさごはん	**asagohan**	breakfast
昼ご□	*	ひるごはん	**hirugohan**	lunch

194 飲	Drink	ノ	𠆢	亽	今	今	刍	食	食
		飣	飲	飲	飲				

Twelve (12) strokes
A drink is food that is poured

■ Trace the gray lines, and then practice on your own.

飲
飲

■ Useful vocabulary: Write the character, and trace the gray ones.

□む	のむ	**nomu**	to drink
□み物	のみもの	**nomimono**	drink

* An asterisk denotes vocabulary with kanji that have not yet been introduced.

Reading 20-B

朝ご飯を食べない人がふえているそうです。ますみさんもその一人です。毎朝おきると、まず何かを食べなければならないと思いますが、何も食べられないのです。その上、このごろつかれて、集中（しゅうちゅう）がないので、ぼーっとしてしまうことが多いです。

さて、今日、ますみさんはびっくりしました。先生の話によると、朝ご飯を食べないと、脳(のう)の働(ばたら)きが悪(わる)くなり、集中力がなくなると聞いたからです。そして、イライラしたり、勉強をする気になれないことがあると教えてもらいました。それだけでなく、いつもつかれたと感(かん)じたり、病気になったりする人もいるそうです。また、そういう生活(せいかつ)をつづけると、太りやすくなったり、体が動かしにくくなったりもするそうです。

そこでますみさんは、健康(けんこう)のために、夜おそくご飯を食べないようにすることにしました。そして、早く寝(ね)て、早く起(お)きる、早寝早起(はやねはやお)きをすることにしました。そうすると、朝おなかがすいて、朝ご飯を食べられるかもしれないと思ったからです。これから、どうなるか楽しみです。

脳(のう) brain　　集中(しゅうちゅう) concentration　　生活(せいかつ) life

Asagohan o tabenai hito ga fuete iru sō desu. Masumi san mo sono hitori desu. Maiasa okiru to, mazu nanika o tabenakereba naranai to omoimasu ga, nanimo taberarenai no desu. Sono ue, kono koro tsukarete, shūchū ga nai node, bōtto shite shimau koto ga ōi desu.

Sate, kyō, Masumi san wa bikkuri shimashita. Asagohan o tabenai to, nō no hataraki ga waruku nari, shūchūryoku ga nakunaru to kiita kara desu. Soshite, iraira shitari, benkyō o suru ki ni narenai koto ga aru to oshiete moraimashita. Sore dake denaku, itsumo tsukareta to kanjitari, byōki ni nattari, suru hito mo iru sō desu. Mata, sō iu seikatsu o tsuzukeru to, futori yasuku nattari, karada ga ugokashi nikuku nattari mo suru sō desu.

Soko de Masumi san wa, kenkō no tame ni, yoru osoku gohan o tabenai yōni suru koto ni shimashita. Soshite, hayaku nete, hayaku okiru, hayane hayaoki o suru koto ni shimashita. Sō suru to, asa onaka ga suite, asagohan o taberareru kamoshirenai to omotta kara desu. Kore kara, dō naru ka tanoshimi desu.

Questions 20-B

1. What health concern is this passage about? (A. people who cannot sleep at night, B. people who eat excessively, C. people who do not eat breakfast, D. people who are always tired)
2. Why was Masumi excited? (A. the alarm clock was very loud, B. breakfast was tasty, C. she found out a possible reason why she feels tired lately, D. she was given a good book)
3. What symptom does the passage describe? (A. irritability, B. sore throat, C. backache, D. nausea)
4. What has Masumi decided? (A. to not eat dinner late at night, B. to not eat dinner at all, C. to diet, D. to go to the gym)

195 味 Flavor

1	2	3	4	5	6	7	8
丨	ㄇ	口	口一	口二	口キ	味	味

Eight (8) strokes
A flavor one has not yet tasted

■ Trace the gray lines, and then practice on your own.

味
味

■ Useful vocabulary: Write the character, and trace the gray ones.

□	あじ	**aji**	flavor
□わう	あじわう	**ajiwau**	to taste
美□しい†	おいしい	**oishii**	delicious
□方	みかた	**mikata**	friend, ally

196 料 Fee, materials

1	2	3	4	5	6	7	8	9	10
丶	丷	䒑	半	米	米	米	米	米	料

Ten (10) strokes
A measure of rice was used as a fee for certain materials

■ Trace the gray lines, and then practice on your own.

料
料

■ Useful vocabulary: Write the character, and trace the gray ones.

□金	りょうきん	**ryōkin**	charge
有□ *	ゆうりょう	**yūryō**	for fee
材□ *	ざいりょう	**zairyō**	ingredients, materials

* An asterisk denotes vocabulary with kanji that have not yet been introduced.
† Note, this is an unusual pronunciation for the kanji.

Reading 20-C

キム： 今度(こんど)、パーティーをします。どんな料理(りょうり)を作ったらいいと思いますか。

本田： そうですね。ピザやバーベキューもいいけれど、健康(けんこう)にいい和食はどうですか。

キム： 和食を食べるのは大好きですが、作ったことがないんです。難(むずか)しいですか。

本田： そんなに難しくない料理もありますよ。たとえば、手巻(ま)きずしや焼(や)き鳥、お好(この)み焼(や)きなどはどうですか。

キム： どれもおいしそうですね。おすすめは何ですか。

本田： そうですね。パーティーに来る人が急(きゅう)にふえても大丈夫だから、手巻きずしがいいと思います。

キム： では、そうします。どんな材料を買ったらいいですか。

本田： お米、のり、さしみ、やさい、たまごなどがあれば、いいですよ。

キム： では、お米やのりは、明後日(あさって)買いに行きます。さしみはパーティの日に買うのがいいですね。

本田： さしみが苦手(にがて)な人のために、ツナやハムなどを使って手巻きずしを作ってもいいですよ。

キム： なるほど。それはいいですね。魚があまり好きではない友達も来るので、そうします。

本田： それでは、パーティーを楽しんでくださいね。質問(しつもん)があったら、いつでも連絡(れんらく)してください。

キム： ありがとうございました。わからないことがあったら、電話します。

連絡(れんらく) question

Kim: Kondo, pātii o shimasu. Donna ryōri o tsukuttara ii to omoimasu ka.
Honda: Sō desu ne. Piza ya bābekyū mo ii keredo, kenkō ni ii washoku wa dō desu ka.
Kim: Washoku o taberu nowa daisuki desu ga, tsukutta koto ga nai n desu. Muzukashii desu ka.
Honda: Sonna ni muzukashikunai ryōri mo arimasu yo. Tatoeba, temakizushi ya yakitori, okonomiyaki nado wa dō desu ka.
Kim: Dore mo oishisō desu ne. Osusume wa nan desu ka.
Honda: Sō desu ne. Pātii ni kuru hito ga kyū ni fuetemo daijōbu da kara, temakizushi ga ii to omoimasu.
Kim: Dewa, sō shimasu. Donna zairyō o kattara ii desu ka.
Honda: Okome, nori, sashimi, yasai, tamago nado ga areba, ii desu yo.
Kim: Dewa, okome ya nori wa, asatte kai ni ikimasu. Sashimi wa pātii no hi ni kau no ga ii desu ne.
Honda: Sashimi ga nigate na hito no tame ni, tsuna ya hamu nado o tsukatte temakizushi o tsukuttemo ii desu yo.
Kim: Naruhodo. Sore wa ii desu ne. Sakana ga amari suki dewa nai tomodachi ga kuru node, sō shimasu.
Honda: Sore dewa, pātii o tanoshinde kudasai ne. Shitsumon ga attara, itsudemo renraku shite kudasai.
Kim: Arigatō gozaimashita. Wakaranai koto ga attara, denwa shimasu.

Questions 20-C

1. Why did Honda suggest cooking Japanese food? (A. because pizza is not so special, B. because BBQ is more expensive, C. because you can impress your friends by cooking something challenging, D. because it is healthy)
2. Why did Honda recommend sushi? (A. because Kim and friends study Japanese, B. because it is the farewell party for friends going to Japan, C. because it is his favorite food, D. because it is ideal when you do not know how many guests are coming)
3. What is Kim going to prepare for those who do not eat raw fish? (A. sandwiches, B. ham and tuna, C. yakitori, D. okonomiyaki)
4. What will Kim do if she has any questions? (A. invite Honda to go shopping with her, B. buy a sushi cookbook, C. contact Honda, D. watch the cooking channel on TV)

197 理 Logic, arrangement

一	T	干	王	王	玎	玾	玾
玾	理	理					

Eleven (11) strokes
A king employs logic to turn earth into fields

■ Trace the gray lines, and then practice on your own.

理
理

■ Useful vocabulary: Write the character, and trace the gray ones.

料理	りょうり	**ryōri**	cooking
日本料理	にほんりょうり	**nihon ryōri**	Japanese cooking
心理学	しんりがく	**shinrigaku**	psychology
理科	りか	**rika**	science

198 由 Reason

丨	冂	巾	由	由			

Five (5) strokes
Oil flowing from a container is a metaphor for one person giving a reason to another person

■ Trace the gray lines, and then practice on your own.

由
由

■ Useful vocabulary: Write the character, and trace the gray ones.

理由	りゆう	**riyū**	reason
自由	じゆう	**jiyū**	free, liberal

Reading 20-D

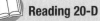

えいようのバランスがいい食事(しょくじ)をしよう

　最近(さいきん)の多くの若い人達(たち)は、好きな物だけを食べていると言われている。しかし、健康(けんこう)のためにも、食事のし方を考(かんが)え直(なお)したほうがいい。ところが、どんな食事を食べればいいか、わからない人が多いので、ここで説明(せつめい)しよう。

まず、バランスの良(よ)い食事は体にいい。それは、ご飯やパンやパスタ、肉や魚、野菜(やさい)、海草(かいそう)などをバランスよく食べる食事のことだ。たとえば、日本の旅館(りょかん)の朝ご飯はえいよう的にとてもいいと言われている。それは、ご飯と味噌汁(みそしる)、魚と野菜と海草などを少しずつ食べる食事のことだ。

また、毎日、果物(くだもの)を食べると良いそうだ。その時に、できれば、朝、果物を食べると一番良い。果物は消化(しょうか)に時間がかからないし、すぐにエネルギーになるからだ。

このように、できるだけ体に良い食べ物を食べて、けんこうになろう。

えいよう　nutrition　　　消化(しょうか)　digestion

Eiyō no baransu ga ii shokuji o shiyō

Saikin no ōku no wakai hito tachi wa, suki na mono dake o tabete iru to iwarete iru. Shikashi, kenkō no tame nimo, shokuji no shikata o kangae naoshita hō ga ii. Tokoro ga, donna shokuji o tabereba ii ka, wakaranai hito ga ōi node, koko de setsumei shiyō.

Mazu, baransu no yoi shokuji wa karada ni ii. Sore wa, gohan ya pan ya pasuta, niku ya sakana, yasai, kaisō nado o baransu yoku taberu shokuji no koto da. Tatoeba, nihon no ryokan no asagohan wa eiyo teki ni totemo ii to iwarete iru. Sore wa, gohan to misoshiru, sakana to yasai to kaisō nado o sukoshi zutsu taberu shokuji no koto da.

Mata, mainichi, kudamono o taberu to yoi sō da. Sono toki ni, dekireba, asa, kudamono o taberu to ichiban yoi. Kudamono wa shōka ni jikan ga kakaranai shi, sugu ni enerugii ni naru kara da.

Kono yōni, dekiru dake karada ni yoi tabemono o tabete, kenkō ni narō.

Questions 20-D

1. What does the passage say about young people today? (A. they are slim, B. they do not cook every day, C. they only eat what they like, D. they are healthy)
2. What is an example of a well-balanced meal? (A. the food at pasta restaurants, B. the food at Japanese traditional inns, C. the food at young peoples' homes, D. the food at cafés in Osaka)
3. What does the article suggest eating in the morning? (A. fruits, B. dairy products, C. meat, D. you should not eat in the morning)
4. This passage is most likely: (A. a letter, B. a folk tale, C. a journal entry, D a newspaper article)

Lesson 20 Practice

A. Kanji Review

Try writing these words in kanji. Use the mnemonic pictures for hints if needed.

 meat, flesh	 against	 meal, cooked rice	 to drink
1.	2.	3.	4.
 flavor	 fee, material	 logic, arrangement	 reason
5.	6.	7.	8.

B. Commonly Mistaken Kanji

Which kanji correctly expresses the meaning of the English word? Circle the most appropriate kanji character.

1.	flavor	妹	未	味	和	末	東
2.	to drink	餅	食	飴	飯	飲	歌
3.	fee, material	科	料	斜	粉	秋	粒
4.	meat, flesh	円	自	内	肉	向	両
5.	logic, arrangement	話	現	規	野	埋	理
6.	against	反	友	坂	戸	広	抜
7.	reason	田	曲	白	由	自	旧
8.	meal, cooked rice	歌	飲	飯	阪	取	販

C. Vocabulary Review

Write these vocabulary and phrases with the appropriate kanji and kana when needed. The number in the parentheses indicates the number of kanji, and an asterisk tells if there are any kana. You may choose from the word bank below.

1. free time (4)*	2. drinks (2)*
3. opposite side (3)	4. reason (2)
5. white rice (2)*	6. beef (2)
7. psychology (3)	8. good taste, flavor (1)*
9. to drink water (2)*	10. to be opposed (2)*
11. Japanese cooking (4)	12. train fare (4)
13. antonym (3)	14. western cooking (4)

牛肉　反対する　反対語　反対がわ　白いご飯　水を飲む　飲み物
いい味　電車料金　日本料理　西洋料理　心理学　理由　自由時間

D. Cooking from Around the World

What types of dishes are typical of Japanese cooking? How about Chinese cooking? Match the following traditional dishes and side dishes with the type of cooking they are associated with. Write the appropriate letters on the blanks.

1. 日本料理 ___ ___
2. 中国料理 ___ ___
3. 韓(かん)国料理 ___ ___
4. インド料理 ___ ___
5. イタリア料理 ___ ___
6. フランス料理 ___ ___

ア.北京(ペキン)ダック	イ.カレー	ウ.すし	エ.スパゲッティ
オ.味噌汁(みそしる)	カ.ギョーザ	キ.エスカルゴ	ク.キムチ
ケ.クロワッサン	コ.ナン	サ.ブルゴギ	シ.ピザ

E. Opposing or Agreeing with School Rules

Many Japanese schools have strict rules. Some of these rules are listed below. Circle 賛成(さんせい)する to express your agreement with, or circle 反対する to express your opposition to, the following rules.

1. 学校には、銃(じゅう)を持ち込(こ)んでは行けません。	賛成(さんせい)する	反対する
2. 制服(せいふく)を着なければなりません。	賛成する	反対する
3. 化粧(けしょう)をしてはいけません。	賛成する	反対する
4. お酒(さけ)を飲んではいけません。	賛成する	反対する
5. 授業(じゅぎょう)中に電話を使ってはいけません	賛成する	反対する
6. アクセサリーをしてはいけません。	賛成する	反対する
7. 人をいじめてはいけません。	賛成する	反対する

銃(じゅう) gun

化粧(けしょう) make up

いじめる to bully (someone)

F. Review Questions

Try writing these sentences in Japanese using kanji whenever appropriate. Each sentence has at least one new kanji from this lesson. Then, compare your translations with the answer key at the end of the book.

1. Do you eat meat every day? ______________________________

____

2. Are you opposed to any of your school rules? Please state one and give a reason.

____

3. Do you like white rice? ____

____

4. Have you tasted Japanese tea before? ____

____

5. Do you like sweet flavors or salty flavors? ____

____

6. Can you make any Japanese foods? ____

____

G. Interview Your Partner

Take turns asking the above questions with your partner. Try to answer as fully and appropriately as you can. For best results, you should elaborate on your answers whenever possible.

H. Read and Respond

Suppose you received the following email from your host family in Japan. Send a reply.

こんにちは。日本に来る日が近(ちか)づいてきましたね。会えるのを楽しみにしています。

さて、今日は食べ物について、質問(しつもん)があります。インフォメーション・シートには、色々な物を食べてみたいと書いてありましたが、もう少し詳(くわ)しく、教(おし)えてください。

どんな食べ物が好きですか。苦手(にが)な食べ物がありますか。アレルギーはありますか。朝ご飯にはたいてい何を食べますか。

お母さんは、日本にいる間に、色々な食べ物を食べてもらいたいと言っています。

お返事を待っています。

山本

199 色	Color	ノ	ク	幺	夕	刍	色		

Six (6) strokes
A person who sees the world through rose-<u>colored</u> classes

■ Trace the gray lines, and then practice on your own.

色
色

■ Useful vocabulary: Write the character, and trace the gray ones.

色	いろ	**iro**	color
色々な	いろいろな	**iroiro na**	various

200 赤	Red	一	十	土	才	赤	赤	赤	

Seven (7) strokes
A <u>red</u> octopus (*aka*-topus; "aka" means red). Also, the character is made up of two radicals; the top is earth (土) and the bottom is a simplified form of fire (火), signifying red colored earthenware, or the color of one's heart when in love.

■ Trace the gray lines, and then practice on your own.

赤
赤

■ Useful vocabulary: Write the character, and trace the gray ones.

赤	あか	**aka**	red
赤い	あかい	**akai**	is red
赤ちゃん	あかちゃん	**akachan**	baby
赤字	あかじ	**akaji**	deficit, loss
赤十字	せきじゅうじ	**sekijūji**	Red Cross
赤道	せきどう	**sekidō**	equator

Reading 21-A

日本の色々な町にある草や木を使(つか)って、糸(いと)や布(ぬの)をそめている人がいる。その人は、「この色がほしい」と思って、草や木を使うことはしない。草や木が持っている色を「いただきたい」と思うそうだ。そめた糸や布がどんな色になるかは、その草や木にまかせる。ただ、できるだけその草木の持っているいいところをいただくようにいのるそうだ。そして、そめる時に使った草や木は、新しい糸や布の中で生きていると考える。その人は、人間は自然(しぜん)に良くないことをしてきたが、それでも自然は人間に色々なことをしてくれる。だから、人間はそれをわすれてはいけないと言っている。

糸(いと)	thread	布(ぬの)	cloth	そめる	to dye
まかせる	up to, leave it to, entrust	自然(しぜん)	nature		

Nihon no iroiro na machi ni aru kusa ya ki o tsukatte, ito ya nuno o somete iru hito ga iru. Sono hito wa, "kono iro ga hoshii" to omotte, kusa ya ki o tsukau koto wa shinai. Kusa ya ki ga motte iru iro o "itadakitai" to omou sō da. Someta ito ya nuno ga donna iro ni naru ka wa, sono kusa ya ki ni makaseru. Tada, dekiru dake sono sōmoku no motte iru ii tokoro o itadaku yō ni inoru sō da. Soshite, someru toki ni tsukatta kusa ya ki wa, atarashii ito ya nuno no naka de ikite iru to kangaeru. Sono hito wa, ningen wa shizen ni yokunai koto o shite kita ga, sore demo shizen wa ningen ni iroiro na koto o shite kureru. Dakara, ningen wa sore o wasurete wa ikenai to itte iru.

Questions 21-A

1. How does the person in the passage extract color pigments? (A. by carefully choosing the grasses and trees to cut, B. by gladly receiving any color pigments extracted, C. by offering incense before cutting the grasses and trees, D. by seeking a fortune teller's advice before cutting the grasses and trees)
2. How does the person decide which colors to use? (A. it depends on the customer, B. it depends on fashion trends, C. he uses chemicals to alter the colors, D. he does not decide, it depends on the type of grasses and trees)
3. Which of the following describes the opinion of the person in the passage? (A. colors have healing properties, B. color can enhance the taste of foods, C. the life of the colors lives on in the materials that are dyed, D. the used grasses and trees should be recycled)
4. What is the main point that the person is trying to make? (A. people should never kill any living thing, B. modern life is too stressful, C. too many disasters are caused by the carelessness of humans, D. people should not forget nature's gifts to them)

201 青	Blue, green	一	十	丰	主	丰	青	青	青

Eight (8) strokes
Green plants and blue well water

■ Trace the gray lines, and then practice on your own.

青									
青									

■ Useful vocabulary: Write the character, and trace the gray ones.

	あお	**ao**	blue
い	あおい	**aoi**	is blue
年	せいねん	**seinen**	youth, young man

202 黒	Black	丨	冂	曰	日	甲	甲	里	里
		黒	黒	黒					

Eleven (11) strokes
Black smoke coming from a fireplace

■ Trace the gray lines, and then practice on your own.

黒									
黒									

■ Useful vocabulary: Write the character, and trace the gray ones.

	くろ	**kuro**	black
い	くろい	**kuroi**	is black
字	くろじ	**kuroji**	profit, surplus

Reading 21-B

ゆうま：お母さん、来月、学校で長野(ながの)にある青年の家に行くことになったよ。

母　　：へえ、そうなの。楽しそうね。いつ行くの。

ゆうま：ええと、六日から九日まで、三泊(ぱく)四日だって。

母　　：そう。ところで、どんなことをするの？

ゆうま：竹で自分のおはしを作ってそれで食事をしたり、カヌーをしたり、ハイキングをしたりするんだって。

母　　：おもしろそうね。

ゆうま：うん。それで、先生が、そばを作りたいか、おやきを作りたいか、決めなさいと言ってたけど、おやきって何？

母　　：おやきというのは、料理のようなおやつのような物よ。おまんじゅうのような形で、中に野菜が入っているものや、あんこが入っているものがあるの。

ゆうま：おいしそうだね。

母　　：昔(むかし)は、焼(や)いてから、いろりの灰(はい)の中に入れて、蒸(む)したそうよ。

ゆうま：へえ、今でもそうするのかなあ。

母　　：じゃあ、おやきにしたらどう。今でも灰の中で蒸すかどうか、聞いてみたら。

ゆうま：そうだね。そうするよ。

いろり　a sunken fireplace (cut in the middle of the floor)
灰(はい)　ash　　蒸(む)す　to steam

Yūma: **Okāsan, raigetsu, gakkō de nagano ni aru seinen no ie ni iku koto ni natta yo.**
Haha : **Hē, sō na no? Tanoshisō ne. Itsu iku no?**
Yūma: **Ēto, muika kara kokonoka made, sanpaku yokka datte.**
Haha : **Sō? Tokoro de, donna koto o suru no?**
Yūma: **Take de jibun no ohashi o tsukutte sore de shokuji o shitari, kanū o shitari, haikingu o shitari suru n datte.**
Haha : **Omoshirosō ne.**
Yūma: **Un. Sore de, sensei ga, soba o tsukuritai ka, oyaki o tsukuritai ka, kimenasai to itte ta kedo, oyaki tte nani?**
Haha : **Oyaki to iu no wa, ryōri no yōna oyatsu no yōna mono yo. Omanjū no yō na katachi de, naka ni yasai ga haitte iru mono ya, anko ga haitte iru mono ga aru no.**
Yūma: **Oishisō da ne.**
Haha : **Mukashi wa, yaite kara, irori no hai no naka ni irete, mushita sō yo.**
Yūma: **Hē, ima demo sō suru no ka nā.**
Haha : **Jā, oyaki ni shitara dō? Ima demo hai no naka de musu kadōka, kiite mitara?**
Yūma: **Sō da ne. Sō suru yo.**

Questions 21-B

1. How long will Yūma be staying at the Nagano Youth Center? (A. three days, B. four days, C. six days, D. nine days)
2. What kinds of activities are there? (A. making a bridge, B. making chopsticks, C. skiing, D. fishing)
3. What is an **oyaki**? (A. a room with a fireplace, B. a name for soba noodles in the Nagano dialect, C. a steamed dumpling eaten as a meal or snack, D. a traditional pork dish)
4. What did Yūma decide to do? (A. make an oyaki, B. eat noodles today, C. take a steaming bath, D. go to Nagano with his mother)

203 茶 Tea

一	十	艹	𠂉	艾	苓	荼	茶
茶							

Nine (9) strokes
A <u>tea</u> house

■ Trace the gray lines, and then practice on your own.

茶
茶

■ Useful vocabulary: Write the character, and trace the gray ones.

	色			ちゃいろ	**chairo**	brown
	色	い		ちゃいろい	**chairoi**	is brown
お				おちゃ	**ocha**	Japanese tea
	道			ちゃどう／さどう	**chadō/sadō**	tea ceremony
	室			ちゃしつ	**chashitsu**	tea room
紅			*	こうちゃ	**kōcha**	black tea

204 黄 Yellow

一	十	廾	龷	𠔉	昔	苗	黄
黄	黄	黄					

Eleven (11) strokes
The <u>yellow</u> color
of a portable shrine
(*mikoshi*)

■ Trace the gray lines, and then practice on your own.

黄
黄

■ Useful vocabulary: Write the character, and trace the gray ones.

	色		きいろ	**kiiro**	yellow
	色	い	きいろい	**kiiroi**	is yellow

* An asterisk denotes vocabulary with kanji that have not yet been introduced.

Reading 21-C

＜お茶について＞

- お茶は中国から日本に伝(つた)わった。
- 最初(さいしょ)、お茶は、薬(くすり)として飲まれていた。
- 日本で千年以上(いじょう)飲まれている。
- お茶を作(つく)るためには、水といい土が必要(ひつよう)だ。
- お茶は作り方によって、大きく、緑(りょく)茶、ウーロン茶、紅(こう)茶に分けられるが、もとは同じ葉(は)からできている。
- 野菜(やさい)や果物(くだもの)を作る時は、日光(にっこう)をあてる。その一方、お茶には日光をあてない作り方もある。それは、日光をあてると、お茶がしぶくなってしまうからだ。日光をあてないと、うまみのある、おいしいお茶になる。
- お茶には、ビタミンやカテキン、カフェインなどがふくまれている。

伝(つた)わる	be introduced into, be conveyed	葉(は)	leaf

<ocha nitsuite>

- **Ocha wa chūgoku kara nihon ni tsutawatta.**
- **Saisho, ocha wa, kusuri toshite nomarete ita.**
- **Nihon de sennen ijō nomarete iru.**
- **Ocha o tsukuru tame niwa, mizu to ii tsuchi ga hitsuyō da.**
- **Ocha wa tsukuri kata niyotte, ōkiku, ryokucha, ūroncha, kōcha ni wakareru ga, moto wa onaji ha kara dekite iru.**
- **Yasai ya kudamono o tsukuru toki wa, nikkō o ateru. Sono ippō, ocha niwa nikkō o atenai tsukuri kata mo aru. Sore wa, nikkō o ateru to, ocha ga shibuku natte shiamau kara da. Nikkō o atenai to, umami no aru, oishii ocha ni naru.**
- **Ocha niwa, bitamin ya katekin, kafein nado ga fukumarete iru.**

Questions 21-C

1. Where is tea originally from? (A. from Japan, B. China, C. England, D. India)
2. What was tea originally used for? (A. a poison, B. a dessert, C. a medicine, D. a delicacy)
3. What do green tea, oolong tea and English tea have in common? (A. they use the same preparation method, B. they use the same leaf, C. they have been used by Japanese for over 1,000 years, D. their tea leaves are grown in the same manner)
4. Some Japanese tea leaves taste better when grown without: (A. water, B. soil, C. sunlight, D. fertilizer)

205 横 Sideways

一	十	才	木	木	木	木	木
村	栟	栟	構	構	横	横	

Fifteen (15) strokes
The sideways beam (wood) used to carry a portable shrine (*mikoshi*)

■ Trace the gray lines, and then practice on your own.

横

横

■ Useful vocabulary: Write the character, and trace the gray ones.

横	よこ	**yoko**	sideways
横浜 *	よこはま	**Yokohama**	Yokohama (city near Tokyo)
横断歩道 *	おうだんほどう	**ōdanhodō**	pedestrian crosswalk

206 銀 Silver

ノ	人	𠆢	亼	全	全	金	金
釒	釒	釒	鉬	鉬	銀		

Fourteen (14) strokes
Silver is a metal that is almost as good as gold (notice one line missing from 良)

■ Trace the gray lines, and then practice on your own.

銀

銀

■ Useful vocabulary: Write the character, and trace the gray ones.

銀	ぎん	**gin**	silver
銀色	ぎんいろ	**giniro**	silver color
銀行	ぎんこう	**ginkō**	bank

* An asterisk denotes vocabulary with kanji that have not yet been introduced.

Reading 21-D

「お茶の水銀行で三百万円ぬすまれる」

昨日の夜 10 時半ごろ、お茶の水銀行の横浜支店で、お金がぬすまれました。

けいさつによると、お金をぬすんだ男の横顔がカメラにうつっていたそうです。その男は、身長 175 センチぐらいで、やせていて、茶色いジャケットを着て、黒のジーンズをはいていました。ぼうしをかぶっていて、かみの毛は短いそうです。三百万円をぬすんだ後、銀行の前にとめてあった黒い車でにげました。

けいさつではこの男がどこにいるかをさがしています。この男について何か知っている人は、ぜひ、けいさつか交番にちょくせつ行くか、電話をして、教えてください。

支店(してん) branch　　ぬすまれる to be stolen
にげる to run away

"Ochanomizu ginkō de sanbyaku manen nusumareru"

Kinō no yoru jūji han goro, ochanomizu ginkō no Yokohama shiten de, okane ga nusumaremashita.

Keisatsu niyoru to, okane o nusunda otoko no yokogao ga kamera ni ututte ita sō desu. Sono otoko wa, shinchō hyaku nanajū go senchi gurai de, yasete ite, chairoi jaketto o kite, kuro no jiinzu o haite imashita. Bōshi o kabutte ite, kami no ke wa mijikai sō desu. Sanbyaku manen o nusunda ato, ginkō no mae ni tomete ita kuroi kuruma de nigemashita.

Keisatsu dewa kono otoko ga doko ni iru ka o sagashite imasu. Kono otoko ni tsuite nanika shitte iru hito wa, zehi, keisatsu ka kōban ni chokusetsu iku ka, denwa o shite, oshiete kusadai.

Questions 21-D

1. What is the passage about? (A. a new bank opening, B. a bank robbery, C. a campaign to encourage bank savings, D. a scandal involving bank officials)
2. How is the person in the passage described? (A. male, B. old, C. heavy set, D. balding)
3. How much money is mentioned in the passage? (A. 30,000,000 yen, B. 3,000,000 yen, C. 300,000 yen, D. 30,000 yen)
4. How are readers encouraged to respond? (A. open a new bank account today, B. call the police, C. write to the local paper, D. call the local TV station)

Lesson 21 Practice

A. Kanji Review

Try writing these words in kanji. Use the mnemonic pictures for hints if needed. Then, see if you can write the hiragana for each one too.

 color	 red	 blue	 black
1.	2.	3.	4.
 brown	 yellow	 sideways	 silver
5.	6.	7.	8.

B. Commonly Mistaken Kanji

Which kanji correctly expresses the meaning of the English word? Circle the most appropriate kanji character.

1.	black	無	魚	黒	思	鼻	里
2.	yellow	横	黄	猫	描	錨	菓
3.	red	寺	青	走	赤	変	魚
4.	brown	花	英	若	草	茶	会
5.	color	晩	魚	勉	色	角	円
6.	silver	鉢	鉄	銀	鈴	銃	飴

7. blue	麦	晴	毒	責	青	漬
8. sideways	柿	枚	相	横	桃	黄

C. Vocabulary Review

Write these vocabulary words in Japanese. You may use the word bank below. The number in the parentheses is the number of kanji, and an asterisk means there is one or more kana characters.

1. tea house (2)	2. young man, youth (2)
3. The Red Cross	4. Yokohama
5. yellow boots	6. various (2)*
7. tea (1)*	8. pedestrian crossing
9. red shoes (1)*	10. black cat (1)*
11. favorite color (2)*	12. gold necklace
13. bank	14. brown jacket (2)*
15. blue shirt (1)*	16. equator (2)
17. tea ceremony (2)	

好きな色　色々な　赤い靴(くつ)　赤ちゃん　赤十字　赤道　銀行青いシャツ　青年　黒ねこ　茶色いジャケット　お茶　茶道　茶室　黄色いブーツ　横浜(はま)　横断(だん)歩道　銀色のネックレス

D. What Color Is It?

Match the items in the list below with the most appropriate color. Write each word under the corresponding color. Some items may fit into more than one color category.

赤	黄	青	黒	白	茶	銀/金

雪	ロ	車のタイヤ	チョコレート	ジーンズ
ジュエリー	レモン	チーズ	コーヒー	フォーク
お金	トマト	ご飯	トースト	海(うみ)

E. Eye Color & Hair Color

Describe your family members' eye color and hair color. You may use the noun or adjective form of the colors.

Example: 父の目の色は青いです。そして、髪(かみ)の色は茶色です。

1. ______________________________

2. ______________________________

3. ______________________________

4. ______________________________

F. Describing What Someone Is Wearing

Choose a famous person or fictitious character, and describe what he/she is wearing. Be sure to use colors in your description. Include a picture with your description.

1. ______________________________

2. ______________________________

3. ______________________________

4. ______________________________

G. Review Questions

Try writing these sentences in Japanese using kanji whenever appropriate. Each sentence has at least one new kanji from this lesson. Then, compare your translations with the answer key at the end of the book.

1. What is your favorite color? ______

2. Do you read various kinds of books? ______

3. Do you remember when you were a baby? ______

4. Who is wearing a blue shirt now? ______

5. Have you studied about the tea ceremony? ______

6. Do you like Japanese tea? ______

7. When you cross the street, do you use the crosswalk? ______

H. Interview Your Partner

Take turns asking the above questions with your partner. Try to answer as fully and appropriately as you can. For best results, you should elaborate on your answers whenever possible.

I. Read and Respond

Imagine your pen pal Shizuku Inaba excitedly wrote to tell you about her brother getting his driver's license. Read the letter below and respond to her questions as fully and appropriately as possible. Use the informal form.

こんにちは。久しぶりだね。

今日は大ニュースがあるよ。お兄ちゃんが先週、車の運転免許を取ったんだよ。大学に入ってからずっとアルバイトをしてお金をためて、教習所で車の運転を習っていたんだ。1回、試験に落ちたけど、2回目で受かったんだよ。それで、日曜日にお兄ちゃんの運転で、海まで行って来たよ。楽しかった！

日本では、運転免許を取ってから１年は、緑と黄色の葉っぱのようなマークを車につけなければならないんだ。それをつけると、「この車を運転している人はまだ運転がそんなに上手じゃないから、気をつけてあげて」ということがほかの車を運転している人にわかるようになんだって。そういうのある？

お兄ちゃんは、今度はまたアルバイトをしてお金をためて、自分の車を買いたいんだって。シルバーがいいか、黒がいいか、それとも白にするか、まよっているみたいだよ。何色がいいと思う？でも新車は高くて買えないんだって。それで、中古の車を買うつもりだから、ほしい色の車があったらラッキーだと思わなきゃいけないんだって。

私もいつか運転免許を取って、自分の車がほしいなあ。自分で好きな時に、好きな所に行けるなんていいよね！どう思う？

返事を待ってるね。

稲葉しずくより

207 春

Spring

Nine (9) strokes
Three people gathered on a sunny day in spring for a picnic

■ Trace the gray lines, and then practice on your own.

春
春

■ Useful vocabulary: Write the character, and trace the gray ones.

□	はる	**haru**	spring
□休み	はるやすみ	**haru yasumi**	spring break
□夏秋冬	しゅんかしゅうとう	**shunkashūtō**	spring, summer, fall, winter
青□	せいしゅん	**seishun**	youth
□分の日	しゅんぶんのひ	**shunbun no hi**	vernal equinox

208 夏

Summer

Ten (10) strokes
A person wearing a hat to shade his eyes from the summer sun, but still dragging his feet in the heat

■ Trace the gray lines, and then practice on your own.

夏
夏

■ Useful vocabulary: Write the character, and trace the gray ones.

□	なつ	**natsu**	summer
□休み	なつやすみ	**natsu yasumi**	summer vacation
□のオリンピック	なつのオリンピック	**natsu no orinpikku**	Summer Olympics

Reading 22-A

けんくんへ、

こんにちは。お元気ですか。夏休みは何をしていますか。私はこの前、オリンピックを見に行きました。すごく良(よ)かったです！

オリンピック会場(じょう)に着(つ)いたら、色々な国の人がたくさんいて、バッジをこうかんしたり、オリンピックのTシャツを買ったり、写真(しゃしん)を撮(と)ったりしていました。それを見て、ぼくもワクワクしました。

ぼくの父が大学生の時に体そうの選手(せんしゅ)だったので、オリンピックでもまず体そうを見に行きました。どの国の選手もとても上手でした。でも、ある選手が体そうをしている時に、ころんでしまったんです。しかし、その選手は、もう一度(ど)立って、やりなおすことにしました。すると、体育館(いくかん)の中から大きな拍手(はくしゅ)がおこったのです。とても感動(かんどう)しました。

オリンピックは、スポーツで色々な国の人が一つになるいい機会(きかい)だと思いました。帰ったら、たくさん見せたい写真があります。会って、話をするのを楽しみにしています。

まさひろより

会場(じょう)	site	ワクワクする	to be excited	拍手(はくしゅ)	hand clapping
感動(かんどう)する	to be moved, to be impressed, to be touched			機会(きかい)	opportunity

Ken kun e,

Konnichiwa, ogenki desu ka. Natsu yasumi wa nani o shite imasu ka. Watashi wa kono mae, orinpikku o mi ni ikimashita. Sugoku yokatta desu!

Orinpikku kaijō ni tsuitara, iroiro na kuni no hito ga takusan ite, bajji o kōkan shitari, orinpikku no tiishatsu o kattari, shashin o tottari shite imashita. Sore o mite, boku mo wakuwaku shimashita.

Boku no chichi ga daigakusei no toki ni taisō no senshu datta node, orinpikku demo mazu taisō o mi ni ikimashita. Dono kuni no senshu mo totemo jōzu deshita. Demo, aru senshu ga taisō o shiteiru toki ni, koronde shimatta n desu. Shikashi, sono senshu wa, mō ichido tatte, yarinaosu koto ni shimashita. Suru to, taiikukan no naka kara ōkina hakushu ga okotta no desu. Totemo kandō shimashita.

Orinpikku wa, supōtsu de iroiro na kuni no hito ga hitotsu ni naru ii kikai da to omoimashita. Kaettara, takusan misetai shashin ga arimasu. Atte, hanashi o suru no o tanoshimi ni shite imasu.

Masahiro yori

Questions 22-A

1. Where did Masahiro go? (A. World Cup, B. Summer Olympics, C. Winter Olympics, D. French Open)
2. What did Masahiro see people doing before the event? (A. selling tickets, B. buying concessions, C. trading badges, D. talking to athletes)
3. What did Masahiro say about his father? (A. he was a tennis player, B. he was a soccer player, C. he was an Olympic runner, D. he was a gymnast)
4. What does Masahiro look forward to doing when he returns? (A. getting some rest, B. watching sports on TV, C. showing pictures to his friend, D. talking to his father)

209 秋	Autumn, fall	ノ	ニ	千	千	禾	禾	禾'	秒
		秋							

Nine (9) strokes
To burn the straw
in the fields
in autumn

■ Trace the gray lines, and then practice on your own.

秋

秋

■ Useful vocabulary: Write the character, and trace the gray ones.

秋	あき	**aki**	autumn, fall
秋分の日	しゅうぶんのひ	**shūbun no hi**	autumn equinox

210 冬	Winter	ノ	ク	夂	冬	冬			

Five (5) strokes
A person dragging
his feet and leaving
footprints in the
snow in the winter

■ Trace the gray lines, and then practice on your own.

冬

冬

■ Useful vocabulary: Write the character, and trace the gray ones.

冬	ふゆ	**fuyu**	winter
冬休み	ふゆやすみ	**fuyu yasumi**	winter vacation
冬のオリンピック	ふゆのオリンピック	**fuyu no orinpikku**	Winter Olympics

Reading 22-B

みなさんは、ドライフルーツが好きですか。スーパーに行くと、一年中(じゅう)、レーズンやアプリコットやマンゴーなど、色々なドライフルーツが売られています。学校のおやつやハイキングに行く時にドライフルーツを持って行く人もたくさんいるでしょう。

さて、日本では秋になると、干(ほ)し柿(がき)が売られます。これはほかのドライフルーツとは少しちがって、おもしろい特長(とくちょう)があるので、ご紹介(しょうかい)します。

まず、日本では、1,300年ぐらい前から干し柿が食べられています。干し柿は、そのままおやつとして食べたり、ドレッシングやサラダに入れたりすることもあります。また、一番おもしろいのは、干し柿には、しぶくて、おいしくないので誰(だれ)も食べない柿(かき)を使うことです。干しておくと、しぶさがあまさに変(か)わるのだそうです。最初(さいしょ)に干し柿を考えた人はすごいですね。

干(ほ)し柿(がき)	dried persimmon	特長(とくちょう)	characteristic
しぶい	astringent, bitter	あまさ	sweetness, a sweet flavor

Minasan wa, doraifurūtsu ga suki desu ka. Sūpā ni iku to, ichinenjū, rēzun ya apurikotto ya mangō nado, iroiro na doraifurūtsu ga urareteimasu. Gakkō no oyastsu ya haikingu ni iku toki ni doraifurūtsu o motte iku hito mo takusan iru deshō.

Sate, nihon dewa aki ni naru to, hoshigaki ga uraremasu. Korewa hoka no doraifurūtsu towa sukoshi chigatte, omoshiroi tokushitsu ga aru node, goshōkai shimasu.

Mazu, nihon dewa, sen sanbyakunen gurai mae kara hoshigaki ga taberarete imasu. Hoshigaki wa, sono mama oyatsu toshite tabetari, doresshingu ya sarada ni iretari suru koto mo arimasu. Mata, ichiban omoshiroi nowa, hoshigaki niwa, shibukute, oishikunai node daremo tabenai kaki o tsukau koto desu. Hoshite oku to, shibusa ga amasa ni kawaru no da sō desu. Saisho ni hoshigaki o kangaeta hito wa sugoi desu ne.

Questions 22-B

1. What are two uses for dried fruits mentioned above? (A. as a school snack and while hiking, B. as a snack while hiking and camping, C. as a snack while camping and traveling, D. as a snack while traveling and as a school snack)
2. What time of the year are dried persimmons sold? (A. summer, B. fall, C. winter, D. spring)
3. What are some of the uses of dried persimmons? (A. artificial sweetener, B. natural ipecac, C. organic additive, D. salad dressing ingredient)
4. What kinds of persimmons are used to make dried persimmons? (A. only the sweetest persimmons, B. any kind of persimmon, C. the persimmons that no one wants to eat, D. carefully selected persimmons)

211 朝 Morning

一	十	𠂇	古	吉	吉	直	卓
𠦝	朝	朝	朝				

Twelve (12) strokes
To see the sun, moon, and stars all in the morning

■ Trace the gray lines, and then practice on your own.

朝
朝

■ Useful vocabulary: Write the character, and trace the gray ones.

☐	あさ	**asa**	morning
毎☐	まいあさ	**maiasa**	every morning
☐ご飯	あさごはん	**asagohan**	breakfast
今☐	けさ	**kesa**	this morning
☐食	ちょうしょく	**chōshoku**	breakfast

212 昼 Daytime, noon

一	コ	尸	尺	尺	昼	昼	昼
昼							

Nine (9) strokes
To draw back the curtains during the daytime

■ Trace the gray lines, and then practice on your own.

昼
昼

■ Useful vocabulary: Write the character, and trace the gray ones.

☐	ひる	**hiru**	noon, daytime
☐寝	ひるね	**hirune**	nap
☐ご飯	ひるごはん	**hirugohan**	lunch
☐食	ちゅうしょく	**chūshoku**	lunch

Reading 22-C

世界には色々な国があって、昼休みのすごし方も様々（さまざま）です。ある国では、学校の昼休みに、教室のカーテンをしめて、みんなで少しの間、昼寝（ひるね）をします。こうすると、午後の授業（じゅぎょう）でねむくならないし、もっと集中（しゅうちゅう）できるからだそうです。また、家に帰（かえ）って昼ご飯を食べて、少し昼寝をしてから、午後の授業をする国もあります。

一般的（いっぱんてき）に、学生や働（はたら）いている人が昼に寝るのはよくないことだと思われています。でも、昼寝をすると、リラックスできます。そして、昼寝をした後は、もっと勉強（べんきょう）や仕事（しごと）ができることが多いです。

昼寝をする時に大切（たいせつ）なのは、長い時間ねむらないことです。人間（にんげん）はたいてい、20 ～ 30 分ねるだけで、元気になることができます。しかし、長い時間ねると、気持ちよくおきることができません。

さあ、あなたもつかれたと思ったら、昼寝をしてみたらどうですか。

様々（さまざま） various　　集中（しゅうちゅう）する to concentrate　　一般的（いっぱんてき）に generally

Sekai niwa iroiro na kuni ga ate, hiruyasumi no sugoshikata mo samazama desu. Aru kuni dewa, gakkō no hiruyasumi ni, kyōshitsu no kāten o shimete, minna de sukoshi no aida, hirune o shimasu. Kō suru to, gogo no jugyō de nemukunaranai shi, motto shūchū dekiru kara da sō desu. Mata, ie ni kaette hirugohan o tabete, sukoshi hirune o shite kara jugyō o suru kuni mo arimasu.

Ippanteki ni, gakusei ya hataraite iru hito ga hiru ni neru no wa yokunai koto da to omowarete imasu. Demo, hirune o suru to, rirakkusu dekimasu. Soshite, hirune o shita ato wa, motto benkyō ya shigoto ga dekiru koto ga ōi desu.

Hirune o suru toki ni taisetsu na no wa, nagai jikan nemuranai koto desu. Ningen wa taitei, nijū kara sanjuppun neru dake de, genki ni naru koto ga dekimasu. Shikashi, nagai jikan neru to, kimochi yoku okiru koto ga dekimasen.

Sā, anata mo tsukareta to omottara, hirune o shite mitara dō desu ka.

Questions 22-C

1. What is the main topic of this passage? (A. length of sleep time in various countries, B. the practice of taking naps, C. the number of working hours of various nations, D. the amount of vacation days of different countries)
2. What is one example of the main topic? (A. in some countries the average amount of sleep exceeds 10 hours per night, B. in some countries adults take naps every day, C. the average work week in some countries is 30 hours, D. some countries have 15 vacation days per month)
3. What does the passage say may help to boost concentration? (A. more frequent vacation days, B. longer vacations, C. taking naps, D. sleeping longer)
4. What does the passage caution against? (A. taking too many vacation days, B. sleeping too long at night, C. taking naps for too long, D. taking vacations that are too long)

213 晩 — Early evening, night

Twelve (12) strokes
The sun escapes from the sky in the evening

■ Trace the gray lines, and then practice on your own.

晩
晩

■ Useful vocabulary: Write the character, and trace the gray ones.

□	ばん	**ban**	early evening, night
今□	こんばん	**konban**	this evening
今□は	こんばんは	**konbanwa**	"Good evening"
□ご飯	ばんごはん	**bangohan**	dinner

214 夜 — Evening, night

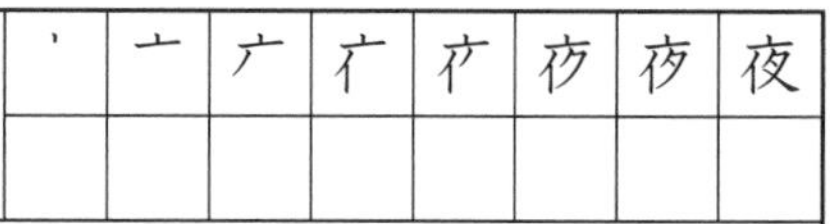

Eight (8) strokes
At night a person can watch the moon trace a path across the sky

■ Trace the gray lines, and then practice on your own.

夜
夜

■ Useful vocabulary: Write the character, and trace the gray ones.

□	よる	**yoru**	evening, night
□中	よなか	**yonaka**	midnight
今□	こんや	**konya**	tonight
□食	やしょく	**yashoku**	evening snack

Reading 22-D

九州(きゅうしゅう)に、お年よりがとても多くて、わかい人が少ない村(むら)がありました。村にはあまり仕事(しごと)の機会(きかい)がないので、その村の高校でバレーボールのコーチをしていた大川さんは、朝から晩まで、どうしたらいいか考(かんが)えました。そして、バレーボールチームの高校生に、さつまいもを作って、それを売ろう。そのお金がたくさんたまったら、みんなで東京に行こうと言いました。バレーボールチームのメンバーは人気があるけれど、遠(とお)くて行ったことがない東京ディズニーランドにいつか行ってみたかったです。だから、練習(れんしゅう)の後から夜くらくなるまで、大川さんを手伝(つだ)うことにしました。

高校生はやる気がありましたが、さつまいもを作ったことがないので、あまり上手にできませんでした。すると、それを聞いた村のお年よりが手伝ってくれて、たくさんおいしいさつまいもができました。そこで、その村では、そのさつまいもでお酒(さけ)を作り、売り始めることにしました。お酒のびんには村のみんなの写真をはりました。すると、おもしろいことをしている村があるとテレビや新聞に取(と)り上げられました。

村のみんなで話し合い、もうけたお金で、足がわるいお年よりのために車いすを買ったり、子どものためにただで勉強を手伝ってあげることにしました。勉強を手伝ってくれた先生へのお金は、もうけたお金からはらいます。その上、村のみんなに一万円ずつボーナスをあげました。村が元気になって、たくさんのわかい人が村にひっこして来ました。そして、今ではとても有名な村になりました。

機会(きかい)	opportunity	さつまいも	sweet potato
やる気	motivation	もうける	to gain profit

Kyūshū ni, otoshiyori ga totemo ōkute, wakai hito ga sukunai mura ga arimashita. Mura niwa amari shigoto no kikai ga nai node, sono mura no kōkō de barēbōru no kōchi o shite ita Ōkawa san wa, asa kara ban made, dō shitara ii ka kangaemashita. Soshite, barēbōru chiimu no kōkōsei ni, Satsumaimo o tsukutte, sore o urō. Sono okane ga takusan tamattara, minna de Tōkyō ni ikō to iimashita. Barēbōru chiimu no menbā wa ninki ga aru keredo, tōkute itta koto ga nai Tōkyō dizuniirando ni itsuka itte mitakatta desu. Dakara, renshū no ato kara yoru kuraku naru made, Ōkawa san o tetsudau koto ni shimashita.

Kōkōsei wa yaruki ga arimashita ga, Satsumaimo o tsukutta koto ga nai node, amari jōzu ni dekimasen deshita. Suru to, sore o kiita mura no otoshiyori ga tetsudatte kurete, takusan oishii satsumaimo ga dekimashita. Soko de, sono mura dewa, sono satsumaimo de osake o tsukuri, urihajimeru koto ni shimashita. Osake no bin niwa mura no minna no shashin o harimashita. Suru to, omoshiroi koto o shite iru mura ga aru to terebi ya shinbun ni toriageraremashita.

Mura no minna de hanashiai, mōketa okane de, ashi ga warui otoshiyori no tame ni kurumaisu o kattari, kodomo no tame ni tada de benkyō o tetsudatte ageru koto ni shimashita. Benkyō o tetsudatte kureta sensei eno okane wa, mōketa okane kara haraimashita. Sono ue, mura no minna ni ichimanen zutsu bōnasu o agemashita. Mura ga genki ni natte, takusan no wakai hito ga mura ni hikkoshite kimashita. Soshite, ima dewa totemo yūmei na mura ni narimashita.

Questions 22-D

1. What kind of fundraiser did the volleyball players participate in? (A. they worked part-time for local farmers, growing sweet potatoes, B. they worked part-time, selling roasted sweet potatoes, C. they worked part-time, growing sweet potatoes, D. they worked part-time, selling vacation packages)
2. How did the local farmers help? (A. they hired the students as part-time workers, B. they taught the students how to grow their own sweet potatoes, C. they bought a large number of vacation packages from the students, D. they bought a large number of roasted sweet potatoes from the students)
3. What did the village do that attracted media attention? (A. the village made sweet potato liquor with the village photo on the bottle, B. the village sent a press release to the local media, C. the village sent pictures of the fundraiser to the local media, D. the village did not get any media attention)
4. What was done with the proceeds from the fundraiser? (A. it was used for new uniforms, B. it was given to the coach, C. it was used for a team trip, D. it was used for various charities and shared among all the villagers)

215 午 Noon

ノ	𠂉	𠂉	午				

Four (4) strokes
Cows in the pasture at noon with heads down, feeding

■ Trace the gray lines, and then practice on your own.

午
午

■ Useful vocabulary: Write the character, and trace the gray ones.

午前	ごぜん	**gozen**	A.M.
午前中	ごぜんちゅう	**gozenchū**	during the morning
午後	ごご	**gogo**	P.M.
正午	しょうご	**shōgo**	noon

216 週 Week

丿	冂	月	円	用	用	周	周
周	凋	週					

Eleven (11) strokes
A stone wall that goes around a property is a metaphor for seven days that cycle through the week

■ Trace the gray lines, and then practice on your own.

週
週

■ Useful vocabulary: Write the character, and trace the gray ones.

一週間	いっしゅうかん	**isshūkan**	for one week
今週	こんしゅう	**konshū**	this week
来週	らいしゅう	**raishū**	next week
先週	せんしゅう	**senshū**	last week
毎週	まいしゅう	**maishū**	every week
週末 *	しゅうまつ	**shūmatsu**	weekend

* An asterisk denotes vocabulary with kanji that have not yet been introduced.

Reading 22-E

マイク： みほさん、今週の週末は何をするつもり？
みほ　： 私は毎月第二土曜日は、午前中ボランティアをしているの。
マイク： すごいね。どこでやってるの？
みほ　： 家の近くの病院で、子供達に本を読んであげているのよ。
マイク： すばらしいね。ぼくもやってみたいな。
みほ　： 本当？それなら、市川さんというリーダーに言っておくわ。
マイク： ありがとう。ところで、日曜日は何をするの？
みほ　： 特に予定はないけど・・・。
マイク： それなら、映画に行かない？
みほ　： いいわね。そうだ、母が今週の日曜日の午前中は映画が特別に安いと言ってたわ。
マイク： どうして？
みほ　： 駅前の映画館が出来て、十年になるからだそうよ。
マイク： 午後は安くならないの？
みほ　： だめみたい。午前中はいそがしい？
マイク： 午前中はいそがしくて、映画に行けないんだ。もしできたら、午後でもいい？
みほ　： いいわよ。じゃあ、何を見る？
マイク： ホラー映画はどう？
みほ　： ホラーはちょっと……。コメディーは？
マイク： そうだね。今、おもしろい映画をやっているらしいよ。時間をしらべておくよ。
みほ　： ありがとう。じゃあ、後で電話をしてくれる？
マイク： うん。晩ご飯の後で、電話するよ。

特別　special

Maiku : Miho san, konshū no shūmatsu wa nani o suru tsumori?

Miho : Watashi wa maitsuki dai ni doyōbi wa, gozenchū borantia o shite iru no.

Maiku : Sugoi ne. Doko de yatte ru no?

Miho : Ie no chikaku no byōin de, kodomo tachi ni hon o yonde agete iru no yo.

Maiku : Subarashii ne. Boku mo yatte mitai na.

Miho : Hontō? Sore nara, Ichikawa san to iu riidā ni itte oku wa.

Maiku : Arigatō. Tokoro de, nichiyōbi wa nani o suru no?

Miho : Toku ni yotei wa nai kedo...

Maiku : Sore nara, eiga ni ikanai?

Miho : Ii wa ne. Sō da, haha ga konshū no nichiyōbi no gozenchū wa eiga ga tokubetsu ni yasui to itte ta wa.

Maiku : Dōshite?

Miho : Ekimae no eigakan ga dekite, jūnen ni naru kara da sō yo.

Maiku : Gogo wa yasuku naranai no?

Miho : Dame mitai. Gozenchū wa isogashii?

Maiku : Gozenchū wa isogashikute, eiga ni ikenain da. Moshi dekitara, gogo demo ii?

Miho : Ii wa yo. Jā, nani o miru?

Maiku : Horā eiga wa dō?

Miho : Horā wa chotto... Komedii wa?

Maiku : Sō da ne. Ima, omoshiroi eiga o yatte iru rashii yo. Jikan o shirabete oku yo.

Miho : Arigatō. Jā, atode denwa o shite kureru?

Maiku : Un. Bangohan no atode, denwa suru yo.

Questions 22-E

1. How often does Miho do volunteer work? (A. every Saturday, B. every other Saturday, C. every second Saturday of the month, D. the last Saturday of the month)
2. What does Miho do for her volunteer work? (A. she makes recordings for audio books, B. she cleans at the local park, C. she reads books to children at the local hospital, D. she helps children with their school studies at the community center)
3. Why are the movie tickets discounted? (A. because of the movie theater's anniversary, B. because they are matinee tickets, C. because Miho's mother got discount coupons at the bookstore, D. because Miho and Mike are elementary students)
4. What is Mike going to find out? (A. the ticket price, B. the movie times, C. which movies are playing, D. the actors in the movie)

217 末 Tip, end

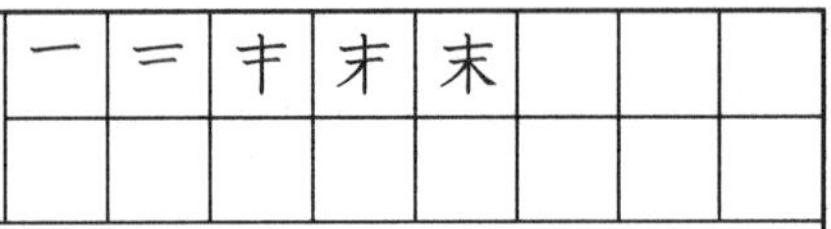

Five (5) strokes
A mature tree with many branches in the tips

■ Trace the gray lines, and then practice on your own.

末
末

■ Useful vocabulary: Write the character, and trace the gray ones.

週 □	しゅうまつ	**shūmatsu**	weekend
後始 □	あとしまつ	**atoshimatsu**	clean-up
十二月 □	じゅうにがつすえ	**jūnigatsu sue**	end of December
□ っ子	すえっこ	**suekko**	last child in the family

218 期 Term, period

Twelve (12) strokes
The four corners of a banner are a metaphor for the four periods (seasons) of the year

■ Trace the gray lines, and then practice on your own.

期
期

■ Useful vocabulary: Write the character, and trace the gray ones.

□ 間	きかん	**kikan**	period of time
□ 待する	きたいする	**kitai suru**	to expect
学 □	がっき	**gakki**	semester
一学 □	いちがっき	**ichigakki**	1st term
□ 末試験 *	きまつしけん	**kimatsu shiken**	end of semester exam

* An asterisk denotes vocabulary with kanji that have not yet been introduced.

Reading 22-F

まりなさん、

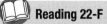

こんにちは。ごぶさたしています。あっという間にもう五月です。私の学校では、あと一週間で期末試験があって、その後は夏休みです。一年は早いですね。

夏休みに、まりなさんが住んでいる日本に行くのを心から楽しみにしています。毎日、まりなさんに会うことばかり考(かんが)えています。いっしょにどこに行こうかとか、日本でどんな食べ物を食べようかとか……。ずっと考えているので、試験(しけん)の勉強も手につかないぐらいです。でも、それではだめですね。本当(とう)は、今、まりなさんに手紙(がみ)を書いていてはいけません。勉強しなければならないからです。でも、一つだけ、質問(しつもん)があります。

私の父も母もまりなさんの家族(ぞく)におみやげを買いたいと言っています。まりなさんはいつもえんりょして、おみやげなんていいよと言いますが、せっかく両親(りょうしん)がそう言っているので、ご家族が好きな物を教えてもらえませんか。アメリカから何かほしい物はないですか。来週、期末試験が終(お)わったら、買い物に行きたいと思っています。だから、それまでに教えてくださいね。

それではまたね！

エレナより

Marina san,

Konnichiwa, Gobusata shite imasu. Atto iu ma ni mō gogatsu desu. Watashi no gakkō dewa, ato isshūkan de kimatsu shaken ga ate, sono ato wa natsu yasumi desu. Ichinen wa hayai desu ne.

Natsu yasumi ni, Marina san ga sunde iru nihon ni iku no o kokoro kara tanoshimi ni shite imasu. Mainichi, Marina san ni au koto bakari kangaete imasu. Isshoni doko ni ikō ka to ka, nihon de donna tabemono o tabeyō ka to ka... Zutto kangaete iru node, shiken no benkyō mo te ni tsukanai gurai desu. Demo, sore dewa dame desu ne. Hontō wa, ima, Marina san ni tegami o kaite ite wa ikemasen. Benkyō shinakereba naranai kara desu. Demo, hitotsu dake, shitsumon ga arimasu.

Watashi no chichi to haha mo Marina san no kazoku ni omiyage o kaitai to itte imasu. Marina san wa itsumo enryō shite, omiyage nante ii yo to iimasu ga, sekkaku ryōshin ga sō itte iru node, gokazoku ga suki na mono o oshiete moraemasen ka. Amerika kara nani-ka hoshii mono wa nai desu ka. Raishū, kimatsu shaken ga owattara, kaimono ni ikitai to omotte imasu. Dakara, sore made ni oshiete kudasai ne.

Sore dewa mata ne.

Erena yori

Questions 22-F

1. When did Elena write this letter? (A. May, B. June, C. July, D. August)
2. Why is Elena having difficulty studying for the end of semester exams? (A. the material is too difficult for her, B. the classes are not in her native language, C. her siblings are very distracting, D. she keeps thinking about her upcoming trip to Japan)
3. What is the main purpose of Elena's letter? (A. to invite Marina to come stay at her home, B. to inform Marina about her graduation, C. to ask Marina a question, D. to tell Marina about her trip to Japan)
4. What do Elena's parents want? (A. to travel to Japan, B. to buy a gift for Marina's family, C. to know when she is welcome to stay at Marina's home, D. to invite Marina's family to come stay at her home)

Lesson 22 Practice

A. Kanji Review

Try writing these words in kanji. Use the mnemonic pictures for hints if needed.

 spring	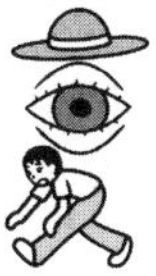 summer	 autumn, fall	 winter	 morning	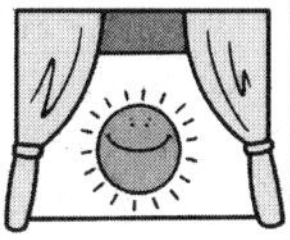 daytime, noon
1.	2.	3.	4.	5.	6.
 evening	 night	 noon	 week	 tip, end	 term, period
7.	8.	9.	10.	11.	12.

B. Commonly Mistaken Kanji

Which kanji correctly expresses the meaning of the English word? Circle the most appropriate kanji character.

1. week	進	近	運	週	道	達
2. evening	喚	晩	勉	色	魚	絶
3. summer	道	顔	頭	直	夏	覚
4. autumn, fall	炊	和	利	私	科	秋
5. night	死	宿	夢	花	荷	夜
6. spring	券	美	春	夫	失	太
7. day time, noon	所	戸	尺	昼	訳	駅
8. noon	午	牛	半	平	年	千

9. end, tip	束	東	未	米	来	末
10. winter	各	冬	久	客	夜	格
11. term, period	旗	明	朝	期	欺	棋
12. morning	朝	転	潮	明	期	幹

C. Vocabulary Review

Write these vocabulary words in Japanese. You may use the word bank below. The number in the parentheses is the number of kanji, and an asterisk means there is one or more kana characters.

1. next week (2)	2. dinner (2)*
3. summer vacation (2)*	4. the end of December (4)
5. last week (2)	6. this evening (2)
7. lunch (2)*	8. period of time (2)
9. weekend (2)	10. spring equinox (3)*
11. nap (2)*	12. (school) semester (2)
13. A.M. (2)	14. this morning (2)
15. spring break (2)*	16. this week (2)
17. breakfast (2)*	18. end of term exam (4)
19. midnight (2)	20. hot summer (1)*
21. every morning (2)	22. one week (3)

23. P.M. (2)	24. Summer Olympics (1)*
25. noon (2)	26. Winter Olympics (1)*
27. autumn equinox (3)*	28. night (1)
29. during the morning (3)	30. cold winter (1)*

春休み　春分の日　あつい夏　夏休み　夏のオリンピック　秋分の日
さむい冬　冬のオリンピック　毎朝　朝ご飯　今朝　昼寝　昼ご飯
今晩　晩ご飯　夜　夜中　午前　午前中　正午　午後　一週間
今週　来週　先週　週末　十二月末　期間　学期　期末試験

D. Annual Events in Japan

Match the following annual events in Japan to the season in which they occur. Write them in Japanese in the most appropriate seasonal categories.

春 (三月～五月)	夏 (六月～八月)	秋 (九月～十一月)	冬 (十二月～二月)

子供(ども)の日	七夕	バレンタインの日	お正月
お盆(ぼん)	体育(いく)の日	成(せい)人の日	花見
七五三	海(うみ)の日	敬老(けいろう)の日	花火大会
節(せつ)分	入学式(しき)	文化祭(さい)	ひな祭(まつ)り

E. Times of the Day

What time of day do high school students usually do the following things? Match the activity to the time of day, and write the activities in Japanese in the most appropriate categories.

朝	昼	晩／夜

パジャマにきがえる	起きる	部活（ぶかつ）
学校に行く	宿題（しゅくだい）をする	寝る
家に帰る	制服（せいふく）にきがえる	教室をそうじする

F. Review Questions

Try writing these sentences in Japanese using kanji whenever appropriate. Each sentence has at least one new kanji from this lesson. Then, compare your translations with the answer key at the end of the book.

1. What did you do during spring break? ____________________

2. Which do you like better, the Summer Olympics or Winter Olympics?

3. Do you know what the days halfway between summer and winter are called?

4. Do you eat breakfast every morning? ____________________

5. Do you sometimes take naps on weekends? ____________________

6. Do you have a lot of homework tonight? ____________________

7. How many hours of TV do you watch per week? ____________________

8. When is your Japanese end of term exam? ____________________

G. Interview Your Partner

Take turns asking the above questions with your partner. Try to answer as fully and appropriately as you can. For best results, you should elaborate on your answers whenever possible.

H. Read and Respond

Suppose you were asked to give advice about using one's time wisely. Read the following instructions and letter from Miss Yamamoto, and then respond with your best advice as fully and appropriately as possible. Use the polite です／ます form.

時間の使い方について

1日は24時間あります。みんな同じだけ持っています。でも、それをどう使うかは、その人次第です。忙しい高校生は、時間の使い方について考えていることが多いでしょう。

さて、ここに、時間がうまく使えなくて困っている人がいます。みなさん、この人にぜひアドバイスをお願いします。

はじめまして。私は山口と言います。高校2年生で、スポーツもボランティアもやっています。楽しいですが、いつも忙しくて、家に帰ると、宿題をしないで、寝てしまうことが多いです。そして、朝起きて、後悔するんです。だから、成績が悪くなってきました。どうしたらいいでしょうか。

人次第（しだい）	up to …	困（こま）る	to be in trouble
後悔（こうかい）	regret	成績（せいせき）	grades

Answers to the Reading Questions

Lesson 1
Reading 1-A: 1.B, 2.C, 3.A, 4.D
Reading 1-B: 1.C, 2.A, 3.B, 4.B
Reading 1-C: 1.B, 2.A, 3.C, 4.C
Reading 1-D: 1.C, 2.B, 3.C, 4.A
Reading 1-E: 1.C, 2.C, 3.A, 4.D
Reading 1-F: 1.B, 2.B, 3.B, 4.D
Reading 1-G: 1.A, 2.C, 3.C, 4.B

Lesson 2
Reading 2-A: 1.B, 2.C, 3.A, 4.D
Reading 2-B: 1.D, 2.D, 3.A, 4.C
Reading 2-C: 1.A, 2.C, 3.D, 4.C
Reading 2-D: 1.B, 2.D, 3.A, 4.B
Reading 2-E: 1.B, 2.C, 3.B, 4.B
Reading 2-F: 1.C, 2.B, 3.C, 4.A

Lesson 3
Reading 3-A: 1.C, 2.A, 3.B, 4.C
Reading 3-B: 1.D, 2.D, 3.C, 4.D
Reading 3-C: 1.B, 2.A, 3.C, 4.D
Reading 3-D: 1.D, 2.A, 3.D, 4.A
Reading 3-E: 1.A, 2.A, 3.B, 4.D

Lesson 4
Reading 4-A: 1.C, 2.A, 3.A, 4.D
Reading 4-B: 1.B, 2.B, 3.A, 4.B
Reading 4-C: 1.B, 2.B, 3.D, 4.C
Reading 4-D: 1.C, 2.D, 3.D, 4.B
Reading 4-E: 1.B, 2.B, 3.C, 4.D
Reading 4-F: 1.A, 2.B, 3.D, 4.C
Reading 4-G: 1.C, 2.B, 3.D, 4.A

Lesson 5
Reading 5-A: 1.A, 2.B, 3.D, 4.A
Reading 5-B: 1.A, 2.D, 3.A, 4.C
Reading 5-C: 1.C, 2.C, 3.C, 4.C
Reading 5-D: 1.C, 2.D, 3.B, 4.B

Lesson 6
Reading 6-A: 1.C, 2.C, 3.C, 4.D
Reading 6-B: 1.D, 2.A, 3.A, 4.C
Reading 6-C: 1.A, 2.C, 3.C, 4.B

Lesson 7
Reading 7-A: 1.D, 2.B, 3.B, 4.A
Reading 7-B: 1.B, 2.B, 3.C, 4.A
Reading 7-C: 1.B, 2.C, 3.A, 4.D
Reading 7-D: 1.B, 2.B, 3.C, 4.B
Reading 7-E: 1.B, 2.A, 3.B, 4.A

Lesson 8
Reading 8-A: 1.C, 2.A, 3.D, 4.B
Reading 8-B: 1.B, 2.A, 3.D, 4.A
Reading 8-C: 1.A, 2.A, 3.B, 4.A
Reading 8-D: 1.B, 2.B, 3.B, 4.C

Lesson 9
Reading 9-A: 1.B, 2.D, 3.D, 4.B
Reading 9-B: 1.C, 2.C, 3.C, 4.B
Reading 9-C: 1.B, 2.C, 3.B, 4.D
Reading 9-D: 1.A, 2.A, 3.B, 4.D
Reading 9-E: 1.B, 2.B, 3.A, 4.C
Reading 9-F: 1.B, 2.C, 3.B, 4.A
Reading 9-G: 1.A, 2.C, 3.A, 4.C

Lesson 10
Reading 10-A: 1.A, 2.A, 3.C, 4.A
Reading 10-B: 1.C, 2.D, 3.D, 4.B
Reading 10-C: 1.B, 2.D, 3.B, 4.D
Reading 10-D: 1.D, 2.D, 3.C, 4.D

Lesson 11
Reading 11-A: 1.C, 2.B, 3.B, 4.D
Reading 11-B: 1.B, 2.B, 3.A, 4.C
Reading 11-C: 1.C, 2.B, 3.D, 4.C
Reading 11-D: 1.D, 2.C, 3.C, 4.C
Reading 11-E: 1.C, 2.C, 3.D, 4.A
Reading 11-F: 1.C, 2.C, 3.A, 4.D

Lesson 12
Reading 12-A: 1.D, 2.D, 3.A, 4.C
Reading 12-B: 1.D, 2.D, 3.B, 4.C
Reading 12-C: 1.B, 2.D, 3.A, 4.B
Reading 12-D: 1.A, 2.B, 3.A, 4.D

Lesson 13
Reading 13-A: 1.B, 2.C 3.D, 4.C
Reading 13-B: 1.B, 2.A, 3.B, 4.B
Reading 13-C: 1.D, 2.A, 3.C, 4.A

Lesson 14
Reading 14-A: 1.A, 2.A, 3.B, 4.B
Reading 14-B: 1.C, 2.B, 3.C, 4.D
Reading 14-C: 1.D, 2.A, 3.D, 4.D
Reading 14-D: 1.B, 2.A, 3.A, 4.D
Reading 14-E: 1.C, 2.C, 3.A, 4.D
Reading 14-F: 1.B, 2.C, 3.A, 4.C
Reading 14-G: 1.D, 2.C, 3.C, 4.C

Lesson 15
Reading 15-A: 1.D, 2.C, 3.C, 4.B
Reading 15-B: 1.C, 2.C, 3.C, 4.A
Reading 15-C: 1.A, 2.C, 3.C, 4.D
Reading 15-D: 1.B, 2.A, 3.B, 4.C
Reading 15-E: 1.D, 2.C, 3.B, 4.D
Reading 15-F: 1.B, 2.A, 3.C, 4.C
Reading 15-G: 1.B, 2.A, 3.C, 4.D

Lesson 16
Reading 16-A: 1.C, 2.B, 3.A, 4.D
Reading 16-B: 1.B, 2.D, 3.C, 4. B
Reading 16-C: 1.C, 2.A, 3.C, 4. D
Reading 16-D: 1.D, 2.D, 3.A, 4. B
Reading 16-E: 1.A, 2.D, 3.B, 4.C
Reading 16-F: 1.C, 2.B, 3.A, 4.B
Reading 16-G: 1.C, 2.D, 3.B, 4.B
Reading 16-H: 1.A, 2.A, 3.B, 4.D

Lesson 17
Reading 17-A: 1.C, 2.C, 3.D, 4.D
Reading 17-B: 1.B, 2.A, 3.C, 4.A
Reading 17-C: 1.B, 2.B, 3.A, 4.C
Reading 17-D: 1.B, 2.A, 3.B, 4.D

Lesson 18
Reading 18-A: 1.D, 2.A, 3.D, 4.C
Reading 18-B: 1.C, 2.C, 3.B, 4.B
Reading 18-C: 1.D, 2.A, 3.D, 4.C

Lesson 19
Reading 19-A: 1.A, 2.C, 3.C, 4.D
Reading 19-B: 1. D, 2.A, 3.D, 4.C
Reading 19-C: 1.C, 2.B, 3.B, 4.D
Reading 19-D: 1.B, 2. A, 3.A, 4.C
Reading 19-E: 1. B, 2.A, 3.D, 4.C
Reading 19-F: 1.B, 2.C, 3.D, 4.A

Lesson 20
Reading 20-A: 1.A, 2.D, 3.A, 4.C
Reading 20-B: 1.C, 2.C, 3.A, 4.A
Reading 20-C: 1.D, 2.D, 3.B, 4.C
Reading 20-D: 1.C, 2.B, 3.A, 4.D

Lesson 21
Reading 21-A: 1.B, 2.D, 3.C, 4.D
Reading 21-B: 1.B, 2.B, 3.C, 4.A
Reading 21-C: 1.B, 2.C, 3.B, 4.C
Reading 21-D: 1.B, 2.A, 3.B, 4.B

Lesson 22
Reading 22-A: 1.B, 2.C, 3.D, 4.C
Reading 22-B: 1.A, 2.B, 3.D, 4.C
Reading 22-C: 1.B, 2.B, 3.C, 4.C
Reading 22-D: 1.C, 2.B, 3.A, 4.D
Reading 22-E: 1.C, 2.C, 3.A, 4.B
Reading 22-F: 1.A, 2.D, 3.C, 4.B

Answers to the Practice Exercises

Lesson 1

A. Kanji Review

1. 一, 2. 二, 3. 三, 4. 四, 5. 五, 6. 六, 7. 七, 8. 八, 9. 九, 10. 十, 11. 百, 12. 千, 13. 万, 14. 円

B. Japanese Vocabulary Related to Numbers

1. 八百や, 2. せかい一, 3. 一つ一つ, 4. 五りん, 5. 三かく, 6. 四かく, 7. だい二, 8. 七めんちょう, 9. 七ころび八おき, 10. せき十じ, 11. しゃく八, 12. 七五三, 13. 十円だま, 14. だい一に

C. Ordering at a Japanese Restaurant

1. (550yen), 2. 625yen, 3. 780yen, 4. 575yen, 5. 675yen, 6. 1,490yen, 7. 830yen, 8. 600yen, 9. Shabushabu (Hot pot), 10. Own answer, 11. Own answer

D. Writing Japanese Addresses

1.	2.	3.	4.
二	一	六	四
|	|	|	|
四	五	三	六
|	|	|	|
十	二	八	二
七	十		十
	九		八

E. Large Numbers in Japanese

A. 七千三百五十万
B. 六百万九千七十
C. 八千二万千百
Mt. Fuji's h. in ft.: 12,388

F. Time and Cost

	Time	Cost
日光 Nikko	二じかん二十ぷん Example: 2 hours 20 minutes	五千六百三十円 Example: 5,630 yen
鎌倉 Kamakura	五十五ふん 55 minutes	八百九十円 890 yen
京都 Kyoto	二じかん二十一ぷん 2 hours 21 minutes	一万三千七百二十円 13,720 yen
横浜 Yokohama	二十四ぷん 24 minutes	四百五十円 450 yen
奈良 Nara	三じかん三十四ぷん 3 hours 34 minutes	一万四千八百三十円 14,830 yen
広島 Hiroshima	三じかん二十五ふん 3 hours 25 minutes	三万五千三百円 35,300 yen
姫路 Himeji	三じかん八ぷん 3 hours 8 minutes	一万九千十円 19,010 yen

G. Most Populous Cities in the World

Ranking	City	Population (Kanji)	Population (Arabic numerals)
四	Sao Paulo, Brazil	千七百七十一万一千人	17,711,000
九	Calcutta, India	千二百九十万人	12,900,000
二	Mexico City, Mexico	千八百十三万人	18,130,000
一	Tokyo, Japan	二千八百二万九千人	28,025,000

八	Los Angeles, USA	千三百十二万九千人	13,129,000
六	Shanghai, China	千四百十七万三千人	14,173,000
五	New York City, USA	千六百六十二万六千人	16,626,000
十	Buenos Aires, Argentina	千二百四十三万一千人	12,431,000
七	Lagos, Nigeria	千三百四十八万八千人	13,488,000
三	Mumbai, India	千八百四万二千人	18,042,000

Lesson 2

A. Kanji Review

1. 日、2. 月、3. 火、4. 水、5. 木、6. 土、
7. 王、8. 金、9. 山、10. 田、11. 川

B. Vocabulary Review

1. 木曜(よう)日、2. 田んぼ、3. 土足(そく)
4. 水着(ぎ)、5. 火山、6. お金、7. 王女、
8. 小(お)川、9. 積(つみ)木、10. 花(はな)火、11. 金魚(ぎょ)、
12. 休(きゅう)日、13. 桜(さくら)の木

C. Campout Story, Fill in the Blank

1. 山、2. 木、3. 川、4. 月、5. 水、6. 火、
7. 金、8. 日、9. 土

D. Guess the Kanji

1. 水、2. 山、3. 金、4. 木、5. 月、6. 田、
7. 川、8. 土、9. 日、10. 火

E. Months of the Year

January 一月	February 二月	March 三月	April 四月
May 五月	June 六月	July 七月	August 八月
September 九月	October 十月	November 十一月	December 十二月

F. Calendar with Kanji

(Own answers)

G. Japanese Last Names

1. 金山、2. 山田、3. 田川、4. 木山、5. 山川、6. 金田、7. 川田、8. 土田、9. 三田

H. Annual Japanese Festivals and Holidays

National Holiday	Date	Festival	Date
New Year's Day 一月一日	January 1st	New Year's 一月一日～三日	January 1st to 3rd
Coming of Age Day 一月のだい二月曜(よう)日	The 2nd Monday of January	Bean Sowing Festival 二月三日	February 3rd
Constitution Day 二月十一日	February 11th	Girls' Day 三月三日	March 3rd
Vernal Equinox 三月二十一日ごろ	Around March 21st	Cherry Blossom Viewing 四月のはじめごろ	Around the beginning of April
Shōwa Day 四月二十九日	April 29th	Golden Week 四月二十九日から一週間	One week beginning April 29

Constitution Day 五月三日	May 3rd	Boys' Day 五月五日	May 5th
Greenery Day 五月四日	May 4th	Star Festival 七月七日	July 7th
Children's Day 五月五日	May 5th	Bon Festival 八月十五日ごろ	Around August 15th
Marine Day 七月だい三月曜(よう)日	The 3rd Monday of July	7-5-3 Festival 十一月十五日	November 15th
Respect for the Aged Day 九月のだい三月曜(よう)日	The 3rd Monday of September	Ōmisoka 十二月三十一日	December 31st
Autumnal Equinox 九月二十三日ごろ	Around September 23rd		
Health and Sports Day 十月のだい二月曜(よう)日	The 2nd Monday of October		
Culture Day 十一月三日	November 3rd		
Labor Thanksgiving Day 十一月二十三日	November 23rd		
Emperor's Birthday 十二月二十三日	December 23rd		

I. Translations of the Review Questions

1. お誕生(たんじょう)日は何(なん)月ですか。
2. つぎの休(やす)みはいつですか。
3. 金曜(よう)日に何(なに)をしますか。
4. 火山を見(み)たことがありますか。

J. Interview Your Partner

(Own answers)

Lesson 3

A. Kanji Review

1. 人、2. 力、3. 男、4. 父、5. 女、6. 母、7. 子、8. 好、9. 方、10. 々

B. Vocabulary Review

1. 子ども、2. お母さん、3. 日本人、4. 好きな、5. 男の子、6. 男の人、7. 父の日、8. 女の人、9. 両方、10. 男子校、11. 父母、12. 女の子、13. 男女、14. 力強い、15. 子犬、16. 人生、17. お父さん、18. 母の日、19. 力持ち、20. 人々

C. Common Japanese Last Names

1. 八田、2. 千田、3. 金子、4. 三好、5. 八木、6. 土田、7. 三木

D. Nationalities

1. オーストラリア人、2. ブラジル人、3. カナダ人、4. 中国(ちゅうごく)人、5. エジプト人、6. フランス人、7. ドイツ人、8. インド人、9. イスラエル人、10. 日本(にほん)人、11. かんこく人、12. メキシコ人、13. サウジアラビア人、14. スペイン人、15. イギリス人、16. アメリカ人

E. Translations of the Review Questions

1. ごかぞくはなん人ですか。
2. 男の子がなん人いますか。

3. お父さんの (お) なまえはなんですか。
4. お父さんは力持ちですか。
5. お父さんとお母さんとではどちらがきびしいですか。
6. あなたはなに人ですか。
7. あなたのがっこうには日本人がいますか。
8. あなたのがっこうで人気のある人はだれですか。
9. 去年の母の日にはお母さんになにをあげましたか。
10. 毎日しゅくだいをしますか。
11. 子犬をかっていますか。
12. いぬとねことではどちらの方が好きですか。
13. クラッシックおんがくとロックミュージックではどちらの方が好きですか。
14. 日本りょうりと、フランスりょうりとではどちらの方が好きですか。
15. 日本りょうりのつくり方をしっていますか。

F. Interview Your Partner
(Own answers)

Lesson 4

A. Kanji Review
1. 小、2. 少、3. 中、4. 大、5. 夕、6. 多、7. 内、8. 外、9. 上、10. 下、11. 工、12. 左、13. 右

B. Opposites
1. 上、2. 女、3. 多、4. 母、5. 小、6. 内、7. 大人、8. 左

C. Vocabulary Review
1. 一日中、2. 小学生、3. 七夕、4. 大事な、5. 年上、6. 多数、7. 工事、8. 下りる、9. 右利き、10. 左利き、11. 下ろす、12. 下さい、13. 大きい、14. 少女、15. 工業、16. 中学校、17. 少数、18. 夕食、19. 上がる、20. 少なくとも、21. 多分、22. 海外、23. 中古、24. 右側、25. 屋内、26. 多目的、27. 外国語、28. 工場、29. 左側、30. 上がる、31. 夕べ、32. 外食

D. Japanese Names
1. 内山、2. 小川、3. 田中、4. 川上、5. 山下、6. 大川、7. 下田、8. 中山、9. 大山、10. 内田、11. 三上、12. 多田、13. 小田、14. 大内、15. 木内、16. 中田、17. 山中、18. 小口、19. 木下

E. How Many?
1. 多い、2. 少ない、3. 少ない、4. 少ない、5. 多い

F. Which One?
1. 七、2. 四、3. 十六、4. 九、5. 十三、6. 一、7. 十八、8. 二十五、9. 十五、10. 二十二

G. Translation of the Review Questions
1. 大きい車 (くるま) と小さい車とでは、どちらの方が好きですか。
2. 左手でひらがなをかくことができますか。
3. あなたは右利 (き) きですか。左利きですか。
4. バックパックの中に何がありますか。
5. こんばん、しゅくだいが多いですか。
6. 夕べ何をしましたか。
7. 映画 (えいが) かんの外で一時間 (じかん) 待 (ま) ったことがありますか。
8. あなたの家 (うち) は大きいですか。小さいですか。
9. あなたはスポーツが上手ですか。
10. どこでうんどうするのが好きですか。外ですか。
11. しゅうまつに、テレビを一日中見 (み) ることがありますか。
12. 大人になっても、テレビゲームをしたいですか。
13. アニメが大好きですか。
14. 七夕を知 (し) っていますか。
15. 日本語 (ご) は多少分 (わ) かりますか
16. あなたは何が下手ですか。
17. この学校 (がっこう) では日本語をとっているせいとが多いですか。
18. 年上のきょうだいがいますか。
19. 大工になりたいですか。

H. Interview Your Partner
(Own answers)

Lesson 5

A. Kanji Review

1. 家、2. 入、3. 出、4. 門、5. 開、6. 閉、7. 所、8. 近、

B. Vocabulary Review

1. 開ける、2. 所、3. 出口、4. 家、5. 入れる、6. 正門、7. 閉める、8. 近代、9. 作家、10. 外出、11. 開会式、12. 名所、13. 校門、14. 閉会式、15. 最近、16. 記入する、17. 出す、18. 開始、19. 専門、20. 台所、21. 閉まる、22. 家庭、23. 場所、24. 出る、25. 近代的、26. 閉店、27. 出来る、28. 入学する、29. 近所、30. 家計、31. 開く、32. 家族、33. 入口、34. 近い

C. Opposites

1. 入、2. 下、3. 閉、4. 右、5. 女、6. 父、7. 大、8. 外

D. Translations of the Review Questions

1. いつこの学校に入学しましたか。
2. あさ何時に家を出ますか。
3. おべんとうをバックパックに入れますか。
4. デパートは何時に開きますか。
5. いつもどこの入口から学校に入りますか。
6. もう今日のしゅくだいを出しましたか。
7. 新しくできたびじゅつかんは近代的なたてものですか。
8. 去年（きょねん）のなつやすみにゆうめいな所に行（い）きましたか。
9. 近所の家は大きいですか。
10. 学校の門（もん）のまえで会（あ）いましょう。
11. あなたの家ではだれがごみを出しますか。
12. レストランのりょうりと家庭（てい）りょうりとでは、どちらの方が好きですか。
13. 日曜日に何時に外出するよていですか。
14. この近くにバードウォッチングができる場所がありますか。
15. からてが出来（き）きますか。
16. オリンピックの開会式（しき）をテレビで見（み）ましたか。

E. Interview Your Partner

(Own answers)

Lesson 6

A. Kanji Review

1. 口、2. 目、3. 耳、4. 手、5. 心

B. Vocabulary Review

1. 左耳、2. 安心する、3. 目下、4. 入口、5. 目上、6. 人口、7. 手品、8. 北口、9. 出口、10. 耳が痛い、11. 目立つ、12. 上手、13. 中心、14. 右耳、15. 下手、16. 入口

C. More Japanese Vocabulary Related to the Body

1. 目がわるい、2. 耳がとおい、3. 目がまわる、4. はや口ことば、5. うんてん手、6. せん手、7. か手、8. から口

D. Guess the Kanji

1. 耳、2. 手、3. 口、4. 目、5. 心

E. Japanese Last Names

1. 山口、2. 川口、3. 田口、4. 水口

F. Translations of the Review Questions

1. 好きな歌手はだれですか。
2. 好きなスポーツ選手がいますか。だれですか。
3. あなたは何が上手ですか。
4. あなたは何が苦手ですか。
5. 私たちの日本語のクラスで目がわるい人はだれですか。
6. 日本語のはや口ことばを知っていますか。
7. 日本語のクラスでは、手をあげなければなりませんか。
8. 手品ができますか。
9. 辛口の料理と甘口の料理とでは、どちらの方が好きですか。
10. パンの耳が好きですか。
11. あなたの町の人口は何人ですか。

G. Interview Your Partner

(Own answers)

Lesson 7

A. Kanji Review

1. 寺、2. 時、3. 半、4. 間、5. 分、6. 今、7. 何(なに)、8. 年、9. 回、10. 毎

B. Vocabulary Review

1. 一時、2. 間に合う、3. 分かる、4. 何時(なんじ)ですか、5. 今日、6. 後(こう)半、7. 清(きよ)水寺、8. 時間、9. 自(じ)分、10. 今朝(けさ)、11. 半島(とう)、12. 金閣(かく)寺、13. 何度(なんど)、14. 半分、15. 十分、16. 何(なに)か

C. Common Japanese Last Names

1. 半田、2. 小出、3. 寺内、4. 寺田、5. 門田、6. 今川、7. 田所、8. 今田

D. Telling Time

1. 3:20, 2. 6:55, 3. 11:40, 4. 8:10, 5. 1:05, 6. 7:35, 7. 4:30, 8. 10:25, 9. 12:50, 10. 9:45

E. Questions Words with 何(なん) (What?)

1. 何才(なんさい)、2. 何年(なんねん)、3. 何時(なんじ)、4. 何月(なんがつ)、5. 何人(なんにん)、6. 何回(なんかい)、7. 何分(なんぷん)、8. 何日(なんにち)、9. 何月(なんがつ)、10. 何時間(なんじかん)、11. 何日(なんにち)、12. 何曜日(なんようび)

F. Ayaka's High School Class Schedule

1. Wednesday and Saturday
2. Six days
3. 9:40
4. Four days
5. Thursday
6. Physical Education
7. 10: 40
8. English
9. 1 hour and 50 minutes
10. Homeroom

G. How Many Times?

(Own answers)

H. Translations of the Review Questions

1. たいてい何時(なんじ)におきますか。
2. いつも一時間目のクラスに間に合いますか。
3. 今日何のクラスがありますか（ありましたか)。
4. (あなたは) 何曜(よう)日に日本語(ご)のクラスがありますか。
5. 日本語のクラスは何時(なんじ)からですか。
6. (あなたの) 日本語のクラスにはせいとが何人いますか。
7. 日本語の先生(せんせい)は何人ですか。
8. スペイン語が分かりますか。
9. 今年のすうがくのしゅくだいはむずかしいですか。
10. 今日三時半から何(なに)をするよていですか。
11. 日本にりょこうをするのに十分なお金がありますか。
12. 毎日ながい時間おんがくをききますか。
13. 自分のへやにテレビがありますか。
14. 小学校の時に学校にあるいて行(い)きましたか。
15. お寺に行ったことがありますか。

I. Interview Your Partner

(Own answers)

Lesson 8

A. Kanji Review

1. 聞、2. 見、3. 思、4. 言、5. 語、6. 話、7. 会

B. Vocabulary Review

1. 見物(ぶつ)、2. 言う、3. 見える、4. 日本語、5. 会話、6. 昔(むかし)話、7. 大会、8. 話す、9. 聞こえる、10. 花(はな)見、11. 思い出す、12. 話、13. 方言、14. 世(せ)話、15. 機(き)会、16. 語る、17. 思う、18. 聞く、19. 意(い)思、20. 物(もの)語、21. 会館(かん)、22. 笑(わら)い話、23. 聞き手、24. 思い出、25. 集(しゅう)会、26. 言語、27. 見る、28. 神(しん)話、29. 単(たん)語、30. 新(しん)聞、31. 会う、32. 外国語

C. Odd One Out

1. ラジオ、2. やきとり、3. あたま、4. 木、5. イヤホン

D. Languages of the World

Rank	Language	Language Name in Japanese	Number of Native-Speakers
五	Arabic	アラビア語	206,000,000
七	Bengali	ベンガル語	171,000,000
一	Chinese (Mandarin)	中国語	873,000,000
四	English	英語	309,350,000
十	German	ドイツ語	95,400,000
二	Hindu	ヒンディー語	366,000,000
九	Japanese	日本語	122,400,000
六	Portuguese	ポルトガル語	177,500,000
八	Russian	ロシア語	145,000,000
三	Spanish	スペイン語	322,300,000

E. Which Part of the Body?

1. 口、2. あたま、3. 目、4. 口、5. 耳、6. 手

F. Commonly Mistaken Kanji

1. 四、2. 人、3. 開、4. 今、5. 中、6. 千、7. 目、8. 大、9. 聞、10. 金、11. 小、12. 思、13. 万、14. 上、15. 回、16. 門、17. 少、18. 火、19. 水、20. 内

G. Verbs, Matching

1 (話す)、8 (会う)、5 (話す)、4 (思う)、11 (聞く)、12 (話す)、6 (聞く)、13 (思う)、3 (見る)、7 (思う)、14 (会う)、15 (聞く)、2 (会う)、16 (思う)、9 (聞く)、10 (見る)

H. Say, Think, and Ask

1 (思う)、8 (言う)、7 (聞いた)、10 (思う)、9 (聞いた)、11 (思う)、2 (言う)、4 (思う)、14 (聞いた)、6 (言った)、15 (聞いた)、13 (言った)、3 (聞く)、12 (言った)、5 (思う)

I. Translations of the Review Questions

1. こわい話が好きですか。
2. 一か月に何回えいがを見ますか。
3. 一日に何時間でんわで話しますか。
4. 一ばんさいしょの思い出は何ですか。
5. 一さいの時のことを思い出すことが出きますか。
6. 何年間日本語をべんきょうしましたか。
7. 何語を話せますか。
8. お母さんは話しやすいですか。
9. お父さんは毎日新聞 (しんぶん) を読 (よ) みますか。
10. あなたのベッドルームのまどから何が見えますか。
11. 日本語のきょうしつから何が見えますか。
12. スポーツの大会に出たことがありますか。
13. 親友 (しんゆう) にはどこで出会いましたか。
14. いつも思っていることをはっきり言いますか。

J. Interview Your Partner

(Own answers)

Lesson 9

A. Kanji Review

1. 生、2. 先、3. 私、4. 友、5. 学、6. 校、7. 本、8. 字、9. 文、10. 対、11. 書、12. 化、13. 公、14. 立

B. Vocabulary Review

1. 生け花、2. 大学、3. 大文字、4. 文学、5. 天文学、6. 目立つ、7. 行き先、8. 私立校、9. 学ぶ、10. 校正、11. 本州、12. 文化、13. お化け、14. 自立、15. 生きる、16. 私たち、17. 学生、18. ローマ字、19. に対して、20. 書く、21. 公立の、22. 人生、23. 日本、24. 小学校、25. 私立大学、26. 先月、27. 友人、28. 先に、29. 友だち、30. 学校、31. 先生

C. Japanese Last Names

(2) Tomoda san, (4) Hitomi san, (1) Futami san, (5) Tsuchimoto san, (3) Kumon san

D. Subjects of Study

1. 科学、2. 文学、3. 数学 4. 天文学、5. 言語学、6. でんき工学、7. 化学、8. どうぶつ学、9. 土木工学、10. ぶつり学、11. しゃ会学

E. Types of Literature

1. ドイツ文学、2. ふつ文、3. 中国文学、4. 英文学、5. 国文学、6. 古文

F. Japanese School System

1. 小学一年、2. 小学二年、3. 小学三年、4. 小学四年、5. 小学五年、6. 小学六年、7. 中学一年、8. 中学二年、9. 中学三年、10. 高一年、11. 高二年、12. 高三年、13. 大学一年、14. 大学二年、15. 大学三年、16. 大学四年

G. Commonly Mistaken Kanji

1. 校、2. 友、3. 書、4. 学、5. 先、6. 対、7. 本、8. 公、9. 字、10. 生、11. 立、12. 文、13. 化、14. 私

H. Translations of the Review Questions

1 どんな本が好きですか。
2 (お)休みに本をよみますか。
3 日本の文学をよんだことがありますか。
4 日本の文化の何が好きですか。
5 生け花を見たことがありますか。
6 英語の先生は、作文をすぐになおしてかえしてくれますか。
7 先生の下のなまえは何ですか。
8 時々日本語をローマ字で書きますか。
9 年をとっている人も外国語を学ぶことができますか。
10 日本人の友だちがいますか。
11 どこで生まれましたか。
12 このまちに私立校は多いですか。
13 公立大学と私立大学とでは、どちらに行きたいですか。
14 ホンダの車をもっている人をしっていますか。
15 日本語で手紙を書いたことがありますか。
16 毎年クリスマスカードを書きますか。
17 お化けがこわいですか。
18 せいようのお化けと　日本のお化けはどこがちがいますか。

I. Interview Your Partner

(Own choices)

J. Read and Respond

(Own choice)

Lesson 10

Let's Review

1. 犬、2. 子犬、3. 鳥、4. 小鳥、5. 馬、6. 子馬、7. 羊、8. 子羊、9. 牛、10. 子牛

A. Kanji Review

1. 犬、いぬ、2. 鳥、とり、3. 馬、うま、4. 羊、ひつじ、5. 牛、うし、6. 魚、さかな、7. 虫、むし

B. Vocabulary Review

1. 本の虫、2. 水虫、3. 鳥肉、4. 馬力、5. 魚屋、6. 泣き虫、7. 牛肉、8. 金魚、9. 番犬、10. 乗馬、11. 羊の肉、12. 白鳥、13. 弱虫、14. 七面鳥、15. 一石二鳥、16. 馬車

C. Zodiac Animals

(Own answers)

D. Japanese Names

1. 犬山、2. 牛島、3. 牛山、4. 鳥山

E. Translations of the Review Questions

1 犬をかっていますか。
2 金魚をかったことがありますか。
3 乗馬が出来ますか。
4 魚つりが上手ですか。
5 魚を食べるのが好きですか。
6 肉をりょうりすることが出来ますか。
7 牛肉と鳥肉とでは、どちらの方が好きですか。
8「一石二鳥」と言うことわざをしっていますか。
9 あなたの家族には本の虫がいますか。
10 虫がきらいですか。
11 あなたは子どもの時、泣き虫でしたか。

F. Interview Your Partner

(Own answers)

G. Read and Respond – Journal Entry

1. Trees, 2. To the right of the house, 3. Sheep, 4. Birds, 5. 14 cows and 2 horses, 6. A river, 7. Fishing

Lesson 11

Let's Review

1. 来る、2. 行く、3. 帰る、4. 待つ、
5. 持つ、6. 食べる、7. 米、8. 良い、
9. 白い、10. 番、11. 物

A. Kanji Review

1. 米、2. 来、3. 番、4. 行、5. 待、6. 持、
7. 帰、8. 白、9. 良、10. 食、11. 物

B. Vocabulary Review

1. 米国(こく)、2. 一番、3. 行う、4. 見物、
5. 食べ物、6. 日帰り、7. 待ち合わせる、
8. 来年、9. 気(き)持ち、10. 面(おも)白い、
11. 良さそう、12. 買(か)物、13. テレビ番組(ぐみ)、
14. 行事(じ)、15. 白黒(くろ)、16. 米屋(や)、17. 来月、
18. 食事(じ)、19. 南(なん)米、20. 良く、21. 和(わ)食、
22. 金持ち、23. 当(とう)番、24. 不(ふ)良品(ひん)、
25. 来客(きゃく)、26. 動(どう)物、27. 番犬、28. 出来る、
29. 期(き)待、30. 帰国(こく)する、31. 旅(りょ)行、32. 荷(に)物、
33. 日米、34. 持って行く、35. 三番目、
36. 夕食、37. 物語

C. Commonly Mistaken Kanji – Lessons 10 & 11

1. 牛、2. 帰、3. 白、4. 犬、5. 良、6. 虫、
7. 待、8. 鳥、9. 物、10. 持、11. 米、12. 馬、
13. 番、14. 魚、15. 来、16. 羊、17. 食、18. 行

D. Opposites

1. 入、2. 来、3. 男、4. 父、5. 外、6. 小、7.
多、8. 上、9. 話、10. 閉、11. 小人、12. 右

E. Japanese Last Names

1. 白川、2. 持田、3. 白鳥、4. 白木、5. 白田

F. Verbs, Matching

１(行く)、４(帰る)、５(来る)、
９(食べる)、３(待つ)、１２(持つ)、
８(来る)、１３(待つ)、１４(食べる)、
１１(持つ)、１５(来る)、７(持つ)、
１０(行く)、１６(帰る)、６(待つ)、
２(食べる)、１７(行く)

G. Translations of the Review Questions

1 和食をよく食べますか。
2 時々和(わ)食を作(つく)りますか。
3 日本の米はどこでかうことが出来ますか。
4 一年に何回旅(りょ)行しますか。
5 人を待てますか。
6 あなたの学校には、どんな行事が行われますか。
7 日本のアニメは面白いと思いますか。
8 あなたは先生が言っていることが良くわかりますか。
9 来年も日本語をべんきょうするつもりですか。
10 一番好きなテレビ番ぐみは何ですか。
11 日本の物語をよんだことがありますか。
12 きょうとを見物をしたいと思いますか。
13 週末(しゅうまつ)は、いつもよりおそく家に帰ってもいいですか。

H. Interview a Partner

(Own answers)

Lesson 12

Let's Review

1. 天気、2.雪、3.雨、4.風、5. 大雨、
6. 風が強い、7. 良い天気、8.台風

A. Kanji Review

1. 雨、2. 雪、3. 電、4. 風、5. 元、6. 天、
7. 気

B. Vocabulary Review

1. 天才、2. 元々、3. 人気がある、4. 電気、5. 病気、6. 気をつける、7. 元日、8. 天使、9. 電池、
10. 気付く、11. 空気、12. 初雪、13. 元気な、14. 電話、15. 足元、16. 雨戸、17. 天国、18. 気持ち、
19. 電車、20. 雨上がり、21. 雪まつり、22.手元

C. Japanese Last Names

1. 山元、2. 風間、3. 中元、4.元木

D. Weather Broadcast

Sapporo	Snow	High: -8 degrees
Niigata	Cloudy, with occasional snow	High: -2 degrees
Sendai	Clear, later cloudy	High: 3 degrees
Tokyo	Clear	High: 9 degrees
Osaka	Cloudy	High: 6 degrees
Hiroshima	Cloudy	High: 7 degrees
Fukuoka	Cloudy, with occasional rain	High: 5 degrees
Okinawa	Cloudy, later rain	High: 17 degrees

E. Translations of the Review Questions

1 今日は一日中、 良い天気ですか。
2 おきなわは、 雨がたくさん降(ふ)りますか。
3 雨の時、 かさをさしますか。
4 台風をけいけんしたことがありますか。
5 雪がふったら、 どんなことをしたいですか。
6 雪であそぶことがありますか。
7 電車にのったことがありますか。
8 一日に何時間電話で話しますか。
9 あなたの兄弟(きょうだい)は、 長(なが)電話をしますか。
10 おじいさんとおばあさんは、 お元気ですか。
11 あなたの家族(かぞく)は、 元日に何(なに)をしますか。何(なに)か、 特別(とくべつ)なしゅうかんがありますか。
12 えびの天ぷらを食べたことがありますか。
13 アインシュタインは本当(ほんとう)に天才(てんさい)でしたか。
14 この学校で、 人気がある人は、 だれですか。
15 あなたは、 病気(びょうき)になったら、 何(なに)をしますか。
16 生徒(と)がガムをかむと、 あなたの先生は気が付きますか。

Lesson 13

A. Kanji Review

1. 石、2. 早、3. 草、4. 花、5. 林、6.森

B. Vocabulary Review

1. 早く、2. 森、3. 早口言葉、4. 熱帯雨林、5. 花見、6. 早合点、7. 森林、8. 早速、9. 石庭、10. 早い、11. 仕草、12. 開花、13. 早めに、14. 花、15. 人口林、16. 林業、17. 生け花、18. 花火、19. 一石二鳥、20. 木を見て森を見ず

C. Commonly Mistaken Kanji Characters (Weather and Nature)

1. 林、2. 雨、3. 電、4. 石、5. 雪、6. 風、7. 早、8. 元、9. 森、10. 天、11. 花、12. 気、13. 草

D. Japanese Last Names

1. 花田、2. 草間、3. 中林、4. 林田、5. 石川、6. 大森、7. 石山、8. 早川、9. 立石、10. 森下、11. 森元、12. 林、13. 森山、14. 大林、15. 立花、16. 白石、17. 石森、18. 森川、19. 上林、20. 今林、21. 森、22. 小林、23. 中森、24. 石田、25. 大石

E. Translations of the Review Questions

1 日本語の早口ことばを知(し)っていますか。
2 「一石二鳥」 は、どういういみ (meaning) ですか。
3 「木を見て森を見ず」 のれい (example) は、 何ですか。
4 学校で熱帯(ねったい)雨林についてべんきょうしましたか。
5 日本の石庭についてどう思いますか。
6 日本とアメリカの国の花は同(おな)じですか。
7 東京(とうきょう)では、さくらは、いつ開花しますか。
8 朝(あさ)早くおきますか。
9 日本人に特有(とくゆう)の仕草は何ですか。

Lesson 14

A. Kanji Review

1. 旅、2. 車、3. 首、4. 道、5. 駅、6. 町、7. 市、8. 京、9. 玉、10. 国、11. 北、12. 南、13. 西、14. 東

B. Commonly Mistaken Kanji

1. 北、2. 旅、3. 車、4. 南、5. 首、6. 京、7. 道、8. 西、9. 玉、10. 駅、11. 町、12. 市、13. 国、14. 東

C. Vocabulary Review

1. 関東、2. 車いす、3. 手首、4. 山道、5. 東京駅、6. 町田、7. 市長、8. 京都、9. 十円玉、10. 中国、11. 北口、12. 南口、13. 西口、14. 東口、15. 旅費、16. 自転車、17. 足首、18. 近道、19. 駅員、20. 町外れ、21. 市立、22. 東京行き、23. 水玉、24. 国内、25. 北部、26. 南アメリカ、27. 西洋、28. 中東、29. 旅行、30. 電車、31. 駅長、32. 港町、33. 市外電話、34. 北京、35. 神道、36. 南アフリカ、37. 大西洋、38. 東洋、39. 旅館、40. 風車、41. 駅名、42. 町内会、43. 市場、44. お手玉、45. 国語、46. 北海道、47. 洗車、48. 書道、49. お年玉、50. 天国、51. 南部、52. 玉ねぎ、53. 母国語

D. Japanese City Names

1. 市川市、四万七千人、2. 犬山市、八万人、3. 上田市、十七万人、4. 大月市、三万人、5. 国立市、七万人、6. 国分寺市、十二万人、7. 下田市、三万人、8. 立川市、十八万人、9. 八王子市、五十七万人、10.町田市、四十二万人

E. Martial Arts and Hobbies

1. じゅう道、4. 書道、6. けん道、8. ぶ道、3. きゅう道、2. 茶道、5. 道じょう、7. あい気道

F. Translations of the Review Questions

1 学校への近道をしっていますか。
2 あなたは自転(じてん)車を持っていますか。
3 学校の近くに駅がありますか。
4 一年に何回旅行をしますか。
5 外国へ旅行をしたいですか。
6 日本のおみやげがありますか。
7 中国りょうりが好きですか。
8 中東へ旅行したことがありますか。
9 北京ダックを食べたことがありますか。
10 あなたの住(す)んでいる市の市長のなまえをしっていますか。
11「書道」とは何(なに)か、知っていますか。
12 あなたの母国語は、何ですか。

Lesson 15

A. Kanji Writing

1. 足、2. 走、3. 起、4. 止、5. 正、6. 歩、7. 休、8. 体、9. 指、10. 背、11. 自、12. 鼻、13.寝

B. Commonly Mistaken Kanji

1. 寝、2. 止、3. 鼻、4. 起、5. 背、6. 歩、7. 足、8. 指、9. 休、10. 走、11. 体、12. 正、13.自

C. Vocabulary Review

1. 二足、2. 正しいこたえ、3. 六時半に起きる、4. ゆっくり歩く、5. 雨が止んだ、6. 指がいたい、7. 背が高い、8. Aを目指す、9. 電車が止まった、10. しあいを中止する、11. 右足、12. 休み時間、13. お正月、14. がっこうに歩いて行く、15. 背中、16. 自分、17. こたえを指す、18. 五千円で足りる、19. つよい体、20. 車を止める、21. 早寝早起き、22. 五キロを走る、23. 寝る時間、24. 休み、25. よく寝る、26. がっこうを休む、27. 鼻水が出る、28. 行き止まり、29. 大体六十才、30. 止まれ！

D. Vocabulary Writing – Parts of the Body

E. Daily Routines

1. 田中さんは、六字半に起きる。2. 七時にあさごはんを食べる、3. 七時半にがっこうに歩いて行く。4. 十一時にとしょかんに行く。5. 四時にサッカーをする。6. 六時に家に帰る。7. 六時半にばんごはんを食べる。8. 七時にテレビを見る。9. 七時半にしゅくだいをする。10.十時に寝る。

F. Translations of the Review Questions

1. 日本への旅行に二しゅう間行くのに、三千ドルで足りますか。
2. 走ることが好きですか。
3. あなたの家の近くにバスが止まりますか。
4. あなたは、時々学校に歩いて行きますか。
5. 今日だれがお休みですか。
6. つぎのお休みには、何(なに)をするつもりですか。
7. どんな人を目指していますか？
8. 早寝早起きしていますか。

G. Interview Your Partner

(Own answer)

H. Read and Respond

(Own answer)

Lesson 16

A. Kanji Review

1. 新、2. 古、3. 美、4. 若、5. 長、6. 太、7. 高、8. 安、9. 楽、10. 明、11. 広、12. 有、13. 名、14. 前、15. 後

B. Commonly Mistaken Kanji

1. 有、2. 太、3. 楽、4. 高、5. 明、6. 新、7. 広、8. 安、9. 古、10. 名、11. 若、12. 前、13. 美、14. 後、15. 長

C. Vocabulary Review

1. 長い足、2. 市長、3. 安い車、4. 安心する、5. 古い本、6. 新聞、7. 長男、8. 楽しじゅぎょう、9. 高校、10. 若い先生、11. 新しい友だち、12. サッカーを楽しむ、13. 明るいへや、14. 長女、15. 長さ、16. 明日、17. 楽ないす、18. 中古、19. 高いくつ、20. 広い家、21. 美しいえ、22. 太っている犬、23. 名所、24. 十年後、25. 私の名前、26. 有名な人27. 学校の後で、28. じゅぎょうの前、29. 三年前

D. Opposites

1. 広い、2. 太っている、3. 安い、4. 楽しい、
5. 美しい、6. 新しい、7. 前、8. 古い、
9. 長い、10. 背が高い、11. 後、12. 若い

E. Common Japanese Last Names

前田、6、B
高木、1、C
広田、5、F
古川、2、E
若林、4、D
太田、3、A

F. Translations of the Review Questions

1 今年新しい友だちができましたか。
2 一週(しゅう)間に何回新聞を読みますか。
3 あなたの英語の教科(きょうか)書は古いですか。
4 中古車を運転していますか。
5 どんな絵(え)が美しいと思いますか。
6 あなたのおじいさんとおばあさんは若いですか。
7 長いかみのけが好きですか。
8 長男／長女で生まれた方がいいと思いますか。
9 太っている人がたくさんいますか。
10 あなたのくつは、 高かったですか。
11 いつこの高校に来ましたか。
12 安い車がほしいですか。
13 あなたの数(すう)学のじゅぎょうは楽しいですか。
14 クラスで一番明るい人はだれですか？どうしてですか。
15 あなたの家は広いですか。
16 駿 宮崎(はやおみやざき)さんと明黒澤(あきらくろさわ)さんでは、だれの方が有名ですか。
17 自分の名前を漢字で書くことができますか。
18 学校の後でたいてい何(なに)をしますか。

G. Interview Your Partner

(Own answers)

H. Read and Respond

(Own answer)

Lesson 17

A. Kanji Review

1. 族、2. 様、3. 主、4. 未、5. 姉、6. 妹、
7.兄、8. 弟

B. Commonly Mistaken Kanji

1. 弟、2. 様、3. 姉、4. 主、5. 族、6. 兄、
7. 妹、8. 未

C. Vocabulary Review

1. 持ち主、2. お姉さん、3. 弟、4. 様、
5. 様々、6. 兄、7. 未来、8. 主人、
9. お兄さん、10. 姉、11. 家族、12. 兄弟、
13. 妹、14. 様子、15. 姉妹、16. 弟子、
17. この様に、18. 父兄、19. 未知、
20. 主に、21. 姉妹校、22. ご主人

D. Vocabulary Writing – Describe Your Family

(Own choice)

E. Translations of the Review Questions

1 ご家族は何人ですか。
2 ここに 田中様はいますか。
3 日本人の様におはしで食べることができますか。
4 大学では、主に何を勉強したいですか。
5 あなたの家の前の持ち主は、だれでしたか。
6 田中さんのご主人は、英語が話せますか。
7 未来の車は電気で走ると思いますか。
8 未知の国に旅行したいですか。
9 あなたの妹さんは、あなたの音楽の本をよくかりますか。
10 お姉さんは、あなたに時々料理をしてくれますか。
11 姉妹校にどんなプレゼントをさしあげましょうか。
12 あなたの弟は、はやく走ることができますか。
13 お兄さんは、けっこんしていますか。
14 兄弟でよくかんかをしますか。

F. Interview Your Partner

(Own answers)

G. Read and Respond

1. Attending a university in Japan,
2. November 23rd,
3. Wednesday,
4. 7:00 to 8:30,
5. Room 103
6. Instructions, information, advice
7. Principal, counselors, and graduates
8. Juniors and seniors
9. In case one has questions about the meeting

Lesson 18

A. Kanji Writing

1. 住、2. 室、3. 和、4. 洋、5. 部、6. 屋

B. Commonly Mistaken Kanji

1. 和、2. 屋、3. 住、4. 部、5. 室、6. 洋

C. Vocabulary Review

1. 和食、2. 私の住所、3. 洋室、4. 東洋、5. 大西洋、6. 私の部屋、7. 日本に住んでいる、8. 先生のお住まい、9. 洋食、10. デパートの屋上、11. 屋外プール、12. 西洋、13. 和室、14. 魚屋、15. 本屋、16. コンピューターの部分 17. ケーキの一部、18. 室内

D. Types of Rooms and Types of Stores

1. パン屋、2. 教室、3. 部屋、4. 花屋、5. 薬(くすり)屋、6. 校長室、7. 肉屋、8. 客(きゃく)室、9. 図書(としょ)室 10. 和菓子(がし)屋、11. 寝室、12. 八百屋、13. 靴(くつ)屋、14. 保健(ほけん)室

E. Japanese Last Names

和田 d, 安部 f, 川部 b, 中屋 c, 土屋 e, 和歌山 a

F. Translations of the Review Questions

1 和食が好きですか。
2 日本人はよく洋食を食べると思いますか。
3 和室に入ったことがありますか。
4 化学の教(きょう)室は、どこにありますか。
5 学校の住所を知っていますか。
6 あなたは、どこに住んでいますか。
7 あなたの部屋にテレビがありますか。
8 今日、本屋に行きましょう。

G. Interview Your Partner

(Own answers)

H. Read and Respond

(Own answer)

Lesson 19

A. Kanji Writing

1. 知、2. 科、3. 教、4. 枚、5. 英、6. 音、7. 勉、8. 強、9. 漢、10. 紙、11. 絵

B. Commonly Mistaken Kanji

1. 強、2. 枚、3. 漢、4. 教、5. 英、6. 絵、7. 科、8. 音、9. 紙、10. 勉、11. 知

C. Vocabulary Review

1. 一枚の紙、2. へんな音楽、3. 英国、
4. 父の知人、5. 知りません、
6. 大好きな科目、7. 漢字を勉強する、
8. うるさい音、9. 教会、10. 和紙、
11. 力強い書き方、12. 先生に知らせる、
13. 白い紙、14. 美しい絵、15. 教科書、
16. 英語、17. 日本語を教える、
18. 友だちへの手紙、19. 強いチーム、
20. 科学の教室

D. Education and Medicine Related Terms

1. 小児(しょうに)科、2. 耳鼻咽喉(じびいんこう)科 3. 家庭科、4. 内科、5. 工学科、6. 外科、7. 英文科、8. 漢方薬(かんぽうやく) 9. 国語科

E. Counters Review

1. 三百円、2. 二回、3. 三千ドル、4. 一時間、5. 二年（間）、6. 二足、7. 二日間、8. 一万円、9. 三分（間）、10. 三枚、11. 一番、12. 一か月

F. Translation of Review Questions

1 一番好きな学校の科目は何ですか。
2 あなたの科学の教室は広いですか。
3 あなたの学校の教科書はおもいですか。
4 漢字は読みにくいと思いますか。
5 毎日日本語を勉強しますか。
6 学校を休む時に先生に知らせますか。
7 英語のレポートを紙で出しますか、それともeメールで出しますか。
8 どんな音楽が好きですか。
9 絵をかくことが、上手ですか。
10 州の知事の名前を知っていますか。

G. Interview Your Partner

(Own answers)

H. Read and Respond

1. わだ/Wada、2. Twenty years ago, 3. Mail correspondence, 4. She could not speak English, so various things were difficult for her, 5. Two, 6. Science

Lesson 20

A. Kanji Review

1. 肉、2. 反、3. 飯、4. 飲、5. 味、6. 料、7. 理、8. 由

B. Commonly Mistaken Kanji

1. 味、2. 飲、3. 料、4. 肉、5. 理、6. 反、7. 由、8. 飯

C. Vocabulary Review

1. 自由時間、2. 飲み物、3. 反対がわ、4. 理由、5. 白いご飯、6. 牛肉、7. 心理学、8. いい味、9. 水を飲む、10. 反対する、11. 日本料理、12. 電車料金、13. 反対語、14. 西洋料理

D. Cooking from Around the World

1. ウ、オ、2. ア、カ、3. ク、サ、4. イ、コ、5. エ、シ、6. キ、ケ

E. Opposing or Agreeing with School Rules

(Own answers)

F. Translations of the Review Questions

Translations of the Review Questions These questions are Japanese translations of the Review Questions on the prior page. Use them to check your translations. Remember there are often many correct ways to translate a sentence.

1. あなたは、毎日肉を食べますか。
2. 学校のきそくに反対ですか 。理由を説明(せつめい)してください 。
3. 白いご飯が好きですか。
4. 日本のお茶を飲んだことがありますか。
5. 甘(あま)いのと塩辛(しおから)いのとでは、どちらの方が好きですか。
6. 日本料理の作り方を知っていますか 。

G. Interview Your Partner

(Own answers)

H. Read and Respond

(Own answer)

Lesson 21

A. Kanji Review

1. 色、いろ、2. 赤、あか、3. 青、あお、4. 黒、くろ、5. 茶、ちゃ、6. 黄、き、7. 横、よこ、8. 銀、ぎん

B. Commonly Mistaken Kanji

1. 黒、2. 黄、3. 赤、4. 茶、5. 色、6. 銀、7. 青、8. 横

C. Vocabulary Review

1. 茶室、2. 青年、3. 赤十字、4. 横浜(はま)、5. 黄色いブーツ 6. 色々、7. お茶、8. 横断歩道(おうだんほどう)、9. 赤い靴(くつ)、10. 黒ねこ、11. 好きな色、12. 金色のネックレス、13. 銀行、14. 茶色いジャケット、15. 青いシャツ、16. 赤道、17. 茶道

D. What Color is it? (Some items may fit into more than more color category)

赤	黄	青	黒	白	茶	銀/金
ロ	レモン	ジーンズ	車のタイヤ	雪	チョコレート	ジュエリー
トマト	チーズ	海(うみ)	コーヒー	ご飯	トースト	フォーク お金

E. Eye Color & Hair Color

(Own answers)

F. Describing What Someone is Wearing

(Own answers)

G. Translations of the Review Questions

1. 一番好きな色は何ですか。
2. 色々な本をよみますか。
3. 赤ちゃんの時をおぼえていますか。
4. 今、青いシャツをきている人は、だれですか。
5. 茶道について勉強したことがありますか。
6. 日本のお茶が好きですか。
7. 道をわたる時に横断歩道を使いますか。

H. Interview Your Partner

(Own answers)

I. Read and Respond

(Own answer)

Lesson 22

A. Kanji Review

1. 春、2. 夏、3. 秋、4. 冬、5. 朝、6. 昼、7. 晩、8. 夜、9. 午、10. 週、11. 末、12. 期

B. Commonly Mistaken Kanji

1. 週、2. 晩、3. 夏、4. 秋、5. 夜、6. 春、7. 昼、8. 午、9. 末、10. 冬、11.期、 12. 朝

C. Vocabulary Review

1. 来週、2. 晩ご飯、3. 夏休み、4. 十二月末、5. 先週、6. 今晩、7. 昼ご飯、8. 期間、9. 週末、10. 春分の日、11. 昼寝、12. 学期、13. 午前、14. 今朝、15. 春休み、16. 今週、17. 朝ご飯、18. 期末試験、19. 夜中、20. 暑い夏、21. 毎朝、22. 一週間、23. 午後、24. 夏のオリンピック、25. 正午、26. 冬のオリンピック、27. 秋分の日、28. 夜、29. 午前中、30. さむい冬

D. Annual Events in Japan

春 (三月〜五月)	夏 (六月〜八月)	秋 (九月〜十一月)	冬 (十二月〜二月)
子供の日	七夕	体育の日	バレンタインの日
花見	お盆	七五三	お正月
入学式	海の日	敬老の日	成人の日
ひな祭り	花火大会	文化祭	節分

E. Times of the Day

朝	昼	晩／夜
起きる	部活	宿題をする
学校に行く	家に帰る	パジャマにきがえる
制服にきがえる	教室をそうじする	寝る

F. Translations of the Review Questions

1. 春休みには、何をしましたか。
2. 夏のオリンピックと冬のオリンピックとでは、どちらの方が好きですか。
3. 夏と冬の真ん中の日は何というか知っていますか。
4. 毎朝、朝食を食べますか。
5. 週末、時々昼寝をしますか。
6. 今晩、宿題がたくさんありますか。
7. 一週間に何時間ぐらいテレビを見ますか。
8. 日本語の期末試験はいつですか。

G. Interview Your Partner

(Own answers)

H. Read and Respond

(Own answer)

Acknowledgements

We would like to thank the many individuals who kindly assisted us in this project. First, thank you to Keiko Yasuno at the American School in Japan for her encouragement and excellent proofreading. Thank you as well to Keiko Ando, Sumino Hirano, Mariko Smisson, and others at ASIJ who have helped. Thank you to the Intermountain Association of Teachers of Japanese (IMATJ), Noriko Okada, and other teachers in Utah for their important feedback. Finally, we want to express thanks to our editor at Tuttle Publishing, Sandra Korinchak, and the others who have guided this project to its successful completion.

Dual-platform disc contains practice software and flash cards. Windows users: If you have difficulty accessing the PDF flash card files on the disc, you may download them from www.tuttlepublishing.com